NEW TITLE — U·X·L® Encyclopedia of World Biography

In 10 volumes, this resource presents 750 biographies of notable historic and current figures from around the world.

Selected from nearly 7,000 entries included in Gale®'s critically acclaimed *Encyclopedia of World Biography,* 2nd Edition, entries include a portrait or illustration; birth and death information; a biographical sketch; and sources for further reading. Features include 750 black-and-white photos and illustrations; a chronology; a table of contents by nationality; and a subject index.

450.00

1st Ed. 1,990 pp. in 10 vols. 2002.
ISBN 0-7876-6465-0. Order #GML00103-182070.
U.S. $~~425.00~~/10-vol. set.

U·X·L
ENCYCLOPEDIA
OF WORLD
BIOGRAPHY

U·X·L
ENCYCLOPEDIA
OF WORLD
BIOGRAPHY

Volume 10

T–Z

Laura B. Tyle, Editor

U·X·L®

THOMSON

GALE

Detroit • New York • San Diego • San Francisco • Cleveland • New Haven, Conn. • Waterville, Maine • London • Munich

THOMSON
★
GALE
™

U•X•L Encyclopedia of World Biography
Laura B. Tyle, Editor, Proof Positive/Farrowlyne Associates, Inc.

Project Editors
Lawrence W. Baker, Elizabeth Shaw Grunow

Editorial
Elizabeth Anderson, Sarah Hermsen

Permissions
Margaret Chamberlain

Imaging and Multimedia
Randy Bassett, Lezlie Light, Dave Oblender, Kelly A. Quin

Product Design
Tracey Rowens

Composition
Evi Seoud

Manufacturing
Rita Wimberley

LIBRARY OF CONGRESS CATALOGING-IN-PUBLICATION DATA

UXL encyclopedia of world biography / Laura B. Tyle, editor.
    p. cm.
        Summary: A collection of 750 biographies and portraits of notable historic and current figures in American and world history, literature, science and math, arts and entertainment, and the social sciences. Includes bibliographical references and index.
        ISBN 0-7876-6465-0 (set hardcover : alk. paper)
        1. Biography—Dictionaries—Juvenile literature. [1. Biography—Dictionaries.] I. Title: Encyclopedia of world biography. II. Tyle, Laura B.
CT103 .U95 2002
920.02—dc21
Revised
                                                  2002004316

ISBN 0-7876-6465-0 (set); 0-7876-6466-9 (v. 1); 0-7876-6467-7 (v. 2); 0-7876-6468-5 (v. 3); 0-7876-6469-3 (v. 4); 0-7876-6470-7 (v. 5); 0-7876-6471-5 (v. 6); 0-7876-6472-3 (v. 7); 0-7876-6473-1 (v. 8); 0-7876-6474-X (v. 9); 0-7876-6475-8 (v. 10)

Printed in the United States of America
10 9 8 7 6 5 4 3 2 1

contents

entries by nationality

English

reader's guide

U•X•L Encyclopedia of World Biography features 750 biographies of notable historic and contemporary figures from around the world. Chosen from American history, world history, literature, science and math, arts and entertainment, and the social sciences, the entries focus on the people studied most often in middle school and high school, as identified by teachers and media specialists.

The biographies are arranged alphabetically across ten volumes. The two- to four-page entries cover the early lives, influences, and careers of notable men and women of diverse fields and ethnic groups. Each essay includes birth and death information in the header and concludes with a list of sources

for further information. A contents section lists biographees by their nationality. Nearly 750 photographs and illustrations are featured, and a general index provides quick access to the people and subjects discussed throughout *U•X•L Encyclopedia of World Biography*.

Special thanks

Much appreciation goes to Mary Alice Anderson, media specialist at Winona Middle School in Winona, Minnesota, and Nina Levine, library media specialist at Blue Mountain Middle School in Cortlandt Manor, New York, for their assistance in developing the entry list. Many thanks also go to the following people for their important editorial contributions: Taryn Benbow-Pfalzgraf (proofreading), Jodi Essey-Stapleton (copyediting and proofing), Margaret Haerens (proofreading), Courtney Mroch (copyediting), and Theresa Murray (copyediting and indexing). Special gratitude goes to Linda Mahoney at LM Design for her excellent typesetting work and her flexible attitude.

Comments and suggestions

We welcome your comments on the *U•X•L Encyclopedia of World Biography*. Please write: Editors, *U•X•L Encyclopedia of World Biography,* U•X•L, 27500 Drake Road, Farmington Hills, MI 48331-3535; call toll-free: 1-800-877-4253; fax to 248-699-8097; or send e-mail via www.gale.com.

U·X·L
ENCYCLOPEDIA
OF WORLD
BIOGRAPHY

MARIA TALLCHIEF

Born: January 24, 1925

Fairfax, Oklahoma

Native American dancer and choreographer

M aria Tallchief is a world-renowned ballerina and one of the premiere (first-ranking) American ballerinas of all time. She was the first American to dance at the Paris Opera and has danced with the Paris Opera Ballet, the Ballet Russe, and the Balanchine Ballet Society, later renamed the New York City Ballet.

Early years

Maria Tallchief was born in Fairfax, Oklahoma, on January 24, 1925. Fairfax is located on the Osage Indian Reservation. Her grandfather had helped negotiate the treaty (agreement) that established the reservation and kept the tribe's right to own any minerals found on the land. When oil was discovered on the reservation, the Osage became the wealthiest Native American tribe in the country.

Maria's father, Alexander Joseph Tall Chief, an Osage Indian, was a wealthy real estate executive. Her mother, Ruth Mary Porter Tall Chief, was of Scottish and Irish ancestry. Eliza Big Heart, her grandmother, frequently took young Maria and her sister, Marjorie, to the ceremonial tribal dances.

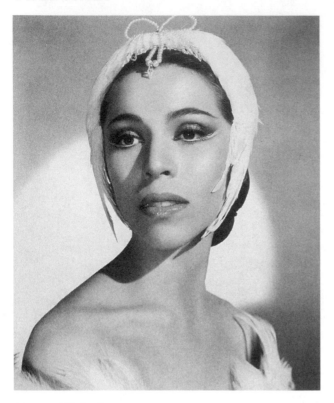

Maria Tallchief.
Reproduced by permission of Archive Photos, Inc.

Tallchief began ballet and piano lessons at the age of three and frequently performed before civic organizations in Osage County. By age eight she and her sister had exhausted the training resources in Oklahoma, and the family moved to Beverly Hills, California. Although her mother hoped she would be a concert pianist, Tallchief devoted more and more of her time to dance. At one of her performances she devoted half of her program to the piano and half to dance.

By age twelve Tallchief was studying under Madame Nijinska, sister of the great Russian ballet dancer Vaslav Nijinsky (1890–1950), and David Lichine, a student of the renowned Russian ballerina Anna Pavlova (1882–1931).

When she was fifteen years old, Tallchief danced her first solo performance at the Hollywood Bowl in a number choreographed by Nijinska. Following her graduation from Beverly Hills High School in 1942, it was apparent that ballet would be Tallchief's life. Instead of college she joined the Ballet Russe de Monte Carlo, a highly acclaimed Russian ballet troupe based in New York City. She made her debut with the company in Canada. It was at this time that Marie Elizabeth Tall Chief changed her name to Maria Tallchief to give herself a more European image.

Early professional career

Initially Tallchief was treated with skepticism (uncertainty) by members of the Russian troupe, who were unwilling to acknowledge the Native American's greatness. When choreographer George Balanchine (1904–1983) took control of the company, however, he recognized Tallchief's talent. He selected her for the understudy role in *The Song of Norway*. Under Balanchine, Tallchief's reputation grew, and she was eventually given the title of ballerina. During this time, Tallchief married Balanchine. When he moved to Paris, France, she went with him.

As had happened with the Ballet Russe, Tallchief was initially treated as an inferior in Paris. Her debut at the Paris Opera was the first ever for any American ballerina, and Tallchief's talent quickly won French audiences over. She later became the first American to dance with the Paris Opera Ballet at the Bolshoi Theatre in Moscow, Russia. She quickly became the ranking soloist and soon after joined the Balanchine Ballet Society, now called the New York City Ballet.

Later career

At the New York City Ballet Tallchief became recognized as one of the greatest dancers in the world. When she became the prima (lead) ballerina, she was the first American dancer to achieve this title. She held that title for eighteen years, until she retired.

Tallchief left the New York City Ballet in 1966. She went on to found the Chicago City Ballet in 1981. She also served as the artistic director of that company through 1987. Tallchief had formed a strong relationship with the Chicago art community when she danced in a production of *Orfeo ed Euridice* with the Lyric Opera of Chicago in 1962.

Tallchief was presented with a National Medal of the Arts award by the National Endowment for the Arts in 1999.

For More Information

Browne, Vee. *Maria Tallchief, Prima Ballerina.* Parsippany, NJ: Modern Curriculum Press, 1994.

Tallchief, Maria, and Larry Kaplan. *Maria Tallchief: America's Prima Ballerina.* New York: Henry Holt, 1997.

Gourley, Catherine. *Who Is Maria Tallchief?* New York: Grosset & Dunlap, 2002.

Lang, Paul. *Maria Tallchief: Native American Ballerina.* Springfield, NJ: Enslow, 1997.

AMY TAN

Born: February 19, 1952
Oakland, California
Asian American writer

Amy Tan is known for her lyrically written (using flowing, melodic language) tales of emotional conflict between Chinese American mothers and daughters separated by generational and cultural differences.

Early life

Amy Ruth Tan was born in Oakland, California, on February 19, 1952. Her father was a Chinese-born Baptist minister; her mother was the daughter of an upper-class family in Shanghai, China. Throughout much of her childhood, Tan struggled with her parent's desire to hold onto Chinese traditions and her own longings to become more Americanized (integrated with American ideals). Her parents wanted Tan to become a neurosurgeon (a doctor who performs surgery on the brain), while she wanted to become a fiction writer. While still in her teens, Tan experienced the loss of both her father and her sixteen-year-old brother to brain tumors and learned that two sisters from her mother's first marriage in China were still alive (one of several autobiographical elements she would later incorporate into her fiction).

Tan majored in English at San Jose State, in California, in the early 1970s rather than fulfill her mother's expectations of becoming a surgeon. After graduate work at the University of California, Berkeley, she began a career as a technical writer (a person who writes about mechanical and computer issues). As a release from the demands of her technical writing career, she turned to fiction writing, having gained inspiration from her reading of Louise Erdrich's novel of Native American family life, *Love Medicine.*

Amy Tan.
Reproduced by permission of Archive Photos, Inc.

First novels

Despite Tan's achievements, her literary career was not planned; in fact, she first began writing fiction as a form of therapy. Considered a workaholic by her friends, Tan had been working ninety hours per week as a freelance technical writer. She became dissatisfied with her work life, however, and hoped to rid herself of her workaholic tendencies through psychological counseling. But when her therapist fell asleep several times during her counseling sessions, Tan quit and decided to cut back her working hours by jumping into jazz piano lessons and writing fiction instead. Tan's first literary efforts were

stories, one of which secured her a position in the Squaw Valley Community of Writers, a fiction writers' workshop. Tan's hobby soon developed into a new career when her first novel, *The Joy Luck Club,* was published in 1989.

Tan's *The Joy Luck Club,* received the Commonwealth Club gold award for fiction and the American Library Association's best book for young adults award in 1989 and stayed on the *New York Times*'s best-seller list for nine months. In 1993, Tan produced and coauthored the screenplay (script for a movie) for *The Joy Luck Club* which was made into a critically acclaimed film. It was adapted for the stage in a production directed by Tisa Chang for Pan Asian Repertory in 1999. Tan's second novel, *The Kitchen God's Wife,* was published in 1991 followed by the children's books *The Moon Lady* (1992) and *The Chinese Siamese Cat* (1994). The year 2001 saw the release of yet another successful novel, *The Bonesetter's Daughter.*

Tan's *The Joy Luck Club* is made up of sixteen stories told by four Chinese immigrant women and their four American-born daughters, linked together by the narrative of June, whose mother had founded a women's social club in China. Nearly forty years later, June's mother has died. The surviving members, the "aunties," recruit June to replace her mother, then send her to China to meet her half-sisters and inform them of the mother's death. When June expresses doubts about her ability to execute this assignment, the older women respond with disappointment. June then realizes the women rightly suspect that she, and their own daughters, know little of the women's lives and the strength and hope they wished to give the next generation.

Throughout the novel, the various mothers and daughters attempt to demonstrate their own concerns about the past and the present and about themselves and their relations.

Critical praise

Amy Tan's novels, *The Joy Luck Club* and *The Kitchen God's Wife,* were enthusiastically received by critics as well as the book-buying public. Focusing on the lives of Chinese American women, Tan's books introduce characters who are uncertain as she once was about their Chinese background. Tan remarked in a *Bestsellers* interview that though she once tried to distance herself from her ethnicity, writing *The Joy Luck Club* helped her discover "how very Chinese I was. And how much had stayed with me that I had tried to deny." Upon *The Joy Luck Club*'s release, Tan quickly became known as a gifted storyteller, a reputation she upheld with the publication of *The Kitchen God's Wife.*

Tan's *The Joy Luck Club* was praised as a thought-provoking, engaging novel. In *Quill and Quire,* Denise Chong wrote: "These moving and powerful stories share the irony, pain, and sorrow of the imperfect ways in which mothers and daughters love each other. Tan's vision is courageous and insightful." In her review for the *Toronto Globe and Mail,* Nancy Wigston declared that Tan's literary debut "is that rare find, a first novel that you keep thinking about, keep telling your friends about long after you've finished reading it." Some critics were particularly impressed with Tan's ear for authentic dialogue. Carolyn See, for instance, wrote in the *Los Angeles Times Book Review* that Tan ranks among the "magicians of language."

Tan's *The Kitchen God's Wife* deals with a young woman in California who realizes a greater understanding of her mother's Chinese background. A generation gap exists between the two heroines: Mother Winnie has only awkwardly adapted to the relatively freewheeling ways of American—particularly Californian—life; daughter Pearl, on the other hand, is more comfortable in a world of sports and fast food than she is when listening, at least initially, to her mother's recollections of her own difficult life in China. As Winnie recounts the secrets of her past, including her mother's mysterious disappearance, her marriage to a psychotic and brutal man, the deaths of her first three children, and her journey to the United States in 1949, Pearl is able to view her mother in a new light and gathers the courage to reveal a secret of her own.

Critics hailed Tan's *The Kitchen God's Wife,* admiring its touching and bittersweet humor. Sabine Durrant, writing in the *London Times,* called the book "gripping" and "enchanting," and Charles Foran, in his review for the *Toronto Globe and Mail,* proclaimed Tan's work "a fine novel" of "exuberant storytelling and rich drama." In a *Washington Post Book World* review, Wendy Law-Yone asserted that Tan exceeded the expectations raised by her first book, declaring that "*The Kitchen God's Wife* is bigger, bolder and, I have to say, better" than *The Joy Luck Club.*

Tan continues to write. In 2001 her novel *The Bonesetter's Daughter* was released to much of the same praise as her earlier books.

For More Information

Bloom, Harold, ed. *Amy Tan.* Philadelphia: Chelsea House, 2000.

Kramer, Barbara. *Amy Tan, Author of* The Joy Luck Club. Springfield, NJ: Enslow, 1996.

Shields, Charles J. *Amy Tan.* Philadelphia: Chelsea House, 2002.

ELIZABETH TAYLOR

Born: February 27, 1932
London, England
American actress

Elizabeth Taylor is one of film's most famous women, having starred in over fifty films and having won two Academy Awards. She also attracted attention because of her eight marriages and her devotion to raising money for research to fight acquired immune deficiency syndrome (AIDS; a virus that destroys the body's ability to fight off infection).

Began acting at nine

Elizabeth Rosemond Taylor was born in London, England, on February 27, 1932, to American parents Francis and Sara Taylor. Her father was a successful art dealer who had his own gallery in London. Her mother was an actress who had been successful before marriage under the stage name Sara Sothern. Taylor has an older brother, Howard, who was born two years earlier. In 1939 the family moved to Los Angeles, California, where Taylor was encouraged and coached by her mother to seek work in the motion picture industry. Taylor was signed by Universal in 1941 for $200 a week.

Success and special treatment

In 1942 Taylor signed a contract with Metro-Goldwyn-Mayer, the biggest and best studio of the time, and landed a part in *Lassie Come Home.* In 1943 she was cast in *National Velvet,* the story of a young woman who wins a horse in the lottery and rides it in England's Grand National Steeplechase. Taylor was so determined to play the role that she exercised and dieted for four months. During filming she was thrown from a horse and suffered a broken back, but she forced herself to finish the project. *National Velvet* became both a critical and commercial success.

Taylor loved her work, the costumes, the makeup, and the attention. Columnist Hedda Hopper, a friend of Taylor's mother, declared that at fifteen Elizabeth was the most beautiful woman in the world. Making films such as *Little Women, Father of the Bride, Cynthia,* and *A Place in the Sun,* Taylor began to gain a reputation as a moody actress who demanded special treatment. In May 1950 she married Conrad N. Hilton Jr., whose family owned a chain of hotels, but the union lasted less than a year. After divorcing Hilton, she married British actor Michael Wilding in February 1952. They had two sons.

Between 1952 and 1956 Elizabeth Taylor played in many romantic films that did not demand great acting talent. In 1956 she played opposite James Dean (1931–1955) in *Giant,* followed by the powerful *Raintree County* (1957), for which she was nominated (put forward for consideration) for an Academy Award for the first time. In *Suddenly Last Summer* (1959) she received five hundred thousand dollars (the most ever earned by an actress for eight weeks of work) and another Academy Award nomination.

Movies and marriages

In 1956 Taylor and Wilding separated, and in February 1957 she married producer Mike Todd. Taylor was shaken by James Dean's death and her friend Montgomery Clift's (1920–1966) near-fatal automobile accident, which occurred when the actor was driving home from a party at her house. In March 1958 her husband Mike Todd died in a plane crash. Taylor began trying to ease her grief with pills and alcohol. Her performance in the film *Cat on a Hot Tin Roof* (1958) won her an Academy Award nomination and led to a relationship with singer Eddie Fisher, who had been Mike Todd's best man at their wedding. Soon after his divorce from actress Debbie Reynolds (1932–), who had been Taylor's matron of honor, Taylor and Fisher were married in May 1959.

In 1960 Taylor turned in one of her best performances in *Butterfield 8,* for which she won an Oscar as Best Actress. A few months later, in 1961, she signed with 20th Century-Fox for $1 million for the film *Cleopatra,* also starring Richard Burton (1925–1984). The two stars were soon romancing off the set as well as on, leading to criticism from the Vatican, which referred to the two stars as "adult children." Upset and confused over her tangled relationships, Taylor attempted suicide in early 1962. By 1964, however, she and Burton had each divorced their spouses and were married.

Taylor won another Oscar for her performance alongside Burton in *Who's Afraid of Virginia Woolf?* (1966). Over a dozen films followed, as did a divorce from Burton. The couple remarried in October 1975 before divorcing for the second and final time in July 1976. In 1978 Taylor married for the seventh time. Her new husband was John Warner, a candi-

Elizabeth Taylor.
Reproduced by permission of Archive Photos, Inc.

date for the U.S. Senate in Virginia. According to one biographer, Taylor broke "all the rules for being a good political wife." She had also gained considerable weight, and the press attacked her about it. After Warner was elected, he and Taylor divorced.

Pain and loss

Taylor then moved to Broadway for the first time in a well-received staging of *The Little Foxes.* She and Richard Burton appeared together in a 1983 production of *Private Lives,* but critics felt that the dramatic spark between them was no longer there. In 1983 Taylor checked into the Betty Ford Clinic in California for treatment for her alcohol addiction. The death of Burton in August 1984, however, combined with back pain and general ill health, led to her return to drinking and drugs.

Taylor was also alarmed as a number of her friends, including actor Rock Hudson (1925–1985) and fashion designer Halston, became ill with AIDS. Taylor began to speak out on behalf of AIDS research. In 1985 she became the cofounder and chair of the American Foundation for AIDS Research (AmFAR). Her "Commitment to Life" benefit of that year was the first major AIDS research fundraiser staged by the Hollywood community.

Taylor returned to the Betty Ford Clinic in 1988, where she met a forty-year old construction worker named Larry Fortensky. Their friendship continued outside the clinic and they married in 1991. In 1993 the Academy of Motion Picture Arts and Sciences honored Taylor with a special humanitarian (supporter of human welfare) award for her years with AmFAR. In 1994 Taylor returned to the movies after a fourteen-year absence for a small part in *The Flintstones*. She then announced her retirement from films. Her marriage to Fortensky ended in 1996.

Later years

In February 1997 Taylor participated in the ABC-TV (American Broadcasting Company-television) special, "Happy Birthday Elizabeth—A Celebration of Life," which marked her sixty-fifth birthday and raised money for AIDS research. The following day she underwent an operation to remove a two-inch tumor from her brain. She also underwent operations on her hip and broke her back in 1998. In the summer of 1999 she fell and suffered a fracture to her spine.

In May 2000 Taylor was dubbed Dame Commander of the Order of the British Empire, the female version of a knight. Queen Elizabeth (1926–) presented her with the award for services to the entertainment industry and to charity. That same year she was given the Marian Anderson Award for her efforts on behalf of the AIDS community. She also returned to the hospital briefly after coming down with pneumonia. Taylor is a beautiful, much-beloved woman with a larger-than-life presence, both on and off the screen.

For More Information

Amburn, Ellis. *The Most Beautiful Woman in the World: The Obsessions, Passions, and Courage of Elizabeth Taylor.* New York: Cliff Street Books, 2000.

Heymann, C. David. *Liz: An Intimate Biography of Elizabeth Taylor.* New York: Carol Publishing Group, 1995.

Kelley, Kitty. *Elizbeth Taylor: The Last Star.* New York: Simon and Schuster, 1981.

Maddox, Brenda. *Who's Afraid of Elizabeth Taylor?* New York: M. Evans, 1977.

Walker, Alexander. *Elizabeth: The Life of Elizabeth Taylor.* New York: G. Weidenfeld, 1991.

PETER ILYICH TCHAIKOVSKY

Born: May 7, 1840
Votkinsk, Russia
Died: November 6, 1893
St. Petersburg, Russia
Russian composer

P eter Ilyich Tchaikovsky was one of the most loved of Russian composers. His music is famous for its strong emotion, and his technical skill and strict work habits helped guarantee its lasting appeal.

Early years

Born on May 7, 1840, in Votkinsk in the Vyatka district of Russia, Peter Ilyich Tchaikovsky was the son of a successful engineer. Peter and his brothers and sister received a sound education from their French governess. His parents sometimes took him to concerts, and after one such evening he complained that he could not fall asleep because of the music stuck in his head. He was devoted to his mother, and at age four he and his sister composed a song for her. Her death when he was fourteen was a huge blow to him.

Tchaikovsky attended law school in St. Petersburg, Russia, and, while studying law and government, he took music lessons, including some composing, from Gabriel Lomakin. Tchaikovsky graduated at the age of nineteen and took a job as a bureau clerk. He worked hard, but he hated the job; by this time he was totally absorbed by music. He soon met the Rubinstein brothers, Anton (1829–1894) and Nikolai (1835–1881), both of whom were composers. Anton was a pianist second only to Franz Liszt (1811–1886) in technical brilliance and fame. In 1862 Anton opened Russia's first conservatory (a school that focuses on teaching the fine arts), under the sponsorship of the Imperial Russian Music Society (IRMS), in St. Petersburg. Tchaikovsky was its first composition student.

Early works

Tchaikovsky's early works were well made but not memorable. Anton Rubinstein was demanding and critical, and when Tchaikovsky graduated two years later he was still somewhat frightened by Anton's harshness. In 1866 Nikolai Rubinstein invited Tchaikovsky to Moscow, Russia, to live with him and serve as professor of composition at the Moscow Conservatory, which he had just established. Tchaikovsky's father was now in financial (money-related) trouble, and the composer had to support himself on his meager earnings from the conservatory. The musical poems *Fatum* and *Romeo and Juliet* that he wrote in 1869 were the first works to show the style he became famous for. *Romeo and Juliet* was redone with Mily Balakirev's (1837–1910) help in 1870 and again in 1879.

During the 1870s and later, there was considerable communication between Tchaikovsky and the Rubinsteins on the one hand and the members of the "Mighty Five" Russian composers—Balakirev, Aleksandr Borodin (1834–1887), Modest Mussorgsky (1839–1881), Nicolai Rimsky-Korsakov (1844–1908), and César Cui—on the other. It was widely reported that the two groups did not get along, but this was not true. Tchaikovsky worked as an all-around musician in the early 1870s, and, as was expected of a representative of the IRMS, he taught, composed, wrote critical essays, and conducted (although he was not a great conductor). In 1875 he composed what is perhaps his most universally known and loved work, the Piano Concerto No. 1. Anton Rubinstein mocked the piece, although he himself often performed it years later as a concert pianist. Also popular was Tchaikovsky's ballet *Swan Lake* (1876). It is the most success-

Peter Ilyich Tchaikovsky.
Courtesy of the Library of Congress.

ful ballet ever written if measured in terms of broad audience appeal.

A disastrous marriage

In 1877 Tchaikovsky married the twenty-eight-year-old Antonina Miliukova, his student at the conservatory. It has been suggested that she reminded him of Tatiana, a character in his opera *Eugene Onegin*. His unfortunate wife, who became mentally ill and died in 1917, not only suffered rejection by her husband but also the vicious criticism of his brother Modeste Tchaikovsky. Modeste, like Peter, was a misogynist (one who hates women). Modeste attacked Antonina in

a biography he wrote about Peter. This was an attempt to shield Peter and mask his weaknesses. Later biographers repeated and even exaggerated Modeste's claim that Antonina was cheap and high-strung.

Tchaikovsky never stuck around to find out what she was like. Within a few weeks he had fled Moscow alone for an extended stay abroad. He made arrangements through his relatives to never see his wife again. In his correspondence of this period—indeed through a large part of his career—he was often morbid (gloomy) about his wife, money, his friends, even his music and himself. He often spoke of suicide. This, too, has been reported widely by Tchaikovsky's many biographers. Even during his life critics treated him unkindly because of his open, emotional music. But he never sought to change his style, though he was dissatisfied at one time or another with most of his works. He also never stopped composing.

Arrangement with Madame von Meck

Tchaikovsky became involved in another important relationship at about the same time as his marriage. Through third parties an unusual but helpful arrangement with the immensely wealthy Nadezhda von Meck was made. She was attracted by his music and the possibility of supporting his creative work, and he was interested in her money and what it could provide him. For thirteen years she supported him at a base rate of six thousand rubles a year, plus whatever "bonuses" he could manage to get out of her. He was free to quit the conservatory, and he began a series of travels and stays abroad.

Von Meck and Tchaikovsky purposely never met, except for one or two accidental encounters. In their correspondence Tchaikovsky discusses his music thoughtfully; in letters to his family he complains about her cheapness. He dedicated his Fourth Symphony (1877) to her. Tchaikovsky finished *Eugene Onegin* in 1879. It is his only opera generally performed outside the Soviet Union. Other works of this period are the Violin Concerto (1881), the Fifth Symphony (1888), and the ballet *Sleeping Beauty* (1889).

Later years

Tchaikovsky's fame and his activity now extended to all of Europe and America. To rest from his public appearances he chose a country retreat in Klin near Moscow. From this he became known as the "Hermit of Klin," although he was never a hermit. In 1890 he finished the opera *Queen of Spades,* based on a story by the Russian poet Aleksandr Pushkin (1799–1837). Tchaikovsky was happy when, despite the criticism of "experts," the opera was well received. In late 1890 Von Meck cut him off. He had reached the point where he no longer depended on her money, but he was still upset by her rejection. Even his brother Modeste expressed surprise at his anger. Tchaikovsky had an immensely successful tour in the United States in 1891.

The Sixth Symphony was first heard in October 1893, with the composer conducting. This work, named at Modeste's suggestion *Pathétique,* was poorly received—very likely because of Tchaikovsky's conducting. Tchaikovsky never knew of its eventual astonishing success, for he contracted cholera (a disease of the small intestine) and died, still complaining about Von Meck, on November 6, 1893.

For More Information

Cencetti, Greta. *Tchaikovsky.* Columbus, OH: Peter Bedrick Books, 2002.

Garden, Edward. *Tchaikovsky.* New York: Oxford University Press, 2000.

Holden, Anthony. *Tchaikovsky: A Biography.* New York: Random House, 1995.

ALFRED, LORD TENNYSON

Born: August 6, 1809
Somersby, England
Died: October 6, 1892
Haslemere, England
English poet

Alfred, Lord Tennyson was regarded by many in his generation as the greatest poet of Victorian England. A superb craftsman in verse, he wrote poetry that ranged from confident assertion to black despair.

His early days

Alfred, Lord Tennyson was born on August 6, 1809, in the village of Somersby, Lincolnshire, England. His parents were the Reverend George Clayton Tennyson and Elizabeth Fytche Tennyson. He had seven brothers and four sisters. His father was an educated man, but was relatively poor. He was a country clergyman (church official). Though he was not very wealthy, he did have a large library. Alfred read widely in this library, and he learned to love reading, especially poetry,

Alfred, Lord Tennyson.
Reproduced by permission of AP/Wide World Photos.

heroic figure) in imitation of Sir Walter Scott (1771–1832). Other models were Lord Byron (1788–1824), and Percy Bysshe Shelley (1792–1822). In 1827 there appeared a small volume entitled *Poems by Two Brothers.* The book, despite its title, included poems by three of the Tennyson brothers, a little less than half of them probably by Alfred. That same year he entered Trinity College, Cambridge University. Tennyson's undergraduate days were a time of intellectual and political turmoil in England. He belonged to a group called the Apostles. The institutions of church and state were being challenged, and the Apostles debated these issues. He also took up the cause of rebels in Spain.

Those who knew Tennyson as a university student were impressed by his commanding physical presence and his youthful literary achievements. In 1831 his father died, and Tennyson left the university without taking a degree.

Love of beauty and obligation to society

In the volume entitled *Poems,* which Tennyson published in 1832, a recurring theme is the conflict between a selfish love of beauty and the obligation to serve society. The collection includes "The Lady of Shalott," a narrative set in the England of King Arthur (a mythical king of England). Tennyson was saddened by some of the reviews of this book and by the death of a close friend. For the next ten years he did not publish anything. In 1840 he invested what money he had inherited in a plan to make woodworking machinery. By 1843 he had lost his small inheritance.

at an early age.

As Tennyson's father grew older, he became more passionate and melancholy (sad). He began drinking heavily, suffered from lapses of memory, and once even tried to kill his eldest son. Misfortune, not surprisingly, haunted the whole Tennyson family. The year he died, the elder Tennyson said of his children, "They are all strangely brought up."

Early poetry and Cambridge

Tennyson began writing poetry as a child. At twelve he wrote a six-thousand-line epic (a long poem about a real or fictional

Turning point

Poems, Two Volumes (1842) signaled a change in Tennyson's fortunes. It contained one of the several poems that would eventually make up the *Idylls of the King.* Other poems in this collection are "Ulysses," a dramatic monologue (speech given by one person) in which the aging king urges his companions to undertake a final heroic journey. In "The Two Voices" he wrote of an interior debate between the wish to die and the will to live. *Poems, Two Volumes* was well received. The prime minister (head of government) of England, who was particularly impressed by "Ulysses," awarded Tennyson a pension (a fixed annual amount of money) that guaranteed him two hundred pounds a year.

In Memoriam

The greatest year of Tennyson's life was 1850. On June 1 he published *In Memoriam,* the long elegy (an artistic piece expressing sadness over someone's death) inspired by the death of his friend Arthur Hallam. Less than two weeks later he married Emily Sellwood, with whom he had fallen in love fourteen years before. Finally, in November, he was appointed poet laureate (official poet of a country) to succeed William Wordsworth (1770–1850). Tennyson's years of uncertainty and financial insecurity were over. He became the highly regarded poetic spokesman of his age.

In Memoriam is a series of 129 lyrics (short poems) of varying length, all composed in the same form. The lyrics may be read individually, rather like the entries in a journal, but the poem has an overall organization. It moves from grief through acceptance to joy. The poem combines private feeling with a confusion over the future of Christianity, which was a feeling many of Tennyson's age group shared.

Although Tennyson was now settled and prosperous, his next book, *Maud and Other Poems* (1855), is notable for another study in sadness. Tennyson described the poem as a "little Hamlet," a reference to the play written by William Shakespeare (1564–1616). It almost certainly expresses some of the author's youthful anxieties as recollected in his middle age. Of the other poems in the 1855 volume, the best-known are "The Charge of the Light Brigade" and "The Ode on the Death of the Duke of Wellington," perhaps the greatest of the poems written by Tennyson in his capacity as poet laureate.

The Idylls of the King

Between 1856 and 1876 Tennyson's principal concern was the composition of a series of narrative poems about King Arthur and the Round Table. He worked on this project for more than twenty years. One section was written as early as 1833. Another part was not published until 1884. As published in 1889, *The Idylls of the King* consisted of twelve blank-verse (unrhymed iambic pentameter [lines of five poetic feet]) narratives (the idylls) that dealt with Arthur, Merlin, Lancelot, Guinevere, and other figures in the court. The individual narratives are linked by a common theme: the destructive effect of incorrect passion on an honorable society. The Round Table is brought down in ruins by the unlawful love of Lancelot and Guinevere.

Some of Tennyson's peers regretted that he had expended so much attention on the legendary past. However, it is clear that this poetic myth of a dying society expressed some of his fears for nineteenth-century England.

Plays and last years

Tennyson had a long and immensely productive literary career. A chronology (list of works by date) shows that he did ambitious work until late in his life. In his sixties he wrote a series of historical verse plays—"Queen Mary" (1875), "Harold" (1876), and "Becket" (1879)—on the "making of England." The plays were intended to revive a sense of national grandeur and to remind the English of their liberation from Roman Catholicism.

Tennyson's last years were crowned with many honors. The widowed Queen Victoria (1819–1901) ranked *In Memoriam* next to the Bible as a comfort in her grief. In 1883 Tennyson was awarded a peerage (rights of nobility).

Tennyson died in Haslemere, England, on October 6, 1892. He was buried in Westminster Abbey after a great funeral. The choir sang a musical setting for "Crossing the Bar," Tennyson's poem that is placed at the end of all collections of his work.

For More Information

Bloom, Harold, ed. *Tennyson.* Broomall, PA: Chelsea House, 1999.

Lang, Cecil Y., and Edgar F. Shannon, eds. *The Letters of Alfred Lord Tennyson.* New York: Oxford University Press, 1981.

Ricks, Christopher. *Tennyson.* 2nd ed. Berkeley: University of California Press, 1989.

Shaw, W. David. *Alfred Lord Tennyson: The Poet in an Age of Theory.* New York: Twayne, 1996.

Tennyson, Hallam. *Alfred, Lord Tennyson: A Memoir.* New York: Macmillan, 1897. Reprint, Boston: Milford House, 1973.

VALENTINA TERESHKOVA

Born: March 6, 1937
Maslennikovo, Russia
Russian cosmonaut

Valentina Tereshkova was the first woman in space, orbiting the earth forty-eight times in *Vostok VI* in 1963. She orbited the Earth for almost three days, showing that women have the same ability in space as men. Later she toured the world promoting Soviet science and feminism. She also served on the Soviet Women's Committee and the Supreme Soviet Presidium (government committee).

Early years

Valentina Vladimirovna "Valya" Tereshkova was born on March 6, 1937, in the Volga River village of Maslennikovo. Her father, Vladimir Tereshkov, was a tractor driver. He had been a Russian Army soldier during World War II (1939–45; a war fought mostly in Europe that pitted Great Britain, France, the United States, and the Soviet Union against Italy, Germany, and Japan). He was killed during the war when Valentina was two. Her mother Elena Fyodorovna Tereshkova was a worker at the Krasny Perekop cotton mill. She single-handedly raised Valentina, her brother Vladimir, and her sister Ludmilla in economically trying conditions. Valentina helped her mother at home and was not able to begin school until she was ten.

Tereshkova later moved to her grandmother's home in nearby Yaroslavl, where she worked as an apprentice at a tire factory in 1954. In 1955 she joined her mother and sister as a loom operator at the cotton mill. Meanwhile, she took correspondence courses (courses taught through the mail) and graduated from the Light Industry Technical School. An ardent communist (believer that there should be no private property), she joined the mill's Komsomol (Young Communist League) and soon advanced to the Communist Party.

Joins space program

In 1959 Tereshkova joined the Yaroslavl Air Sports Club and became a skilled amateur (nonprofessional) parachutist. Inspired by the flight of Yuri Gagarin (1934–1968), the first man in space, she volunteered for the Soviet space program. Although she had no experience as a pilot, her achievement of 126 parachute jumps gained her a position as a cosmonaut (Russian astronaut) in 1961. At the time the Russian space program was looking for people with parachuting experience, because cosmonauts had to parachute from their capsules after they came back into Earth's atmosphere.

Valentina Tereshkova.
Reproduced by permission of the Corbis Corporation.

Five candidates were chosen for a one-time woman-in-space flight. Tereshkova received a military rank in the Russian air force. She trained for eighteen months before becoming chief pilot of the *Vostok VI*. All candidates underwent a rigorous (difficult) course of training, which included tests to determine the effects of being alone for long periods, tests with machines made to create extreme gravity conditions, tests made to duplicate the zero gravity weightless conditions in space, and parachute jumps.

Admiring fellow cosmonaut Yuri Gagarin was quoted as saying, "It was hard for her to master rocket techniques, study spaceship designs and equipment, but she tackled the job stubbornly and devoted much of her own time to study, poring over books and notes in the evening."

Into space

At 12:30 P.M. on June 16, 1963, Junior Lieutenant Tereshkova became the first woman to be launched into space. Using her radio callsign (nickname) Chaika (Seagull), she reported, "I see the horizon. A light blue, a beautiful band. This is the Earth. How beautiful it is! All goes well."

Tereshkova was later seen smiling on Soviet and European TV, pencil and logbook floating weightlessly before her face. Vostok VI made forty-eight orbits (1,200,000 miles) in 70 hours, 50 minutes, coming within 3.1 miles of the previously launched *Vostok V,* which was piloted by cosmonaut Valery Bykovsky. By comparison, the four American astronauts who had been in space before this flight had a combined total of thirty-six orbits.

Tereshkova's flight confirmed Soviet test results that women had the same resistance as men to the physical and psychological stresses of space. In fact, tests showed that women could actually tolerate G-forces (gravitational forces) better than men.

Upon her return Tereshkova and Bykovsky were hailed in Moscow's Red Square, a large plaza in Moscow used for official celebrations. On June 22 at the Kremlin she was named a Hero of the Soviet Union. Presidium Chairman Leonid Brezhnev (1906–1982) decorated her with the Order of Lenin and the Gold Star Medal.

A symbol of the liberated Soviet woman, Tereshkova toured the world as a goodwill ambassador, promoting the equality of the sexes in the Soviet Union. She received a standing ovation at the United Nations. With Gagarin, she traveled to Cuba in October as a guest of the Cuban Women's Federation and then went to the International Aeronautical Federation Conference in Mexico.

Unfortunately, Tereshkova and the other female Russian cosmonauts were not taken as seriously inside the Soviet Union as they were outside. The Russians used the female cosmonauts for publicity purposes to show how women were treated equally in their country.

In truth, however, they were never thought of as the equals of the "regular," that is, male, cosmonauts, and they never received the same quality of flight assignments.

After Tereshkova's flight

On November 3, 1963, Tereshkova married Soviet cosmonaut Colonel Andrian Nikolayev, who had orbited the earth sixty-four times in 1962 in the *Vostok III.* Their daughter, Yelena Adrianovna Nikolayeva, was born on June 8, 1964. Doctors, who were fearful of her parents' space exposure, carefully studied the girl, but no ill effects were found.

Tereshkova, after her flight, continued as an aerospace engineer in the space program. She also worked in Soviet politics, feminism, and culture. She was a deputy to the Supreme Soviet between 1966 and 1989, and a people's deputy from 1989 to 1991. Meanwhile, she was a member of the Supreme Soviet Presidium from 1974 to 1989. During the years from 1968 to 1987, she also served on the Soviet Women's Committee, becoming its head in 1977. Tereshkova headed the USSR's International Cultural and Friendship Union from 1987 to 1991, and later chaired the Russian Association of International Cooperation.

Tereshkova summarized her views on women and science in an article titled "Women in Space," which she wrote in 1970 for the American journal *Impact of Science on Society.* In that article she said, "I believe a woman should always remain a woman and nothing feminine should be alien to her. At the same time I strongly feel that no work done by a woman in the field of science or culture or whatever, however vigorous or demanding, can enter into conflict with her ancient 'wonderful mission'—to love, to be loved—and with her craving for the bliss of motherhood. On the contrary, these two aspects of her life can complement each other perfectly."

Valentina Tereshkova still serves as a model not only for the women of her native country, but for women throughout the world who wish to strive for new goals.

For More Information

Lothian, A. *Valentina: First Woman in Space.* Edinburgh: Pentland Press, 1993.

O'Neill, Lois Decker. "Farthest Out of All: The First Woman in Space," in *Women's Book of World Records and Achievements.* Garden City, NY: Doubleday/Anchor Press, 1979, pp. 739–740.

Sharpe, Mitchell R. *"It Is I, Sea Gull": Valentina Tereshkova, First Woman in Space.* New York: Crowell, 1975.

WILLIAM MAKEPEACE THACKERAY

Born: July 18, 1811
Calcutta, India
Died: December 24, 1863
London, England
English novelist

The English novelist William Makepeace Thackeray created unrivaled panoramas (thorough and complete studies of subjects) of English upper-middle-class life, crowded with memorable characters displaying the realistic mixture of virtue, vanity, and vice.

Early life

William Makepeace Thackeray was born on July 18, 1811, in Calcutta, India. He was the only child of Richmond and Anne Thackeray. His family had made its fortunes in the East India Company for two generations. In 1817, after the death of his father, five-year-old Thackeray was sent to England to live with his aunt while he received his education. He was a precocious (showed the characteristics of an older person at a young age) child and showed a talent for drawing.

Around 1818 Thackeray's mother married Major Carmichael Smyth, an engineer and author. In 1821 the two moved back to England and reunited with Thackeray, who developed a close relationship with his stepfather. When Thackeray was eleven, he was sent to the prestigious Charterhouse School. Schoolmates described him as a student who was not too serious, but very sociable. Also, he did not enjoy or participate in any sports or games. However, he did learn about gentlemanly conduct—an ideal that later he both criticized and upheld.

Education

In 1829 Thackeray entered Trinity College at Cambridge University, where he was only an average student. He left the university the next year, convinced that it was not worth his while to spend more time in pursuit of a second-rate degree under an unsuitable educational institution. A six-month stay in Weimar, Germany, gave Thackeray a more

William Makepeace Thackeray.
Courtesy of the Library of Congress.

sophisticated polish, as well as a more objective view of English manners. After Thackeray returned to London, he began studying law at the Middle Temple. He seemed more devoted to the fashionable but expensive habits of drinking and gambling that he had acquired at Cambridge, however.

At the age of twenty-one Thackeray rejected law and went to Paris, France, to study French, to draw, and to attend plays. The inheritance he acquired at that age soon disappeared into bad business ventures, bad investments, and loans to needy friends. Unfortunately, he was unable to distinguish himself as an artist. He met Isabella Shawe

while in Paris, and they married in 1836. They had two daughters.

Magazine writing

Between 1837 and 1844 Thackeray wrote critical articles on art and literature for numerous papers and journals, but he contributed most of his fiction of this period to *Fraser's Magazine.* In *The Memoirs of C. J. Yellowplush,* which appeared in a series from 1837 to 1838, he parodied (humorously wrote in the style of) the high-flown language of "fashnabble" novels. In *Catherine* (1839–1840) he parodied the popular criminal novel. "A Shabby Genteel Story" (1840) and other short compositions explored the world of rogues (dishonest people) and fools in a spirit of extreme and bitter disappointment. *The Irish Sketch Book* (1843) and *Notes of a Journey from Cornhill to Cario* (1845), supposedly written by the confirmed Londoner Mr. M. A. Titmarsh, were in a lighter vein.

In the fall of 1840 Thackeray's wife suffered a mental breakdown from which she never recovered. This experience profoundly affected his character and work. He became more sympathetic and less harsh in his judgments, and came to value domestic affection as the greatest good thing in life. These new attitudes emerged clearly in the best of his early stories, "The History of Samuel Titmarsh and the Great Hoggarty Diamond" (1841). In this tale an obscure (not distinct) clerk rises to sudden success and wealth but finds true happiness only after ruin has brought him back to hearth and home.

Adopting the mask of an aristocratic (upper-class) London bachelor and clubman named George Savage Fitz-Boodle, Thackeray next wrote a number of papers satirizing (pointing out and devaluing sin or silliness) his way of life. The series called "Men's Wives," which was written at the same time, shows a maturing sense of comedy and tragedy. With *The Luck of Barry Lyndon* (1844) Thackeray returned to an earlier subject, the gentleman scoundrel. His central theme is the ruin of a young man's character by false ideals of conduct and worldly success.

As a regular contributor to the satiric magazine *Punch* between 1844 and 1851, Thackeray finally achieved widespread recognition. His most famous contribution was *The Snobs of England, by One of Themselves* (1846–1847). It was a critical survey of the manners of a period in which the redistribution of wealth and power caused by industrialism (the rise of industry) had shaken old standards of behavior and social relationships.

Thackeray's novels

Vanity Fair (1847–1848) established Thackeray's fame permanently. Set in the time just before and after the Battle of Waterloo (1815; a battle that ended French domination of Europe), this novel is a portrait of society and centers on three families interrelated by acquaintance and marriage. In the unrestrained and resourceful Becky Sharp, Thackeray created one of fiction's most engaging characters.

In *Pendennis* (1849–1850) Thackeray concentrated on one character. The story of the development of a young writer, the first part draws on Thackeray's own life at school, at college, and as a journalist. The second half, which he wrote after a severe illness, lost the novel's focus. It presents only a superficial (having insincere and shallow qualities) analysis of character in Pen's struggle to choose between a practical, worldly life and one of domestic virtue.

The History of Henry Esmond (1852), Thackeray's most carefully planned and executed work, is a historical novel set in the eighteenth century. He felt a temperamental sympathy with this age of satire and urbane wit. *Esmond* presents a vivid and convincing realization of the manners and historical background of the period. It contains some of Thackeray's most complex and firmly controlled characters.

The Newcomes (1854–1855) is another serial. Supposedly written by the hero of *Pendennis*, it chronicles the moral history of four generations of an English family. The most massive and complex of Thackeray's social panoramas, it is also the darkest in its relentless portrayal of the defeat of humane feeling by false standards of respectability.

Later career

Thackeray, feeling that he had written himself out, returned to earlier works for subjects for his later novels. *The Virginians* (1858–1859) follows the fortunes of Henry Esmond's grandsons in the United States, and *The Adventures of Philip* (1862) continues "A Shabby Genteel Story." His later career included an unsuccessful campaign for Parliament as a reform candidate in 1857, and two lecture trips to the United States in 1852 and 1855. A founding editor of the *Cornhill Magazine,* he served it from 1859 to 1862.

Thackeray was 6 feet 3 inches tall, and a pleasant and modest man, fond of good food and wine. In the years of his success he openly took great pleasure in the comforts of the society that he portrayed so critically in his novels. Thackeray died on December 24, 1863, in London, England.

When William Makepeace Thackeray began his literary career, Charles Dickens (1812–1870) dominated English prose (having to do with the common language) fiction. Thackeray's writing style was formed in opposition to Dickens's accusation of social evils, and against the artificial style and sentimentality (emotionalism) of life and moral (having to do with right and wrong) values of the popular historical romances. Although critical of society, Thackeray remained basically conservative (a person who prefers to preserve existing social and political situations without change). He was one of the first English writers of the time to portray the commonplace with greater realism. This approach was carried on in the English novel by Anthony Trollope (1815–1882).

For More Information

Peters, Catherine. *Thackeray's Universe: Shifting Worlds of Imagination and Reality.* New York: Oxford University Press, 1987.

Shillingsburg, Peter L. *William Makepeace Thackeray: A Literary Life.* New York: Palgrave, 2001.

Taylor, D. J. *Thackeray.* London: Chatto & Windus, 1999.

TWYLA THARP

Born: July 1, 1941
Portland, Indiana
American dancer and choreographer

Dancer and choreographer (one who develops and directs dances) Twyla Tharp is known for developing a unique style that merged ballet and modern dance techniques with various forms of American vernacular (everyday) dance.

Early years

Twyla Tharp was born in Portland, Indiana, on July 1, 1941, the daughter of Lecile and William Tharp. Her grandparents on both sides were Quakers and farmers. She was named after Twila Thornburg, the "Princess" of the eighty-ninth Annual Muncie Fair in Indiana. Her mother changed the "i" to "y" because she thought it would look better on a marquee (a sign outside a theater). Twyla was the eldest of four children. She had twin brothers and a sister, Twanette. Her mother, a piano teacher, began giving Twyla lessons when she was eighteen months old.

When Tharp was eight years old, the family moved to the desert town of Rialto, California, where her parents built and operated the local drive-in movie theater. The house her father built in Rialto included a playroom with a practice section featuring a built-in floor for tap dancing, ballet barres (rails used for dance exercises and stretches), and closets filled with acrobatic mats, batons, ballet slippers, castanets (mini-sized percussion instruments that are attached to the thumb and forefinger), tutus, and capes for matador routines. Her well-known tendency as a workaholic and a perfectionist began with her heavily scheduled childhood.

Tharp began her dance lessons at the Vera Lynn School of Dance in San Bernardino, California. Then she studied with the Mraz sisters. She also studied violin, piano, drums, Flamenco dancing, castanets, cymbals, and baton twirling with Ted Otis, a former world champion. At age twelve she began studying ballet. She attended Pacific High School and spent her summers working at the family drive-in.

Young adulthood

Tharp entered Pomona College as a freshman, moving to Los Angeles, California, that summer to continue her dance training with Wilson Morelli and John Butler. At midterm of her sophomore year she transferred to Barnard College in New York City. She studied ballet with Igor Schwezoff at the American Ballet Theater, then with Richard Thomas and his wife, Barbara Fallis. She began attending every dance concert she could and studied with Martha Graham (1893–1991), Merce Cunningham (1919–), and Eugene "Luigi" Lewis, the jazz teacher.

In 1962 Tharp married Peter Young, a painter whom she had met at Pomona College. Her second husband was Bob Huot, an artist. Both marriages ended in divorce. Huot and Tharp had one son, Jesse, who was born in 1971.

Start as an artist

Tharp graduated from Barnard College in 1963 with a degree in art history. She made her professional debut that year with the Paul Taylor dance company, billed as Twyla Young. In the following year, at age twenty-three, she formed her own company and began experimenting with movement in an improvisatory (made up on the spot) manner.

For the first five years Tharp and her dancers struggled, but by the early 1970s she

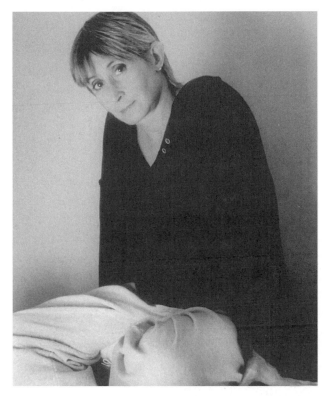

Twyla Tharp.
Reproduced by permission of Archive Photos, Inc.

began to be recognized for the breezy style of dance that added irreverent squiggles, shrugged shoulders, little hops, and jumps to conventional dance steps, a technique she called the "stuffing" of movement phrases.

Among the most creative of her early pieces is *The Fugue* (1970) for four dancers, set to the percussive beat of their own feet on a floor set up with microphones. In 1971 she choreographed *Eight Jelly Rolls* to music by Jelly Roll Morton (1890–1941) and *The Bix Pieces* to music by jazz musician Bix Beiderbecke (1903–1931).

Tharp performed as a member of her company until the mid-1980s. She stopped dancing to concentrate on her many projects for television and film, as well as for her company. She returned to performing in 1991. Other works for her company include *Sue's Leg* (1975), *Baker's Dozen* (1979), *In the Upper Room* (1986), and *Nine Sinatra Songs* (1982) set to the music of Frank Sinatra (1915–1998).

Beyond her own dance company

In 1973 Tharp created a work for the Joffrey Ballet, her first for a company other than her own and her first work for dancers on pointe (on the tip of the toe). Tharp used the Joffrey dancers and her own company in a work entitled *Deuce Coupe,* set to music by the Beach Boys. Teenage graffiti artists created the setting on stage each night. It was a huge success.

Tharp then went on to create *As Time Goes By* (1973) for the Joffrey; five works for the American Ballet Theater, including *Push Comes to Shove* (1976) and *Sinatra Suite* (1984), both with leading roles for Mikhail Baryshnikov (1948–); *Brahms-Handel* (1984) in collaboration with Jerome Robbins for the New York City Ballet; and *Rules of the Game* (1989) for the Paris Opera Ballet.

Tharp's work for her own company and for the ballet troupes made her among the first to demand a "crossover" dancer, one who would be equally at home in ballet and modern dance technique. With the success of *Deuce Coupe,* Tharp was in demand everywhere for her irreverent, funky-look choreography that appealed to the widest array of audiences in the United States.

New projects

Tharp made her first television program for the Public Broadcasting Service (PBS) series *Dance in America* (1976). She continued in television with *Making Television Dance* (1980), *Scrapbook Tapes* (1982), *The Catherine Wheel* (1983) for the British Broadcasting Corporation (BBC), and the television special *Baryshnikov by Tharp* (1985). Her film work began in 1978 with *Hair,* followed by *Ragtime* (1980), *Amadeus* (1984), and *White Nights* (1985). Tharp directed two full-evening productions on Broadway: *The Catherine Wheel* (1981) and the stage adaptation of the film *Singing in the Rain* (1985).

By 1987 Tharp was forced to disband her company because raising money to keep her dancers on salary was getting difficult. She was also interested in various other projects. She was invited to join the American Ballet Theater as artistic associate with Baryshnikov. When he departed the American Ballet Theater in 1989, she left as well, taking her ballets from the theater's repertory (the works regularly presented by a performance company). After that her works were presented by the Boston (Massachusetts) Ballet and the Hubbard Street Dance Company, based in Chicago, Illinois.

Work in the 1990s

After leaving the American Ballet Theater, Tharp embarked on a variety of endeavors that kept her in the forefront of American dance, including an autobiography (a book written by oneself about oneself), *Push Comes to Shove,* published in 1992; a series of tours with pick-up companies of dancers recruited mainly from the ballet troupes where she had worked; and a new work for the Boston Ballet, which premiered in April 1994. Tharp continued to tour nationally and internationally with her assistant, Shelley Washington Whitman, often working without a company of her own or a permanent support base.

In 1996 she choreographed *Born Again,* a trio of new dances. They were performed by a group of thirteen young unknown dancers, who were selected in a series of nationwide auditions and trained by Tharp and Whitman. She returned to the American Ballet Theater in 1995 with successful revisions of two recent works, *Americans We* (1995) and *How Near Heaven* (1995), and a new work, *The Elements.*

In 2000 Tharp choreographed a new work for the New York City Ballet based on Beethoven's (1770–1827) seventh and eighth symphonies. In 2001 Tharp made the Lafayette Presbyterian Church in New York City the permanent home for her company. This was her first permanent base in her thirty-five-year career.

Tharp is the recipient of many awards, including a creative citation in dance from Brandeis University (1972), the MacArthur "Genius" Award (1992), and five honorary (earned without completing the usual requirements) doctorates. She has established her own unique style, combining various dance and musical styles.

For More Information

Livet, Anne, ed. *Contemporary Dance.* New York: Abbeville Press, 1978.

Rogosin, Elinor. *The Dance Makers: Conversations with American Choreographers.* New York: Walker, 1980.

Tharp, Twyla. *Push Comes to Shove.* New York: Bantam, 1992.

CLARENCE THOMAS

Born: June 23, 1948
Pin Point, Georgia
American Supreme Court justice

President George Bush (1924–) named Clarence Thomas to the U.S. Supreme Court in 1991. Since joining the Court, Thomas—the second African American to serve on the court—has often voted with the more conservative justices.

Georgia childhood

Clarence Thomas was born in the tiny coastal town of Pin Point, Georgia, on June 23, 1948. As a very young boy he lived in a one-room shack with dirt floors and no plumbing. When Thomas was two years old, his father walked out on the family. As a result, at the age of seven he and his younger brother were sent to live with their grandfather, Myers Anderson, and his wife in Savannah, Georgia. Anderson, a devout Catholic and active member of the National Association for the Advancement of Colored People (NAACP), sent Thomas to a Catholic school staffed by nuns.

In remarks reported by *Jet* magazine, Thomas has said that he grew up speaking Gullah, a creole dialect spoken by African Americans on the coastal islands of the southeastern United States. Unlike other Supreme Court justices, he rarely asks questions from the bench during court proceedings. He has said that he developed this habit of silent listening when he was young because he found it a struggle to speak "stan-

Clarence Thomas.
Courtesy of the Supreme Court of the United States.

dard English" correctly in school. Nevertheless, he was always a strong student.

In 1964 Thomas's grandfather withdrew him from the all-black religious high school he was attending and sent him to an all-white Catholic boarding school in Savannah. Despite being confronted with racism (a dislike or disrespect of a person based on his or her race), Thomas made excellent grades and played on the school's football team. Thomas's grandfather next sent him to Immaculate Conception Seminary (a place for religious education) in northwestern Missouri after his graduation from high school in 1967. Although Thomas was not the only African American student, he still was troubled by poor race relations. A racist remark he overheard about the assassination of Martin Luther King Jr. (1929–1968) caused him to decide that he would not become a priest.

Turning to the law

Thomas left the seminary and enrolled at Holy Cross, a college in Worcester, Massachusetts. There he was a devoted student who also participated on the track team, did volunteer work in the community, and helped found the Black Student Union at Holy Cross. He also met Kathy Ambush, whom he married after graduating in 1971. The couple had one son, but divorced in 1984. (Thomas married his second wife, Virginia Lamp, in 1987.)

Thanks to his excellent academic record, Thomas was admitted to the law schools at Yale, Harvard, and the University of Pennsylvania. He chose Yale because of the financial support it offered him as part of its affirmative action policy to attract students from racial and ethnic minorities. At Yale he continued to do well academically, and he appeared to fit in socially as well. Yet, years later, he described his "rage" and loneliness at feeling snubbed by white people who viewed him as someone who could only attend Yale through an affirmative action program.

First government posts

Thomas graduated from Yale law school in 1974 and accepted a position on the staff of Missouri's Republican attorney general, John Danforth (1936–). In 1979 he moved to Washington, D.C., and became a legislative assistant to Danforth on the condition that he not be assigned to civil rights issues. His resentment toward some aspects of affirmative action, combined with his grandfather's lessons on self-sufficiency and independence, had moved Thomas into a circle of African American conservatives.

Thomas's conservative ideas soon brought him to the attention of the presidential administration of Ronald Reagan (1911–). In 1981 Thomas was appointed assistant secretary for civil rights in the U.S. Department of Education. Thomas openly stated that minority groups must succeed by their own merit. He asserted that affirmative action programs and civil rights legislation do not improve living standards.

In 1982 Thomas became the chairman of the U.S. Equal Employment Opportunity Commission (EEOC), which was designed to enforce laws against discrimination (unequal treatment based on age, disability, nationality, race, religion, or sex) in the workplace. Thomas served two consecutive terms as chairman, despite having previously sworn he would never work at the EEOC.

Supreme Court nomination

In 1990 President George Bush (1924–) appointed Thomas to the Washington, D.C., circuit of the United States Court of Appeals, a common stepping stone to the Supreme Court. Thomas served on this court for only one year. Despite this relatively limited experience, Bush nominated Thomas to replace retiring Supreme Court Justice Thurgood Marshall (1908–1993) on July 1, 1991.

Senate hearings to confirm Thomas's nomination appeared to be moving along smoothly until allegations by Anita Hill, a former EEOC employee, were made public. On October 8, Hill held a press conference in which she made public the main points of testimony she previously had given the Federal Bureau of Investigation (FBI). Protests by some women's groups led the Senate confirmation committee to publicly review Hill's charges.

Anita Hill's charges

Hill charged that while she worked at the EEOC nearly a decade earlier Thomas pestered her for dates and told stories in her presence about pornographic film scenes and his own sexual ability. Hill claimed that Thomas's actions made it difficult for her to do her job and caused physical distress. Nevertheless, she continued to contact Thomas voluntarily even after he helped arrange for her appointment as a law professor at the University of Oklahoma.

Hill, Thomas, and witnesses on both sides testified about the allegations during the televised confirmation hearings, which were among the most widely viewed political events in television history. Thomas denied any wrongdoing. He remarked that the process had been a harrowing personal ordeal for him and his wife. Referring to the acts of violence by which whites had terrorized blacks in the American South in which he grew up, Thomas characterized the televised hearings as a "high-tech lynching." In the end, Thomas was confirmed by a 52-48 margin, the smallest—according to *Time* magazine—by which any justice has been confirmed in the past century.

Hill's allegations helped to make sexual harassment a major political issue. The phrase itself had varying and even conflicting definitions. Nevertheless, local, state, and national laws were passed to stop workplace practices that could make other employees uncomfortable. Meanwhile, articles and books continued to debate whether Hill's specific charges against Thomas were valid.

The quiet justice

After joining the Supreme Court, Thomas voted frequently with Justice Antonin Scalia (1936–) and Chief Justice William Rehnquist (1924–), thereby siding with the court's leading conservatives (people who resist change and prefer to keep traditions). Although generally silent during oral arguments at court proceedings, Thomas has been visible in his opinion writing from the beginning. Reviewers of his legal essays and opinions (the written arguments by which court justices explain the reasons for their ruling or their disagreement with the ruling) agree that they are clear, well researched, and consistent. However, African American political groups criticized Thomas for maintaining his conservative values in cases affecting minorities.

For the first few years after his appointment, Thomas tended to keep a low public profile. Starting in 1996, however, he began to make occasional appearances before conservative political groups. Since the election of George W. Bush (1946–) as president in 2000, he has been increasingly hailed as a judicial hero by American conservatives.

For More Information

Danforth, John. *Resurrection: The Confirmation of Clarence Thomas.* New York: Free Press, 1994.

Gerber, Scott Douglas. *First Principles: The Jurisprudence of Clarence Thomas.* New York: New York University Press, 1999.

Greenya, John. *Silent Justice: The Clarence Thomas Story.* Ft. Lee, NJ: Barricade Books, 2001.

Halliburton, Warren J. *Clarence Thomas, Supreme Court Justice.* Hillside, NJ: Enslow, 1993.

Smith, Christopher E., and Joyce A. Baugh. *The Real Clarence Thomas: Confirmation Veracity Meets Performance Reality.* New York: P. Lang, 2000.

Thomas, Andrew Peyton. *Clarence Thomas: A Biography.* San Francisco: Encounter Books, 2001.

DYLAN THOMAS

Born: October 27, 1914
Swansea, Carmarthenshire, Wales
Died: November 9, 1953
New York, New York
Welsh poet

The Welsh poet Dylan Thomas has been hailed as one of the most important poets of the century. His lyrics rank among the most powerful and captivating of modern poetry.

Welsh childhood

Dylan Marlais Thomas was born in the Welsh seaport of Swansea, Carmarthenshire, Wales, on October 27, 1914. His father, David John, was an English teacher and a would-be poet from whom Dylan inherited his intellectual and literary abilities. From his mother, Florence, a simple and religious woman, Dylan inherited his mood, temperament, and respect for his Celtic heritage. He had one older sister, Nancy. He attended the Swansea Grammar School, where he received all of his formal education. As a student he made contributions to the school magazine and was keenly interested in local folklore (stories passed down within a culture). He said that as a boy he was "small, thin, indecisively active, quick to get dirty, curly." During these early school years, Thomas befriended Daniel Jones, another local schoolboy. The two would write hundreds of poems together, and as adults Jones would edit a collection of Thomas's poetry.

After leaving school, Thomas supported himself as an actor, reporter, reviewer, scriptwriter, and with various odd jobs. When he was twenty-two years old, he married Caitlin Macnamara, by whom he had two sons, Llewelyn and Colm, and a daughter, Aeron. After his marriage, Thomas moved to the fishing village of Laugharne, Carmarthenshire.

Dylan Thomas.
Reproduced by permission of AP/Wide World Photos.

Begins writing career

To support his growing family, Thomas was forced to write radio scripts for the Ministry of Information (Great Britain's information services) and documentaries for the British government. He also served as an aircraft gunner during World War II (1939–45; a war fought between Germany, Japan, and Italy, the Axis powers; and England, France, the Soviet Union, and the United States, the Allies). After the war he became a commentator on poetry for the British Broadcasting Corporation (BBC). In 1950 Thomas made the first of three lecture tours through the United States—the others were in 1952 and 1953—in which he gave more than one hundred poetry readings. In these appearances he half recited, half sang the lines in his "Welsh singing" voice.

Thomas's poetic output was not large. He wrote only six poems in the last six years of his life. A grueling lecture schedule greatly slowed his literary output in these years. His belief that he would die young led him to create "instant Dylan"—the persona of the wild young Welsh bard, damned by drink and women, that he believed his public wanted. When he was thirty-five years old, he described himself as "old, small, dark, intelligent, and darting-doting-dotting eyed . . . balding and toothlessing."

During Thomas's visit to the United States in 1953, he was scheduled to read his own and other poetry in some forty university towns throughout the country. He also intended to work on the libretto (text) of an opera for Igor Stravinsky (1882–1971) in the latter's California home. Thomas celebrated his thirty-ninth birthday in New York City in a mood of gay exhilaration, following the extraordinary success of his just-published *Collected Poems*. The festivities ended in his collapse and illness. On November 9, 1953, he died in St. Vincent's Hospital in New York City. Some reports attribute his death to pneumonia brought on by alcoholism, others to encephalopathy, a brain disease. His body was returned to Laugharne, Wales, for burial.

Literary works

Thomas published his first book of poetry, *Eighteen Poems* (1934), when he was not yet twenty years old. "The reeling excitement of a poetry-intoxicated schoolboy smote the Philistine as hard a blow with one small book as Swinburne had with *Poems and Ballads*," wrote Kenneth Rexroth. Thomas's second and third volumes were *Twenty-five Poems* (1936) and *The Map of Love* (1939). The poems of his first three volumes were collected in *The World I Breathe* (1939).

By this time Thomas was being hailed as the most spectacular of the surrealist poets, or poets who used fantastic imagery of the subconscious in their verse. He acknowledged his debt to James Joyce (1882–1941) and dotted his pages with invented words and puns (the use of two or more words that sound the same, usually for humorous pur-

poses). Thomas also acknowledged his debt to Sigmund Freud (1856–1939), stating: "Poetry is the rhythmic, inevitably narrative, movement from an overclothed blindness to a naked vision. . . . Poetry must drag further into the clear nakedness of light more even of the hidden causes than Freud could realize."

A Portrait of the Artist as a Young Dog (1940) is a collection of humorous autobiographical (having to do with writing about oneself) sketches. Thomas loved the wild landscape of Wales, and he put much of his childhood and youth into these stories. He published two more new collections of poetry, both of which contained some of his finest work: *Deaths and Entrances* (1946) and *In Country Sleep* (1951). *Collected Poems, 1934–1953* (1953) contains all of his poetry that he wished to preserve.

Themes and style

Thomas claimed that his poetry was "the record of my individual struggle from darkness toward some measure of light. . . . To be stripped of darkness is to be clean, to strip of darkness is to make clean." He also wrote that his poems "with all their crudities, doubts, and confusions, are written for the love of man and in praise of God, and I'd be a damned fool if they weren't." Passionate and intense, vivid and violent, Thomas wrote that he became a poet because "I had fallen in love with words." His sense of the richness and variety and flexibility of the English language shines through all of his work.

The theme of all of Thomas's poetry is the celebration of the divine (godly) purpose he saw in all human and natural processes. The cycle of birth and flowering and death, of love and death, are also found throughout his poems. He celebrated life in the seas and fields and hills and towns of his native Wales. In some of his shorter poems he sought to recapture a child's innocent vision of the world.

Thomas was passionately dedicated to his "sullen art," and he was a competent, finished, and occasionally complex craftsman. He made, for example, more than two hundred versions of "Fern Hill" before he was satisfied with it. His early poems are relatively mysterious and complex in sense but simple and obvious in pattern. His later poems, on the other hand, are simple in sense but complex in sounds.

Under Milk Wood, a radio play commissioned by the BBC (published 1954), was Thomas's last completed work. This poem-play is not a drama but a parade of strange, outrageous, and charming Welsh villagers. During the twenty-four hours presented in the play, the characters remember and ponder the casual and crucial moments of their lives. *Adventures in the Skin Trade and Other Stories* (1955) contains all the uncollected stories and shows the wit and humor that made Thomas an enchanting companion.

For More Information

Brinnin, John Malcolm. *Dylan Thomas in America.* New York: Paragon House, 1989.

Ferris, Paul. *Dylan Thomas: The Biography.* Washington, DC: Counterpoint, 2000.

Fryer, Jonathan. *Dylan: The Nine Lives of Dylan Thomas.* London: K. Cathie, 1993.

Goodby, John, and Chris Wigginton, eds. *Dylan Thomas.* New York: Palgrave, 2001.

Thomas, David N. *Dylan Thomas: A Farm, Two Mansions and a Bungalow.* Bridgend, Wales: Saren, 2000.

Thomas, Dylan. *Portrait of the Artist as a Young Dog.* Norfolk, CT: New Directions, 1940.

HENRY DAVID THOREAU

Born: July 12, 1817
Concord, Massachusetts
Died: May 6, 1862
Concord, Massachusetts
American writer

Henry David Thoreau was an accomplished American writer, as well as an outstanding transcendentalist, a person who seeks to rise above common thought or ideas. He is best known for his classic book, *Walden.*

New England childhood

Henry David Thoreau was born on July 12, 1817, in Concord, Massachusetts, and lived there most of his life; it became, in fact, his universe. His parents were permanently poor, as his father failed in several business ventures. Thoreau was raised along with three siblings, but his brother's death in 1842 and a sister's death in 1849 deeply affected him. He attended Concord Academy, where his record was good but not outstanding. Nevertheless, he entered Harvard University in 1833 as a scholarship student. Young as he was he established a reputation at Harvard

Henry David Thoreau.
Courtesy of the Library of Congress.

for being an individualist, one who follows his own will. He was friendly enough with his fellow students, yet he soon saw that many of their values could never become his.

After Thoreau graduated in 1837, he faced the problem of earning a living. He taught briefly in the town school, taught for a longer while at a private school his brother John had started, and also made unsuccessful efforts to find a teaching job away from home. Meanwhile, he was spending a good deal of time writing—he had begun a journal in 1837, which ran to fourteen volumes of close-packed print when published after his death. He wanted, he decided, to be a poet.

Enchanted by nature

America was not supportive of its poets as a rule. Thoreau spent much of his life attempting to do just what he wanted while at the same time surviving, for he wanted to live as a poet as well as to write poetry. He loved nature and could stay indoors only with effort. The beautiful woods, meadows, and waters of the Concord neighborhood attracted him like a drug. He wandered among them by day and by night, observing the world of nature closely and sympathetically. He named himself, half humorously, "inspector of snow-storms and rainstorms."

Thoreau's struggles were watched with compassion by an older Concord neighbor, who was also one of America's great men— Ralph Waldo Emerson (1803–1882). Emerson proved to be Thoreau's best friend. In 1841 Emerson invited Thoreau to live at his home and to make himself useful there only when it would not interfere with his writing. In 1843 he got Thoreau a job tutoring in Staten Island, New York, so that he could be close to the New York City literary market.

Most of the time, however, Thoreau lived at home. A small room was all he needed. He never married, and he required little. At one point he built a cabin at Walden Pond just outside Concord, on land owned by Emerson, and lived in it from 1845 to 1846. There, he wrote much of his book *Walden*.

Literary works

Thoreau wrote nature essays both early and late in his career. They range from the "Natural History of Massachusetts" (1842), which is supposedly a review but seems to be a delightful discussion on the world of nature around him, to the poetic "Autumnal Tints" and "Walking" (both 1862), which appeared shortly after his death. He also wrote three rather slender volumes that might be termed travel books: *The Maine Woods* (1864), *Cape Cod* (1865), and *A Yankee in Canada* (1866). Each was made up of essays and was first serialized (arranged and distributed at set times by a publisher) in a magazine. They were published in book form after Thoreau's death on May 6, 1862.

Thoreau's two most interesting books are hard to classify, or sort. They are not travel books, nor are they polemics (arguments to oppose an accepted opinion). The first is *A Week on the Concord and Merrimack Rivers* (1849), issued at his own expense. As a framework he used two river adventures he and his brother John had made, and he drew heavily from his journal of that time. He filled out the book with other journalizing (keeping a record of), bits of poetry, old college themes, and youthful philosophizing (seeking knowledge). The result was a book that a few enthusiasts (people who follow a special interest) hailed but that the public ignored.

Walden (1854), however, attracted followers from the beginning, and today editions of it crowd the bookshelves of the world. Though basically it is an account of Thoreau's stay beside Walden Pond, it is also many other things. It is a how-to-do-it book, for it tells how to live one's life with a minimum of distasteful labor. It is an apologia, or formal defense. It is a spiritual (or rather, philosophical) autobiography (a book written about oneself). It is a book of seasons. And it is a defiant declaration to the world, for Thoreau was crowing in triumph at his ability to live as he pleased.

The transcendentalist

Thoreau was, so to speak, a working transcendentalist. Thoreau put his personal stamp on those higher ideals of transcendentalism and translated them into action. For example, when a neighbor wanted to hire him to build a wall, Thoreau asked himself whether this was the best way to use his time and decided it was much better to walk in the woods. Transcendentalists regarded nature, both as symbol and actuality. Thoreau made Mother Nature into something like a deity, or god, and he spent more time in the world of nature than any other transcendentalist.

As Thoreau grew into middle age, he inevitably made a few changes. He had to take over the little family business after his father died, since there was no one else to do it. He did some surveying (mapping out land for development) and he became more of a botanist (one who studies plants) and less of a transcendentalist. His spells of illness increased during the 1850s. By December 1861 he no longer left the Thoreau house. By the next spring he could hardly talk above a whisper. He died on May 6, 1862. In spite of the painful last years of his life, his end was peaceful. "Never saw a man dying with so much pleasure and peace," one of his townsmen observed.

During an elegy (a poem to praise the dead) for Thoreau, Emerson characterized him as a hermit and stoic (unaffected by pleasure or pain), but added that he had a softer side that showed especially when he was with young people he liked. Furthermore, Thoreau was resourceful and ingenious—he had to be, to live the life he wanted. He was patient and had to be to get the most out of nature. He could have been a notable leader, given all of those qualities, but, Emerson remarked sadly, Thoreau chose a different path. Nevertheless, Thoreau was a remarkable man, and Emerson gave him the highest possible praise by calling him wise. "His soul," said Emerson in conclusion, "was made for the noblest society."

For More Information

Anderson, Charles R. *The Magic Circle of Walden*. New York: Holt, Rinehart, and Winston, 1968.

Harding, Walter. *The Days of Henry Thoreau*. New York: Knopf, 1965. Reprint, Princeton, NJ: Princeton University Press, 1992.

Paul, Sherman. *The Shores of America: Thoreau's Inward Exploration*. Urbana: University of Illinois Press, 1958. Reprint, New York, Russell & Russell, 1971.

Richardson, Robert D. *Henry Thoreau: A Life of the Mind*. Berkeley: University of California Press, 1986.

Salt, Henry Stephens. *The Life of Henry David Thoreau*. London: R. Bentley & Son, 1890.

Thoreau, Henry David. *Walden*. Boston: Ticknor and Fields, 1862. Multiple reprints.

JIM THORPE

Born: May 28, 1888
Bellemonta, Oklahoma
Died: March 28, 1953
Lomita, California
American football player, baseball player, and Olympic athlete

American track star and professional football and baseball player Jim Thorpe was the hero of the 1912 Olympic Games in Stockholm, Sweden, but had his gold medals taken from him for his status as a professional athlete.

Athletic youth

James Francis Thorpe (Native American name, Wa-tho-huck, or Bright Path) was born south of Bellemonta, near Prague, Oklahoma, on May 28, 1888. He was the son of Hiran P. Thorpe, of Irish and Sac-Fox Indian descent, and Charlotte View, of Potowatomi and Kickapoo descent. He grew up with five siblings, although his twin brother, Charlie, died at the age of nine. Jim's athletic abilities showed at a very early age, when he learned to ride horses and swim at the age of three. Thorpe first attended the Sac-Fox Indian Agency school near Tecumseh, Oklahoma, before being sent to the Haskell Indian School near Lawrence, Kansas, in 1898.

When Thorpe was sixteen, he was recruited to attend a vocational school (a school to learn a trade) for Native Americans, the Carlisle Indian School in Pennsylvania. His track potential was obvious in 1907, when he cleared the high jump bar at 5 feet 9 inches while dressed in street clothes. Glenn S. "Pop" Warner, the school's legendary track and football coach, asked him to join the track team. That fall Thorpe made the varsity football team, playing some but starting the next year as a running back. In 1908 Thorpe was awarded third team All-American status, the highest honor for a collegiate athlete.

Following the spring of 1909, when Thorpe starred in track, he left the Carlisle school with two other students to go to North

Carolina, where they played baseball at Rocky Mount in the Eastern Carolina Association. Thorpe pitched and played first base for what he said was $15 per week. The next year he played for Fayetteville, winning ten games and losing ten games pitching, while batting .236. These two years of paid performances in minor league baseball would later tarnish his 1912 amateur Olympic status.

Thorpe had matured to almost six feet in height and 185 pounds and led Carlisle to outstanding football seasons in 1911 and 1912. In 1911, against Harvard University's undefeated team led by the renowned coach Percy Houghton, Thorpe kicked four field goals—two over 40 yards—and the game ended in a stunning 18-15 victory. Carlisle lost only two games in 1911 and 1912, against Penn State and Syracuse University, but conquered such teams as the U.S. Army, Georgetown University, Harvard, and the University of Pittsburgh. In his last year he scored twenty-five touchdowns and 198 points, and for the second year in a row he was named All-American by football pioneer Walter Camp (1859–1925).

Star of the 1912 Olympics

During the summer of 1912, before Thorpe's last year at Carlisle, he was chosen to represent the United States at the Stockholm Olympics in the decathlon (ten track events) and the pentathlon (five track events). He was an easy victor in the pentathlon, winning four of the five events (broad jump, 200 meter dash, discus, and 1,500 meter race), losing only the javelin. In the decathlon Thorpe set an Olympic mark of 8,413 points that would stand for two

Jim Thorpe.
Reproduced by permission of Archive Photos, Inc.

decades. King Gustav of Sweden addressed Thorpe as the "greatest athlete in the world" and presented him with several gifts, including one from Czar Nicholas of Russia (1868–1918)—a silver, 30-pound likeness of a Viking ship, lined with gold and containing precious jewels.

The gold medal ceremony for the decathlon, Thorpe said, was the proudest moment of his life. A half-year later charges against Thorpe for professionalism led to Thorpe's confession that he had been paid to play baseball in North Carolina in 1909 and 1910. (Actually, Thorpe had been paid cash by coach "Pop" Warner as an athlete at

Carlisle before that.) Shortly thereafter the Amateur Athletic Union (AAU) and the American Olympic Committee declared Thorpe a professional, asked Thorpe to return the medals won at the Olympics, and erased his name from the record books.

Thorpe, a great athlete but not a great baseball player, almost immediately signed a large $6,000-per-year, three-year contract with the New York Giants, managed by John J. McGraw. Thorpe was to be mainly as a gate attraction. His six-year major league career resulted in a .252 batting average with three teams: the New York Giants, the Cincinnati Reds, and the Boston Braves. He batted .327 in 1919, his last year in the majors.

Thorpe signed to play professional football in 1915 with the Canton Bulldogs for the "enormous" sum of $250 a game. Attendance at Canton immediately skyrocketed, and Thorpe led Canton to several championships over its chief rival, the Massillon Tigers. In 1920 he was appointed president of the American Professional Football Association, which would become the National Football League. Thorpe was the chief drawing power in professional football until Red Grange (1903–1991) entered the game in 1925.

The campaign to restore his medals

Honors for past athletic achievements kept coming to Thorpe. At mid-century the Associated Press (AP) polled sportswriters and broadcasters to determine the greatest football player and most outstanding male athlete of the first half of the twentieth century. Thorpe outdistanced Red Grange and Bronko Nagurski (1908–1990) for the title of the greatest football player. He led Babe Ruth (1895–1948) and Jack Dempsey (1896–

1983) for the most outstanding male athlete, being paired with Babe Didrikson Zaharias (1914–1956), the outstanding female athlete.

This recognition, however, did not influence the United States Olympic Committee to help restore Thorpe's Olympic medals. There had been an attempt in 1943 by the Oklahoma legislature to get the AAU to reinstate Thorpe as an amateur. Thirty years later the AAU did restore his amateur status. In 1952, shortly before his death, there was an attempt by Congressman Frank Bow of Canton, Ohio, to get Avery Brundage, president of the United States Olympic Committee (USOC) to use his good offices to restore Thorpe's medals to him. This effort failed. Following Brundage's death in 1975, the USOC requested the International Olympic Committee to restore Thorpe's medals, but it was turned down. Not until 1982, when USOC president William E. Simon met with the International Olympic Committee president Juan Antonio Samaranch, was the action finally taken.

Outside of athletics, Thorpe's life had much more tragedy than two gold medal losses. Besides his twin brother Charlie's death when he was nine years old, his mother died of blood poisoning before he was a teenager. Four years later, shortly after Thorpe entered Carlisle, his father died. Following his marriage to Iva Miller in 1913, their first son died at the age of four from polio, a life-threatening disease that affects development in children. Twice divorced, he had one boy and three girls from his first marriage, and four boys from his second marriage in 1926 to Freeda Kirkpatrick. His third marriage was to Patricia Askew in 1945. His place in sports history, though, was established well before he died of a heart attack on March 28, 1953 in Lomita, California, at the age of sixty-four.

For More Information

Birchfield, D. L. *Jim Thorpe, World's Greatest Athlete.* Parsippany, NJ: Modern Curriculum Press, 1994.

Farrell, Edward. *Young Jim Thorpe: All-American Athlete.* Mahweh, NJ: Troll Associates, 1996.

Lipsyte, Robert. *Jim Thorpe: 20th-Century Jock.* New York: HarperCollins, 1993.

Richards, Gregory B. *Jim Thorpe, World's Greatest Athlete.* Chicago: Children's Press, 1984.

Wheeler, Robert W. *Jim Thorpe: World's Greatest Athlete.* Norman: University of Oklahoma Press, 1979.

JAMES THURBER

Born: December 8, 1894
Columbus, Ohio
Died: November 2, 1961
New York, New York
American writer and artist

James Thurber was an American writer and artist. One of the most popular humorists (writers of clever humor) of his time, Thurber celebrated in stories and in cartoons the comic frustrations of eccentric yet ordinary people.

Early life in Ohio

James Grove Thurber was born on December 8, 1894, in Columbus, Ohio, to Charles Leander and Mary Agnes Thurber. The family soon moved to Virginia where Charles was employed as a secretary to a congressman. While playing with his older brother, Thurber was permanently blinded in his left eye after being shot with an arrow. Problems with his eyesight would plague Thurber for much of his life. After Charles's employer lost a reelection campaign, the Thurbers were forced to move back to Ohio. Thurber attended the local public schools and graduated high school with honors in 1913. He went on to attend Ohio State University—though he never took a degree— and worked for some years afterwards in Ohio as a journalist.

Life in New York City

Thurber moved to New York City in 1926 and a year later he met writer E. B. White (1899–1985) and was taken onto the staff of the *New Yorker* magazine. In collaboration with White he produced his first book, *Is Sex Necessary?* (1929). By 1931 his first cartoons began appearing in the *New Yorker.* These primitive yet highly stylized characterizations included seals, sea lions, strange tigers, harried men, determined women, and, most of all, dogs. Thurber's dogs became something like a national comic institution, and they dotted the pages of a whole series of books.

Thurber's book *The Seal in the Bedroom* appeared in 1932, followed in 1933 by *My Life and Hard Times.* He published *The Middle-aged Man on the Flying Trapeze* in 1935, and by 1937, when he published *Let Your*

James Thurber.
Reproduced by permission of AP/Wide World Photos.

Later years

The last twenty years of Thurber's life were filled with material and professional success in spite of his handicap. He published at least fourteen more books, including *The Thurber Carnival* (1945), *Thurber Country* (1953), and the extremely popular account of the life of the *New Yorker* editor Harold Ross, *The Years with Ross* (1959). A number of his short stories were made into movies, including "The Secret Life of Walter Mitty" (1947), which is also regarded as one of the best short stories written in the twentieth century.

Thurber died of pneumonia (an infection of the lungs) on November 2, 1961, just weeks after suffering a stroke. Thurber left behind a peculiar and unique comic world that was populated by his curious animals, who watched close by as aggressive women ran to ground apparently spineless men. But beneath their tame and defeated exteriors, Thurber's men dreamed of wild escape and epic adventure and, so, in their way won out in the battle of the sexes.

For More Information

Bernstein, Burton. *Thurber: A Biography.* New York: Dodd, Mead, 1975. Reprint, New York: Arbor House, 1985.

Fensch, Thomas. *The Man Who Was Walter Mitty: The Life and Work of James Thurber.* The Woodlands, TX: New Century Books, 2000.

Grauer, Neil A. *Remember Laughter: A Life of James Thurber.* Lincoln: University of Nebraska Press, 1994.

Kinney, Harrison. *James Thurber: His Life and Times.* New York: H. Holt, 1995.

Mind Alone!, he had become so successful that he left his position on the *New Yorker* staff to become a freelance writer and to travel abroad.

The Last Flower appeared in 1939; that year Thurber collaborated with White on a play, *The Male Animal.* The play was a hit when it opened in 1940. But this was also the year that Thurber was forced to undergo a series of eye operations for cataract and trachoma, two serious eye conditions. His eyesight grew steadily worse until, in 1951, it was so weak that he did his last drawing. He spent the last decade of his life in blindness.

Thurber, James. *My Life and Hard Times*. New York: Harper, 1933. Reprint, New York: Perennial Classics, 1999.

MARSHAL TITO

Born: May 25, 1892
Kumrovec, Croatia
Died: May 4, 1980
Ljubljana, Yugoslavia
Yugoslav politician and president

The Yugoslav statesman Marshal Tito became president of Yugoslavia in 1953. He directed the rebuilding of a Yugoslavia devastated in World War II and the bringing together of Yugoslavia's different peoples until his death in 1980.

Brief history of Yugoslavia

From its creation in 1918 until the country broke apart in the early 1990s, Yugoslavia was a multinational state composed of many ethnic (cultural) and religious groups. The various ethnic groups were dissatisfied with their status in the new state, opposed the domination of one ethnic group, the Serbs, and called for greater national and political rights. The country's economy was unstable and the country was surrounded by enemy states dedicated to its destruction.

Because of these conditions, many groups found support for their activities and sought to destroy order. Two of these groups were the fascists, who believed in a strong central government headed by a dictator, or sole ruler, and the communists, who believed that goods and services should be owned and distributed among the people. Among the communists who supported a revolutionary change was Josip Broz, who is commonly known as Marshal Tito.

Tito's early years

Tito was born Josip Broz on May 25, 1892, the seventh of fifteen children of a peasant (poor farmer) family of Kumrovec, a village near Zagreb, Croatia. Tito began working on his family's farm when he was just seven years old. At the same time, he attended an elementary school where he studied until he was twelve years old. When he was fifteen years old, he began training to become a locksmith. During this time he also went to night school where he studied subjects including geography, history, and languages.

After spending several years working as a mechanic in Croatia, Slovenia, Austria, and Germany, Tito was drafted into the Austro-Hungarian army at the outbreak of World War I (1914–18) where German-led forces fought for control of Europe. He was wounded and captured by the Russians, and spent time in a prisoner-of-war camp. Tito soon joined the Red Army, the Communist group that rose to power after the Russian Revolution of October 1917 and would ultimately lead to the creation of the Communist Soviet Union.

In 1920 Tito returned to Croatia and joined the Communist Party of Yugoslavia. In 1928 he was sentenced to five years' imprisonment for Communist activity. After spending several years in the Soviet Union (the name of Communist Russia), in 1934 he was

Marshal Tito.

Tito was able to develop the Yugoslav Communist Party into a powerful political and military organization during World War II (1939–45), where the Axis powers of Germany, Italy, and Japan clashed with the Allied powers of America, Great Britain, and the Soviet Union.

After the Axis invasion of Yugoslavia in April 1941 and Germany's attack on the Soviet Union in June, Tito ordered the Communist Party to activate a small force to resist the Axis powers. At the same time, a movement headed by Colonel (later General) Draza Mihajlovic gained the support of the Yugoslav king Peter II. Allied officers reported that Tito's movement supported national unity rather than communism, and at the same time reported that Mihajlovic's forces had been cooperating with the Axis troops. This conflict between the two resistance leaders led to a bloody civil war.

Communist revolution in Yugoslavia

Tito's greatest accomplishment during World War II was the organization of perhaps the most effective resistance movement in the history of communism. While resisting the Axis forces, he embarked upon a communist revolution. His forces proceeded to destroy the class structure, destroy the old social and economic order, and lay the foundations for a postwar communist state system. By the end of the war, the communist military force was expanded into a large army (the National Liberation Army).

Basic policies of the Communist Party regarding the new Yugoslav state, such as federal organization of the country, were partially begun during the war. Tito provided the country with a system of temporary revolu-

elected to the Central Committee and Politburo of the Yugoslav Party, the top offices of the Communist Party. In 1937 he was appointed secretary general of the Yugoslav Party after many other untrustworthy members were executed.

World War II

Tito was able to revive the Yugoslav Party and to make it a highly disciplined organization. He cleaned the ranks of disloyal members and gave the party a clear-cut and realistic policy to unite the country. For the first time, the party firmly supported the preservation rather than the breakup of Yugoslavia.

tionary government—the Committee for the National Liberation of Yugoslavia. Skillfully he took advantage of every social opportunity to pursue communist political and military goals. Neither his domestic rivals nor the powerful forces of nations that occupied Yugoslavia were able to cope with the widespread activities of Tito's followers.

In December 1943 the Allies, ignoring King Peter who was exiled (forced to live) in London, declared that Tito's supporters would lead the Yugoslav forces against the occupying Axis troops. Tito's forces and those of the Soviet Union entered Belgrade, Yugoslavia, on October 20, 1944. Tito's men, however, drove the Germans from the country essentially by their own efforts, an event of the greatest importance in the future history of Yugoslavia. Unlike communist leaders of other East European countries, Tito himself had commanded the forces defeating the Axis troops and had not entered his country with the victorious Red Army. In August 1945 the Federal Republic of Yugoslavia was created.

Postwar years

From 1945 to 1953 Tito acted as prime minister and minister of defense in the government, whose most dramatic political action was the capture, trial, and execution of General Mihajlovic in 1946. Between 1945 and 1948 Tito led his country through an extreme form of dictatorship (rule by one all-powerful person) in order to mold Yugoslavia into a state modeled after the Soviet Union. In January 1953, he was named first president of Yugoslavia and president of the Federal Executive Council. In 1963 he was named president for life.

By 1953 Tito had changed Yugoslavia's relationship with the Soviet Union. He refused to approve Soviet leader Joseph Stalin's (1879–1953) plans for integrating Yugoslavia into the East European Communist bloc (a group aligned for a common cause). He now started on his own policies, which involved relaxing of central control over many areas of national life, and putting it back into the control of the citizens. Although relations between the Soviet Union and Yugoslavia improved when Soviet leader Nikita Khrushchev (1894–1971) visited Belgrade after Stalin's death in 1955, they never returned to what they were before 1948.

Tito attempted to build a bloc of "nonaligned" countries after Stalin's death. Under his leadership, Yugoslavia maintained friendly ties with the Arab states and criticized Israeli aggression in the Arab-Israeli War of 1967. He protested the Soviet invasion of Hungary in 1956 and Czechoslovakia in 1968, and maintained friendly relations with Romania after Nicolae Ceausescu (1918–1989) became its leader in 1965. Under Tito's leadership Yugoslavia was a very active member of the United Nations (UN), a multinational organization aimed at world peace.

Tito was married twice and had two sons. His first wife was Russian. After World War II he married Jovanka, a Serbian woman from Croatia many years younger than him. His wife often accompanied him on his travels. President for life, Tito ruled until his death in Ljubljana, Yugoslavia, on May 4, 1980, maintaining several homes, where he entertained a wide variety of international visitors and celebrities.

For More Information

Dedijer, Vladimir. *The Battle Stalin Lost: Memoirs of Yugoslavia, 1948–53.* New York: Viking, 1970.

Dedijer, Vladimir. *Tito.* New York: Simon and Schuster, 1952. Reprint, New York: Arno Press, 1972.

Pavlowitch, Stevan K. *Tito—Yugoslavia's Great Dictator: A Reassessment.* Columbus: Ohio State University Press, 1992.

West, Richard. *Tito: And the Rise and Fall of Yugoslavia.* New York: Carroll & Graf, 1995.

J. R. R. TOLKIEN

Born: January 3, 1892
Bloemfontein, South Africa
Died: September 2, 1973
Bournemouth, England
English writer, essayist, poet, and editor

J. R. R. Tolkien gained a reputation during the 1960s and 1970s as a cult figure (a person with a devoted following amongst a small group of people) among youths discouraged by war and the technological age from his work *The Hobbit* and the trilogy that followed, *The Lord of the Rings.*

Early life

John Ronald Reuel Tolkien was born on January 3, 1892, the son of English-born parents in Bloemfontein, in the Orange Free State of South Africa, where his father worked as a bank manager. To escape the heat and dust of southern Africa and to better guard the delicate health of Ronald (as he was called), Tolkien's mother moved back to a small English village with him and his younger brother when they were very young boys. Tolkien would later use this village as a model for one of the locales in his novels. Within a year of this move their father, Arthur Tolkien, died in Bloemfontein, and a few years later the boys' mother died as well.

The Tolkien boys lodged at several homes from 1905 until 1911, when Ronald entered Exeter College, Oxford. Tolkien received a bachelor's degree from Oxford in 1915 and a master's degree in 1919. During this time he married his longtime sweetheart, Edith Bratt, and served for a short time on the Western Front with the Lancashire Fusiliers (a regiment in the British army that used an older-style musket) during World War I (1914–18), when Germany led forces against much of Europe and America).

Begins writing

In 1917, Tolkien was in England recovering from "trench fever," a widespread disease transmitted through fleas and other bugs in battlefield trenches. While bedridden Tolkien began writing "The Book of Lost Tales," which eventually became *The Silmarillion* (1977) and laid the groundwork for his stories about Middle Earth, the fictional world where Tolkien's work takes place.

After the war Tolkien returned to Oxford, where he joined the staff of the *Oxford English Dictionary* and began work as a freelance tutor. In 1920 he was appointed Reader in English Language at Leeds University. The following year, having returned to

Oxford as Rawlinson and Bosworth Professor of Anglo-Saxon, Tolkien became friends with the novelist C. S. Lewis (1898–1963). They shared an intense enthusiasm for the myths, sagas, and languages of northern Europe, and to better enhance those interests, both attended meetings of the "Coalbiters," an Oxford club, founded by Tolkien, at which Icelandic sagas were read aloud.

During the rest of Tolkien's years at Oxford—twenty as Rawlinson and Bosworth Professor of Anglo-Saxon, fourteen as Merton Professor of English Language and Literature—Tolkien published several well-received short studies and translations. Notable among these are his essays "Beowulf: The Monsters and the Critics" (1936), "Chaucer as a Philologist [a person who studies language as it relates to culture]: The Reeve's Tale" (1934), and "On Fairy-Stories" (1947); his scholarly edition of *Ancrene Wisse* (1962); and his translations of three medieval poems: "Sir Gawain and the Green Knight," "Pearl," and "Sir Orfeo" (1975).

The Hobbit

As a writer of imaginative literature, though, Tolkien is best known for *The Hobbit* and *The Lord of the Rings,* tales which were formed during his years attending meetings of the "Inklings," an informal gathering of like-minded friends and writers, that began after the Coalbiters dissolved. The Inklings, which was formed during the late 1930s and lasted until the late 1940s, was a weekly meeting held in Lewis's sitting room at Magdalen College, at which works-in-progress were read aloud and discussed and critiqued by the attendees. Having heard Tolkien's first hobbit story read aloud at a meeting of the

J. R. R. Tolkien.
Reproduced by permission of AP/Wide World Photos.

Inklings, Lewis urged Tolkien to publish *The Hobbit,* which appeared in 1937.

Tolkien retired from his professorship in 1959. While the unauthorized publication of an American edition of *The Lord of the Rings* in 1965 angered him, it also made him a widely admired cult figure in the United States, especially among high school and college students. Uncomfortable with this status, he and his wife lived quietly in Bournemouth for several years, until Edith's death in 1971. In the remaining two years of his life, Tolkien returned to Oxford, where he was made an honorary fellow of Merton College and awarded a doctorate of letters. He was at the height of his fame as a scholarly and imaginative writer when he died in 1973, though critical study of his fiction continues and has increased in the years since.

The world of Middle Earth

Tolkien, a devoted Roman Catholic throughout his life, began creating his own languages and mythologies at an early age and later wrote Christian-inspired stories and poems to provide them with a narrative framework. Based on bedtime stories Tolkien had created for his children, *The Hobbit* concerns the efforts of a hobbit, Bilbo Baggins, to recover a treasure stolen by a dragon. During the course of his mission, Baggins discovers a magical ring which, among other powers, can render its bearer invisible. The ability to disappear helps Bilbo fulfill his quest; however, the ring's less obvious powers prompt the evil Sauron, Dark Lord of Mordor, to seek it. The hobbits' attempt to destroy the ring, thereby denying Sauron unlimited power, is the focal point of the *Lord of the Rings* trilogy, which consists of the novels *The Fellowship of the Ring* (1954), *The Two Towers* (1954), and *The Return of the King* (1955). In these books Tolkien rejects such traditional heroic qualities as strength and size, stressing instead the capacity of even the humblest creatures to win against evil.

Throughout Tolkien's career he composed histories, genealogies (family histories), maps, glossaries, poems, and songs to supplement his vision of Middle Earth. Among the many works published during his lifetime were a volume of poems, *The Adventures of Tom Bombadil and Other Verses from the Red Book* (1962), and a fantasy novel, *Smith of Wootton Major* (1967). Though many of his stories about Middle Earth remained incomplete at the time of Tolkien's death, his son, Christopher, rescued the manuscripts from his father's collections, edited them, and published them. One of these works, *The Silmarillion*, takes place before the time of *The Hobbit* and tells the tale of the first age of Holy Ones (earliest spirits) and their offspring.

Nonetheless, Tolkien implies, to take *The Lord of the Rings* too seriously might be a mistake. He once stated that fairy stories in itself should be taken as a truth, not always symbolic of something else. He went on to say, "but first of all [the story] must succeed just as a tale, excite, please, and even on occasion move, and within its own imagined world be accorded literary belief. To succeed in that was my primary object."

Nearly thirty years after his death, the popularity of Tolkien's work has hardly slowed. In 2001 *The Lord of the Rings: The Fellowship of the Ring* was released as a major motion picture. The magic of Tolkien's world won over both the critics and public alike as the movie was nominated in thirteen categories, including Best Picture, at the Academy Awards; it won four awards. Two more films are scheduled for release by the end of 2003.

For More Information

Bloom, Harold, ed. *J. R. R. Tolkien*. Philadelphia: Chelsea House, 2000.

Carpenter, Humphrey. *J. R. R. Tolkien: A Biography*. London: Allen & Unwin, 1977. Reprint, Boston: Houghton Mifflin, 1988.

Grotta, Daniel. *J. R. R. Tolkien: Architect of Middle Earth*. Philadelphia: Running Press Book Publishers, 2002.

Neimark, Anne E. *Myth Maker: J. R. R. Tolkien.* San Diego: Harcourt Brace, 1996.

Pearce, Joseph. *Tolkien: Man and Myth.* San Francisco: Ignatius Press, 1998.

Shippey, T. A. *J. R. R. Tolkien: Author of the Century.* Boston: Houghton Mifflin, 2001.

LEO TOLSTOY

Born: August 28, 1828
Tula Province, Russia
Died: November 9, 1910
Astapovo, Russia
Russian novelist

The Russian novelist and moral philosopher (person who studies good and bad in relation to human life) Leo Tolstoy ranks as one of the world's great writers, and his *War and Peace* has been called the greatest novel ever written.

Early years

Leo (Lev Nikolayevich) Tolstoy was born at Yasnaya Polyana, his family's estate, on August 28, 1828, in Russia's Tula Province, the youngest of four sons. His mother died when he was two years old, whereupon his father's distant cousin Tatyana Ergolsky took charge of the children. In 1837 Tolstoy's father died, and an aunt, Alexandra Osten-Saken, became legal guardian of the children. Her religious dedication was an important early influence on Tolstoy. When she died in 1840, the children were sent to Kazan, Rus-

sia, to another sister of their father, Pelageya Yushkov.

Tolstoy was educated at home by German and French tutors. He was not a particularly exceptional student but he was good at games. In 1843 he entered Kazan University. Planning on a diplomatic career, he entered the faculty of Oriental languages. Finding these studies too demanding, he switched two years later to studying law. Tolstoy left the university in 1847 without taking his degree.

Tolstoy returned to Yasnaya Polyana, determined to become a model farmer and a "father" to his serfs (unpaid farmhands). His charity failed because of his foolishness in dealing with the peasants (poor, working class) and because he spent too much time socializing in Tula and Moscow. During this time he first began making amazingly honest diary entries, a practice he maintained until his death. These entries provided much material for his fiction, and in a very real sense the collection is one long autobiography.

Army life and early literary career

Nikolay, Tolstoy's eldest brother, visited him at in 1848 in Yasnaya Polyana while on leave from military service in the Caucasus. Leo greatly loved his brother, and when he asked him to join him in the south, Tolstoy agreed. After a long journey, he reached the mountains of the Caucasus, where he sought to join the army as a Junker, or gentleman-volunteer. Tolstoy's habits on a lonely outpost consisted of hunting, drinking, sleeping, chasing the women, and occasionally fighting. During the long lulls he first began to write. In 1852 he sent the autobiographical sketch *Childhood* to the leading journal of the day, the *Contemporary.* Nikolai Nekrasov, its

Leo Tolstoy.
Courtesy of the Library of Congress.

graphical trilogy. He also wrote the three *Sevastopol Tales* at this time, revealing the distinctive Tolstoyan vision of war as a place of unparalleled confusion and heroism, a special space where men, viewed from the author's neutral, godlike point of view, were at their best and worst.

When the city fell, Tolstoy was asked to make a study of the artillery action during the final assault and to report with it to the authorities in St. Petersburg, Russia. His reception in the capital was a triumphant success. Because of his name, he was welcomed into the most brilliant society. Because of his stories, he was treated as a celebrity by the cream of literary society.

Golden years

In September 1862, Tolstoy married Sofya Andreyevna Bers (or Behrs), a woman sixteen years younger than himself. Daughter of a prominent Moscow doctor, Bers was beautiful, intelligent, and, as the years would show, strong-willed. The first decade of their marriage brought Tolstoy the greatest happiness; never before or after was his creative life so rich or his personal life so full. In June 1863 his wife had the first of their thirteen children.

The first portion of *War and Peace* was published in 1865 (in the *Russian Messenger*) as "The Year 1805." In 1868 three more chapters appeared, and in 1869 he completed the novel. His new novel created a fantastic outpouring of popular and critical reaction.

Tolstoy's *War and Peace* represents a high point in the history of world literature, but it was also the peak of Tolstoy's personal life. His characters represent almost everyone he

editor, was ecstatic, and when it was published (under Tolstoy's initials), so was all of Russia. Tolstoy then began writing *The Cossacks* (finished in 1862), an account of his life in the outpost.

From November 1854 to August 1855 Tolstoy served in the battered fortress at Sevastopol in southern Ukraine. He had requested transfer to this area, a sight of one of the bloodiest battles of the Crimean War (1853–1956; when Russia battled England and France over land). As he directed fire from the Fourth Bastion, the hottest area in the conflict for a long while, Tolstoy managed to write *Youth,* the second part of his autobio-

had ever met, including all of his relations on both sides of his family. Balls and battles, birth and death, all were described in amazing detail. In this book the European realistic novel, with its attention to social structures, exact description, and psychological rendering, found its most complete expression.

From 1873 to 1877 Tolstoy worked on the second of his masterworks, *Anna Karenina,* which also created a sensation upon its publication. The concluding section of the novel was written during another of Russia's seemingly endless wars with Turkey. The novel was based partly on events that had occurred on a neighboring estate, where a nobleman's rejected mistress had thrown herself under a train. It again contained great chunks of disguised biography, especially in the scenes describing the courtship and marriage of Kitty and Levin. Tolstoy's family continued to grow, and his royalties (money earned from sales) were making him an extremely rich man.

Spiritual crisis

The ethical quest that had begun when Tolstoy was a child and that had tormented him throughout his younger years now drove him to abandon all else in order to seek an ultimate meaning in life. At first he turned to the Russian Orthodox Church, visiting the Optina-Pustyn monastery in 1877. But he found no answer.

In 1883 Tolstoy met V. G. Chertkov, a wealthy guard officer who soon became the moving force behind an attempt to start a movement in Tolstoy's name. In the next few years a new publication was founded (the *Mediator*) in order to spread Tolstoy's word in tract (pamphlets) and fiction, as well as to make good reading available to the poor. In six years almost twenty million copies were distributed. Tolstoy had long been watched by the secret police, and in 1884 copies of *What I Believe* were seized from the printer.

During this time Tolstoy's relations with his family were becoming increasingly strained. The more of a saint he became in the eyes of the world, the more of a devil he seemed to his wife. He wanted to give his wealth away, but she would not hear of it. An unhappy compromise was reached in 1884, when Tolstoy assigned to his wife the copyright to all his works before 1881.

Tolstoy's final years were filled with worldwide acclaim and great unhappiness, as he was caught in the strife between his beliefs, his followers, and his family. The Holy Synod (the church leaders) excommunicated (kicked him out) him in 1901. Unable to endure the quarrels at home he set out on his last pilgrimage (religious journey) in October 1910, accompanied by his youngest daughter, Alexandra, and his doctor. The trip proved too much, and he died in the home of the stationmaster of the small depot at Astapovo, Russia, on November 9, 1910. He was buried at Yasnaya Polyana.

For More Information

Rancour-Laferriere, Daniel. *Tolstoy on the Couch: Misogyny, Masochism, and the Absent Mother.* New York: New York University Press, 1998.

Troyat, Henri. *Tolstoy.* Garden City, NY: Doubleday, 1967. Reprint, New York: Grove Press, 2001.

Wilson, A. N. *Tolstoy.* London. H. Hamilton, 1988.

HENRI DE TOULOUSE-LAUTREC

Born: November 24, 1864
Albi, France
Died: September 9, 1901
Malromé, France
French painter

The French painter Henri de Toulouse-Lautrec depicted the Parisian night life of cafés, bars, and brothels (houses of prostitution, where sexual acts are traded for money)—the world that he inhabited at the height of his career.

Crippled childhood

Henri de Toulouse-Lautrec, a direct descendant of an aristocratic family of a thousand years, was born on November 24, 1864, at Albi, France, to Alphonse-Charles and Adèle Zoë. His wild and colorful father lived in moderate luxury, hunting with falcons and collecting exotic weapons. Henri began to draw at an early age and found the arts an escape from his loving but over-protective family.

In 1878 Toulouse-Lautrec suffered a fall and broke one femur (thigh bone). A year later he fell again and broke the other one. His legs did not heal properly. His torso developed normally, but his legs stopped growing and were permanently deformed. Many attribute his health problems to the fact that his parents were first cousins.

In 1882, encouraged by his first teachers—the animal painters René Princeteau and John Lewis Brown—Toulouse-Lautrec decided to devote himself to painting, and that year he left for Paris. Enrolling at the École des Beaux-Arts, he entered the studio of Fernand Cormon. In 1884 Toulouse-Lautrec settled in Montmartre, an area in north Paris, where he stayed from then on, except for short visits to Spain, where he admired the works of El Greco (1541–1614) and Diego Velázquez (1599–1660). In England he visited celebrated writer Oscar Wilde (1854–1900) and painter James McNeill Whistler (1834–1903). At one point Toulouse-Lautrec lived near painter Edgar Degas (1834–1917), whom he valued above all other contemporary artists (artists from his time) and by whom he was influenced. From 1887 his studio was on the rue Caulaincourt next to the Goupil printshop, where he could see examples of the Japanese prints of which he was so fond.

By habit Toulouse-Lautrec stayed out most of the night. He frequented many entertainment spots in Montmartre, especially the Moulin Rouge cabaret (a nightclub with entertainment). He also drank a great deal. His loose lifestyle caught up with him—he suffered a breakdown in 1899. His mother had him committed to an asylum, a hospital for the mentally ill, at Neuilly, France. He recovered and set to work again, but not for very long. He died on September 9, 1901, at the family estate at Malromé, France.

The influence of Parisian nightlife

Toulouse-Lautrec moved freely among the dancers, the prostitutes, the artists, and the intellectuals of Montmartre. From 1890 on his tall, lean cousin, Dr. Tapié de Celeyran, accompanied him, and the two, depicted in *At the Moulin Rouge* (1892), made a colorful pair. Despite his deformity,

Toulouse-Lautrec was extremely social and readily made friends and inspired trust. He came to be regarded as one of the people of Montmartre, for he was an outsider like them, fiercely independent, but with a great ability to understand everything around him.

Among the painter's favorite subjects were the cabaret dancers Yvette Guilbert, Jane Avril, and La Goulue and her partner, Valentin le Désossé, the contortionist (an acrobat who demonstrates extraordinary bodily positions). Through the seriousness of his intention, Toulouse-Lautrec depicted his subjects in a style bordering on, but rising above, caricature (exaggeration). He took subjects who often dressed in disguise and makeup as a way of life and stripped away all that was not essential, thus revealing each as an individual—but a prisoner of his own destiny.

The two most direct influences on Toulouse-Lautrec's art were the Japanese print, as seen in his slanted angles and flattened forms, and Degas, from whom he derived the tilted perspective, cutting of figures, and use of a railing to separate the spectator from the painted scene, as in *At the Moulin Rouge*. But the genuine feel of a world of wickedness and the harsh, artificial colors used to create it were Toulouse-Lautrec's own.

Unusual types performing in a grand show attracted Toulouse-Lautrec. In his painting *In the Circus Fernando: The Ringmaster* (1888) the nearly grotesque (distorted and ugly), strangely cruel figure of the ringmaster is the center around which the horse and bareback rider must revolve. From 1892 to 1894 Toulouse-Lautrec produced a series of interiors of brothels, where he actually lived for a while and became the companion of the women. As with his paintings of cabarets, he

Henri de Toulouse-Lautrec.
Reproduced by permission of the Corbis Corporation.

caught the feel of the brothels and made no attempt to glamorize them. In the *Salon in the Rue des Moulins* (1894) the prostitutes are shown as ugly and bored beneath their makeup; the madam (woman in charge) sits quietly in their midst. He neither sensationalized nor drew a moral (having to do with right and wrong) lesson but presented a certain interpretation of this side of society for what it was—no more and no less.

Color lithography and the poster

Toulouse-Lautrec broadened the range of lithography (the process of printing on metal) by treating the tone more freely. His strokes became more summary (executed quickly) and the planes more unified. Sometimes the ink was speckled on the surface to bring about a great textural richness. In his posters he combined flat images (again the influence of the Japanese print) with type. He realized that if the posters were to be successful their message had to make an immediate and forceful impact on the passerby. He designed them with that in mind.

Toulouse-Lautrec's posters of the 1890s established him as the father of the modern large-scale poster. His best posters were those advertising the appearance of various performers at the Montmartre cabarets, such as the singer May Belfort, the female clown Cha-U-Kao, and Loïe Fuller of the Folies-Bergère.

In an 1893 poster of dancer Jane Avril, colored partially in bright red and yellow, she is pictured kicking her leg. Below her, in gray tones so as not to detract attention, is the diagonally placed hand of the violinist playing his instrument. There is some indication of floorboards but no furniture or other figures. The legend reads simply "Jane Avril" in white letters and "Jardin de Paris" in black letters.

For More Information

Cooper, Douglas. *Henri de Toulouse-Lautrec*. London: Thames and Hudson, 1988.

Frey, Julia. *Toulouse-Lautrec: A Life*. New York: Viking, 1994.

Frey, Julia. *Toulouse-Lautrec: A Life*. New York: Viking, 1994.

Heller, Reinhold. *Toulouse-Lautrec: The Soul of Montmartre*. New York: Prestel, 1997.

EIJI TOYODA

Born: September 12, 1913
Kinjo, Nishi Kasugai, Japan
Japanese businessman and engineer

Eiji Toyoda is a former chairman of the Toyota Motor Company. His family-run business made revolutionary changes in the way automobiles were made.

Family business

Eiji Toyoda was born September 12, 1913, in Kinjo, Nishi Kasugai, Aichi, Japan, the son of Heikichi and Nao Toyoda. Toyoda's uncle, Sakichi, founded the original family business, Toyoda Automatic Loom Works, in 1926 in Nagoya, about 200 miles west of Tokyo, Japan. The family was so involved in the business that Eiji's father Heikichi (younger brother of Sakichi) even made his home inside the spinning factory. Such an early exposure to machines and business would have a significant effect on Toyoda's life.

Sakichi ultimately sold the patents (documents that give a person the legal right to control the production of an invention for a specific period of time) for his design to an English firm for two hundred fifty thousand dollars, at a time when textiles was Japan's top industry and used the money to pay for his eldest son Kiichiro's venture into auto making in the early 1930s.

After graduating in 1936 with a mechanical engineering degree from the University of Tokyo—training ground for most of Japan's future top executives—the twenty-three-year-old Toyoda joined the family spinning business as an engineering trainee and transferred a year later to the newly formed Toyota Motor Company. The company was a relative newcomer to the auto business in Japan. Eiji worked on the A1 prototype, the forerunner of the company's first production model, a six-cylinder sedan that borrowed heavily from Detroit automotive technology and resembled the radically styled Chrysler Airflow model of that period. During those early years, Toyoda gained lots of hands-on experience.

Expansion

In this spare time, Eiji Toyoda studied rockets and jet engines and, on the advice of his cousin, even researched helicopters. World War II (1939–45)—when Japan fought alongside Germany and Italy against France, Great Britain, the Soviet Union, and the United States—left Japan's industry in a shambles, and the automaker began rebuilding its production facilities from scratch. But while Kiichiro Toyoda was rebuilding the manufacturing operations, Japan's shattered economy left the company with a growing bank of unsold cars. By 1949, the firm was unable to meet its payroll, and employees began a devastating fifteen-month strike (where workers walk out in protest)—the first and only walkout in the company's history—which pushed Toyota to the brink of bankruptcy. In 1950 the Japanese government forced Toyota to reorganize and split its sales and manufacturing operations into separate companies, each headed by a nonfamily member. Kiichiro Toyoda and his executive staff all resigned. Kiichiro died less than two years later.

Eiji Toyoda, meanwhile, had been named managing director of the manufacturing arm,

Eiji Toyoda.
Reproduced by permission of AP/Wide World Photo.

Toyota Motor Company. He was sent to the United States in 1950 to study the auto industry and return to Toyota with a report on American manufacturing methods. After touring Ford Motor's U.S. facilities, Toyoda turned to the task of redesigning Toyota's plants to incorporate advanced techniques and machinery.

President of Toyota

In 1967 Toyoda was named president of Toyota Motor Company—the first family member to assume that post since Kiichiro resigned in 1950. A year later, the two branches of the company were unified in the new Toyota Motor Corporation, with Eiji

Toyoda as chairman and Shoichiro Toyoda as president and chief executive officer.

The Toyodas led their company to a record year in 1984. Toyota sold an all-time high 1.7 million vehicles in Japan and the same number overseas and profits peaked at $2.1 billion in 1985. While that performance would certainly earn Toyota a mention in automotive history books, Eiji Toyoda and his company may be better remembered for a unique management style that has been copied by hundreds of Japanese companies and is gaining growing acceptance in the United States. The Toyota approach, adopted at its ten Japanese factories and twenty-four plants in seventeen countries, has three main objectives: keeping inventory to an absolute minimum through a system called *kanban,* or "just in time;" insuring that each step of the assembly process is performed correctly the first time; and cutting the amount of human labor that goes into each car.

What Toyoda accomplished for Toyota Motor was dazzling success at a time when Detroit automakers were struggling to stay profitable. Toyota, Japan's number one automaker, spearheaded the tidal wave of small, low-priced cars that swept the United States after successive energy crises in the mid- and late-1970s. In addition to running the largest corporation in Japan—and the world's third largest automaker, behind General Motors (GM) and Ford—Toyota has overseen the development of a highly efficient manufacturing system that is being copied worldwide. Although Eiji Toyoda gave up his post as chairman in 1994, he continues to hold the title of honorary chair of the company.

For More Information

Toyoda, Eiji. *Toyota: Fifty Years in Motion.* New York: Kodansha International, 1987.

HARRY S. TRUMAN

Born: May 8, 1884
Lamar, Missouri
Died: December 26, 1972
Kansas City, Missouri
American president, vice president, and senator

Harry S. Truman (1884–1972), thirty-third president of the United States, led America's transition from wartime to peacetime economy, created the Truman doctrine, and made the decision to defend South Korea against communist invasion.

A shy start

Harry S. Truman was born in Lamar, Missouri, on May 8, 1884. He went to high school in Independence, Missouri. From 1900 until 1905 he held various small business positions, then for the next twelve years he farmed on his parents' land. In 1917, soon after the United States entered World War I (1914–18; a war fought in Europe between the Central Powers—Germany, Austria-Hungary, and Turkey—and the Allies—France, Great Britain, Russia, Italy, Japan, and, after 1917, the United States), he enlisted in the artillery, serving in France. After returning from the war, he married Bess Wallace

(1885–1982) in 1919. The couple had one child, Margaret.

As Truman grew to manhood, he achieved a notable change. As president he would be known for his outgoing personality and for his use of such tough-talking phrases as "The buck stops here!" and "If you can't stand the heat, get out of the kitchen." As a boy, however, Truman was anything but tough and outgoing. He was accident-prone and sickly, and his poor vision and thick glasses forced him to avoid the rough activities in which other boys engaged. Instead, he stayed indoors, taking piano lessons and reading. One of his favorite books as a boy, *Great Men and Famous Women,* detailed the lives of influential historical and political figures.

Political beginnings

A loyal Democrat, Truman entered politics in the 1920s. He was elected as a Jackson County, Missouri, judge in 1922 and served until 1924. He was presiding judge from 1926 to 1934, giving close attention to problems of county administration.

In the national election of 1934, Truman, who was a firm supporter of President Franklin Roosevelt (1882–1945), was chosen U.S. senator from Missouri. Reelected in 1940, he gained national attention as chairman of the Senate Committee to Investigate the National Defense Program. He kept his chairmanship loyal to the Roosevelt administration. When Roosevelt was nominated for a fourth presidential term in June 1944, he chose Truman for vice president.

Thrust into the presidency

Roosevelt was reelected, but after Truman had served only eighty-two days as his

Harry S. Truman.
Courtesy of the Library of Congress.

vice president, Roosevelt died suddenly on April 12, 1945. Truman then became the president. He quickly took command, and in his first address to Congress he promised to continue Roosevelt's policies. That July he attended the Potsdam Conference, Germany, at which the United States, Great Britain, and the Soviet Union set terms for the administration of Germany after World War II (1939–45; a war fought between the Axis powers—Germany, Italy, and Japan—and the Allied powers—mainly Great Britain, France, the Soviet Union, and after 1942, the United States). Later in the summer he authorized the dropping of the atomic bomb on Hiroshima, Japan, on August 6, 1945, and approved the surrender of the Japanese in a treaty signed on September 2, 1945.

The Truman administration quickly took steps to dismantle the military forces and the agencies set up to conduct the war, as well as to resume production of peacetime goods. Truman was soon forced to tackle inflation (a steep rise in the cost of living) and new demands by labor unions. He showed his power of quick decision declaring wage increases that were needed to cushion the blows from changes in the economy. He also sternly opposed measures to restrict labor organizations and acted to maintain union rights.

Truman also called for a broad program of social welfare. Although sharp friction developed between the Truman administration and conservatives (people who resist change and prefer to keep traditions) in Congress, he pushed measures through Congress for clearing away slums, construction of low-cost housing, health insurance, and the establishment of the Council of Economic Advisers to help citizens gain full employment.

In his foreign policy, Truman was alarmed by the growing power of the Soviet Union, a communist nation. He feared the spread of Soviet influence in eastern Europe and Asia, and he supported strong Western reaction to the threat of Soviet expansion. As Soviet aggressiveness made the international scene stormier, he gave vigorous support to the establishment of the United Nations.

Truman Doctrine

In the wake of World War II, Turkey and Greece seemed to be at risk of economic collapse and communist takeover. To prevent this from happening, Truman backed the leaders of his State Department in their stand for continued American support to democracy abroad and asked Congress for $400 million in funds to sustain Turkey and Greece. He also announced the Truman Doctrine (March 12, 1947), declaring that the United States would support all free peoples who were resisting attempts to dominate them, either by armed minorities at home or aggressors outside their borders.

Truman's policy made it possible for members of his state department to push through Congress the important measure known as the Marshall Plan, which began in April 1948. The plan provided for the transfer of large amounts economic aid from Western nations to countries in Europe and Asia that were threatened by communist domination. The presidential campaign of 1948 came as the Marshall Plan gathered widespread support from democratic governments in Europe, South America, Africa, and elsewhere.

Reelection

In 1948 Truman entered the presidential contest and fought a stubborn battle against Republican Thomas E. Dewey (1902–1971). Truman faced heavy odds in this presidential race. Besides the Democratic and Republican candidates, the entry of two new political parties into the battle made the outcome doubtful.

As the election drew near most newspapers seemed confident that Dewey would win. Public opinion polls also indicated a Dewey victory. On election night, Truman went to bed as the *Chicago Tribune* published a special issue with the headline "Dewey Defeats Truman!" The next morning, however, Truman awoke to find the he had not only carried the country by more than two million votes but had also brought in a Democratic Congress.

Korean War

On Sunday, June 25, 1950, the Korean War (1950–53) began when North Korean Communist forces invaded the Republic of South Korea. Truman at once summoned an emergency conference and announced that he would pledge American armed strength for the defense of South Korea. By September 15, American troops, supported by other forces of the United Nations, were in action in Korea. Truman held firm in the costly war that followed but hesitated to approve a major advance across the Yalu River on the northwest border of North Korea and China. China had entered the war on North Korea's side partly to protect its territory in this area.

In April 1951, amid national frustration over the war, Truman dismissed General Douglas MacArthur (1880–1964) as head of the Far East Command of the U.S. Army. He took this action on the grounds that MacArthur—a national hero of World War II (1939–45)—had repeatedly challenged the Far Eastern policies of the administration and had recommended the use of bombs against Chinese forces north of the Yalu. Such an attack against the Chinese might have provoked open war with the Soviet Union and cost the United States the support of important allies in the war. Nevertheless, MacArthur's dismissal was highly controversial, and Truman announced that he would not run again for the presidency. He retired to private life, publishing two volumes of memoirs (memories) in 1955 and 1956.

Lasting popularity

Truman died on December 26, 1972, but his popularity continued to soar long after his death. New books and movies about him have continued to appear, and he has been commemorated with a U.S. postage stamp.

For More Information

Ferrell, Robert H. *Harry S. Truman: A Life.* Columbia: University of Missouri Press, 1994.

Hamby, Alonzo L. *Man of the People: A Life of Harry S. Truman.* New York: Oxford University Press, 1995.

Leavell, J. Perry. *Harry S. Truman.* New York: Chelsea House, 1988.

McCoy, Donald R. *The Presidency of Harry S. Truman.* Lawrence: University Press of Kansas, 1984.

McCullough, David S. *Truman.* New York: Simon and Schuster, 1992.

Schuman, Michael. *Harry S. Truman.* Springfield, NJ: Enslow, 1997.

Truman, Harry S. *The Autobiography of Harry S Truman.* Edited by Robert H. Ferrell. Boulder: Colorado Associated University Press, 1980.

DONALD TRUMP

Born: 1946
New York, New York
American businessman and real estate developer

An American real estate developer, Donald Trump became one of the best known and most controversial businessmen of the 1980s and 1990s.

Donald Trump.
Reproduced by permission of Archive Photos, Inc.

ing to be a star athlete and student leader by the time he graduated in 1964.

During the summers, Trump worked for his father's company at the construction sites. He entered Fordham University and then transferred to the Wharton School of Finance at the University of Pennsylvania, from which he graduated in 1968 with a degree in economics.

Trump seems to have been strongly influenced by his father in his decision to make a career in real estate development, but the younger man's personal goals were much grander than those of his father. After graduating college, Trump joined the family business, the Trump Organization. In 1971 Trump moved his residence to Manhattan, where he became familiar with many influential people. Convinced of the economic opportunity in the city, Trump became involved in large building projects in Manhattan that would offer opportunities for earning high profits, utilizing attractive architectural design, and winning public recognition.

Privileged childhood

Donald John Trump was born in 1946 in Queens, New York City, the fourth of five children of Frederick C. and Mary MacLeod Trump. Frederick Trump was a builder and real estate developer who specialized in constructing and operating middle income apartments in the Queens, Staten Island, and Brooklyn sections of New York. Donald Trump was an energetic and bright child, and his parents sent him to the New York Military Academy at age thirteen, hoping the discipline of the school would channel his energy in a positive manner. Trump did well at the academy, both socially and academically, ris-

Building an empire

When the Pennsylvania Central Railroad entered bankruptcy, Trump was able to obtain an option (a contract that gives a person the authority to sell something for a specific price during a limited time frame) on the railroad's yards on the west side of Manhattan. When plans for apartments were refused because of a poor economic climate, Trump promoted the property as the location of a city convention center, and the city government selected it over two other sites in 1978. Trump's offer to drop a fee if the center were named after his family, however, was turned down, along with his bid to build the complex.

In 1974 Trump obtained an option on one of the Penn Central's hotels, the Commodore, which was unprofitable but in an excellent location near Grand Central Station. The next year he signed a partnership agreement with the Hyatt Hotel Corporation, which did not have a large downtown hotel. Trump then worked out a complicated deal with the city to revamp the hotel. Renamed the Grand Hyatt, the hotel was popular and an economic success, making Trump the city's best known and most controversial developer.

In 1977 Trump married Ivana Zelnickova Winklmayr, a New York fashion model who had been an alternate on the 1968 Czech Olympic Ski Team. After the birth of the first of the couple's three children in 1978, Donald John Trump, Jr., Ivana Trump was named vice president in charge of design in the Trump Organization and played a major role in supervising the renovation of the Commodore.

In 1979 Trump rented a site on Fifth Avenue next to the famous Tiffany & Company as the location for a monumental $200 million apartment-retail complex designed by Der Scutt. It was named Trump Tower when it opened in 1982. The fifty-eight-story building featured a six-story courtyard lined with pink marble and included an eighty-foot waterfall. The luxurious building attracted well-known retail stores and celebrity renters and brought Trump national attention.

Atlantic City

Meanwhile Trump was investigating the profitable casino gambling business, which was approved in New Jersey in 1977. In 1980 he was able to acquire a piece of property in Atlantic City, New Jersey. He brought in his younger brother Robert to head up the complex project of acquiring the land, winning a gambling license, and obtaining permits and financing. Holiday Inns Corporation, the parent company of Harrah's casino hotels, offered a partnership, and the $250 million complex opened in 1982 as Harrah's at Trump Plaza. Trump bought out Holiday Inns in 1986 and renamed the facility Trump Plaza Hotel and Casino. Trump also purchased a Hilton Hotels casino-hotel in Atlantic City when the corporation failed to obtain a gambling license and renamed the $320 million complex Trump's Castle. Later, while it was under construction, he was able to acquire the largest hotel-casino in the world, the Taj Mahal at Atlantic City, which opened in 1990.

Back in New York City, Trump had purchased an apartment building and the Barbizon-Plaza Hotel in New York City, which faced Central Park, with plans to build a large condominium tower on the site. The tenants of the apartment building, however, who were protected by the city's rent control and rent stabilization programs, fought Trump's plans and won. Trump then renovated the Barbizon, renaming it Trump Parc. In 1985 Trump purchased seventy-six acres on the west side of Manhattan for $88 million to build a complex to be called Television City, which was to consist of a dozen skyscrapers, a mall, and a riverfront park. The huge development was to stress television production and feature the world's tallest building, but community opposition and a long city approval process delayed construction of the project. In 1988 he acquired the Plaza Hotel for $407 million and spent $50 million renovating it under his wife Ivana's direction.

Declining wealth

It was in 1990, however, that the real estate market declined, reducing the value of and income from Trump's empire; his own net worth plummeted from an estimated $1.7 billion to $500 million. The Trump Organization required massive loans to keep it from collapsing, a situation that raised questions as to whether the corporation could survive bankruptcy. Some observers saw Trump's decline as symbolic of many of the business, economic, and social excesses from the 1980s.

Yet Trump climbed back and was reported to be worth close to $2 billion in 1997. Donald Trump's image was tarnished by the publicity surrounding his controversial separation and the later divorce from his wife, Ivana. But Trump married again, this time to Marla Maples, a fledgling actress. The couple had a daughter two months before their marriage in 1993. He filed for a highly publicized divorce from Maples in 1997, which became final in June 1999.

On October 7, 1999, Trump announced the formation of an exploratory committee to inform his decision of whether or not he should seek the Reform Party's nomination for the presidential race of 2000, but backed out because of problems within the party.

A state appeals court ruled on August 3, 2000, that Trump had the right to finish an 856-foot-tall condominium on New York City's east side. The Coalition for Responsible Development had sued the city, charging it with violation of zoning laws by letting the building reach heights that towered over everything in the neighborhood. The city has since moved to revise its rules to prevent more of such projects. The failure of Trump's opponents to obtain an injunction (a court order to stop) allowed him to continue construction.

For More Information

Blair, Gwenda. *The Trumps: Three Generations That Built an Empire.* New York: Simon & Schuster, 2000.

Hurt, Harry, III. *The Lost Tycoon: The Many Lives of Donald J. Trump.* New York : W. W. Norton, 1993.

O'Donnell, John R., with James Rutherford. *Trumped!: The Inside Story of the Real Donald Trump.* New York: Simon & Schuster, 1991.

Tucille, Jerome. *Trump: The Saga of America's Master Builder.* New York: D. I. Fine, 1985.

SOJOURNER TRUTH

Born: 1797
Ulster County, New York
Died: November 26, 1883
Battle Creek, Michigan
African American abolitionist

One of the most famous nineteenth-century black American women, Sojourner Truth was an uneducated former slave who actively opposed slavery. Though she never learned to read or write, she became a moving speaker for black freedom and women's rights. While many of her fellow black abolitionists (people who campaigned for the end of slavery) spoke only to blacks, Truth spoke mainly to whites. While they spoke of violent uprisings, she spoke of reason and religious understanding.

Sojourner Truth was born Isabella Baumfree around 1797 on an estate owned by Dutch settlers in Ulster County, New York. She was the second youngest in a slave family of the ten or twelve children of James Baumfree and his wife Elizabeth (known as "Mau-Mau Bett"). When her owner died in 1806, Isabella was put up for auction. Over the next few years, she had several owners who treated her poorly. John Dumont purchased her when she was thirteen, and she worked for him for the next seventeen years.

In 1817 the state of New York passed a law granting freedom to slaves born before July 4, 1799. However, this law declared that those slaves could not be freed until July 4, 1827. While waiting ten years for her freedom, Isabella married a fellow slave named Thomas, with whom she had five children. As the date of her release approached, she realized that Dumont was plotting to keep her enslaved. In 1826 she ran away, leaving her husband and her children behind.

Wins court case to regain son

Three important events took place in Isabella's life over the next two years. She found refuge with Maria and Isaac Van Wagenen, who bought her from Dumont and gave her freedom. She then underwent a religious experience, claiming from that point on she could talk directly to God. Lastly, she sued to retrieve her son Peter, who had been sold illegally to a plantation owner in Alabama. In 1828, with the help of a lawyer, Isabella became the first black woman to take a white man to court and win.

Sojourner Truth.
Reproduced by permission of Archive Photos, Inc.

Soon thereafter, Isabella moved with Peter to New York City and began following Elijah Pierson, who claimed to be a prophet. He was soon joined by another religious figure known as Matthias, who claimed to be the Messiah. They formed a cult known as the "Kingdom" and moved to Sing Sing (renamed Ossining) in southeast New York in 1833. Isabella grew apart from them and stayed away from their activities. But when Matthias was arrested for murdering Pierson, she was accused of being an accomplice. A white couple in the cult, the Folgers, also claimed that Isabella had tried to poison them. For the second time, she went to court.

She was found innocent in the Matthias case, and decided to file a slander suit against the Folgers. In 1835 she won, becoming the first black person to win such a suit against a white person.

Changes name

For the next eight years, Isabella worked as a household servant in New York City. In 1843, deciding her mission was to preach the word of God, Isabella changed her name to Sojourner Truth and left the city. Truth traveled throughout New England, attending and holding prayer sessions. She supported herself with odd jobs and often slept outside. At the end of the year, she joined the Northampton Association, a Massachusetts community founded on the ideas of freedom and equality. It is through the Northampton group that Truth met other social reformers and abolitionists, including Frederick Douglass (1817–1895), who introduced her to their movement.

During the 1850s, the issue of slavery heated up in the United States. In 1850 Congress passed the Fugitive Slave Law, which allowed runaway slaves to be arrested and jailed without a jury trial. In 1857 the U.S. Supreme Court ruled in the case of Dred Scott (1795?–1858) that slaves had no rights as citizens and that the government could not outlaw slavery in new territories.

Lectures to hostile crowds

The results of the Scott case and the unsettling times did not frighten Truth away from her mission. Her life story, *Narrative of Sojourner Truth,* cowritten with Olive Gilbert, was published in 1850. She then headed west and made stops in town after town to speak about her experiences as a slave and her eventual freedom. Her colorful and down-to-earth style often soothed the hostile crowds she faced. While on her travels, Truth noted that while women could be leaders in the abolitionist movement, they could neither vote nor hold public office. Realizing she was discriminated against on two fronts, Truth became an outspoken supporter of women's rights.

By the mid-1850s, Truth had earned enough money from sales of her popular autobiography to buy land and a house in Battle Creek, Michigan. She continued her lectures, traveling throughout the Midwest. When the Civil War began in 1861, she visited black troops stationed near Detroit, Michigan, offering them encouragement. Shortly after meeting U.S. president Abraham Lincoln (1809–1865) in October 1864, she decided to stay in the Washington area to work at a hospital and counsel freed slaves.

Continues fight for freed slaves

Following the end of the Civil War, Truth continued to work with freed slaves. After her arm had been dislocated by a streetcar conductor who had refused to let her ride, she fought for and won the right for blacks to share Washington streetcars with whites. For several years she led a campaign to have land in the West set aside for freed blacks, many of whom were poor and homeless after the war. She carried on her lectures for the rights of blacks and women throughout the 1870s. Failing health, however, soon forced Truth to return to her Battle Creek home. She died there on November 26, 1883.

For More Information

Gilbert, Olive. *Narrative of Sojourner Truth.* Boston: Self-published, 1850. Reprint, New York: Penguin Books, 1998.

Krass, Peter. *Sojourner Truth.* New York: Chelsea House, 1988.

Mabee, Carleton, with Susan Mabee Newhouse. *Sojourner Truth: Slave, Prophet, Legend.* New York: New York University Press, 1993.

McKissack, Patricia, and Fredrick McKissack. *Sojourner Truth: A Voice for Freedom.* Hillside, NJ: Enslow, 1992.

Painter, Nell Irvin. *Sojourner Truth: A Life, a Symbol.* New York: Norton, 1996.

Rockwell, Anne F. *Only Passing Through: The Story of Sojourner Truth.* New York: Alfred A. Knopf, 2000.

TU FU

Born: c. 712
Kung-hsien, China
Died: c. 770
Tanzhou, China
Chinese poet

Tu Fu was a great Chinese poet of the T'ang dynasty, a family that ruled China from 618 to 907. He is known as a poet-historian for his portrayal of the social and political disorders of his time and is also noted for his artistry and craftsmanship.

The life of Tu Fu

Born in Kung-hsien, Honan, of a scholar-official family, Tu Fu lost his mother in early childhood. His father, a minor district official, remarried, and the boy lived for some time with his aunt in Loyang, the eastern capital. In his youth he traveled widely in the Yangtze River and Yellow River regions. He first met the poet Li Po (c. 701–762) in 744 in North China and formed a lasting friendship with him. In 746 Tu Fu went to Ch'ang-an, the capital, in search of an official position, but he failed to pass the literary examination or to win the support of influential people. In 751 he sent a *fu* (rhymed prose) composition to the emperor for each of three grand state ceremonials. While the emperor appreciated Tu Fu's literary talents, he failed to award the poet an office or payment.

After a long, uneventful wait in Ch'ang-an, where Tu Fu's resources were exhausted and his health declined, he was offered a minor position at court. Just then the An Lu-shan rebellion broke out (December 755). The country was thrown into chaos when rebels tried to overthrow the T'ang Dynasty. The rebels captured Tu Fu, but he escaped. He lived the life of a refugee (someone forced away from home for political reasons) for some time before he was able to join the new emperor's court in exile, a court set up in foreign lands after being ousted. As a reward for his loyalty, he was appointed "Junior Reminder" in attendance upon the emperor. In late 757 he returned with the court to Ch'ang-an, which had been recovered from the rebels, but he did not stay there long. He had offended the emperor with his advice and was banished (sent away) to a provincial post, or a remote border post. He soon gave it

Tu Fu.
Reproduced by permission of the Picture Desk, Inc.

tary in the Board of Works. Upon Yen Wu's death in 765, Tu Fu left Ch'eng-tu for a trip that took him to a number of places along the Yangtze River. Three years later he reached Hunan. After having roamed up and down the rivers and lakes there for almost two years (768–770), he died of sickness on a boat in the winter of 770.

Tu Fu's poetry

The rich and varied experiences in Tu Fu's life went into the making of a great poet. His works reveal his loyalty and love of the country, his dreams and frustrations, and his sympathy for the sad status of the common people. He was an eyewitness to the historical events in a critical period that saw a great, prosperous nation ruined by military rebellions and wars with border tribes. Eager to serve the country, Tu Fu was helpless in stopping its disasters and could only faithfully record in poems his own observations and feelings. While some of his poems reflect his mood in happier moments, most of them tell of his poverty, his separation from and longings for his family, his terrible life during the war, and his encounters with refugees, draftees, and recruiting officers.

Tu Fu possesses a remarkable power of description, with which he clearly presents human affairs and natural scenery. Into his poetry he introduces an intense, dramatic, and touching personalism through the use of symbols and images, irony and contrast. Above all, he has the ability to rise above the world of reality to the world of imagination. An artist among poets, he excelled in a difficult verse-form called *lü-shih* (regulated verse), of which he is considered a master.

up and in the fall of 759 started a long journey away from the capital.

Tu Fu spent the next nine years (759–768), the most fruitful period of his poetic career, in various cities in Szechwan, China. He settled down with his family in Ch'eng-tu, the provincial capital, where he built a thatched cottage and led a quiet, happy, though still extremely poor life. Occasionally he had to go from one city to another to seek employment or to escape uprisings within the province. For a year or so, he was appointed by Yen Wu, the governor general of Ch'eng-tu district, as military adviser in the governor's headquarters and assistant secre-

For More Information

Davis, A. R. *Tu Fu*. New York: Twayne Publishers, 1971.

Tu Fu. *A Little Primer of Tu Fu*. Edited by David Hawkes. Oxford, England: Clarendon Press, 1967.

Tu Fu. *Tu Fu: The Autobiography of a Chinese Poet*. Edited by Florence Ayscough. Boston: Houghton Mifflin, 1929.

Tu Fu. *Tu Fu: Selected Poems*. Edited by Rewi Alley. Peking, China: Foreign Language Press, 1990.

TUTANKHAMEN

Born: c. 1370 B.C.E.
Died: c. 1352 B.C.E.
Egyptian king and pharaoh

Tutankhamen was the twelfth king of the eighteenth Egyptian dynasty (reigned 1361–1352 B.C.E.). Although his reign was relatively unimportant, Tutankhamen became the most famous of the pharaohs (Egyptian kings) when his treasure-filled tomb was discovered in the early twentieth century. The vast and untouched contents of his tomb offered historians great insight into the ancient Egyptian culture.

Early life

Little is known of Tutankhamen's childhood; even the identity of his parents remains a mystery. Historian believe Tutankhamen was the son of either Amenophis III or Akhenaten. His mother was probably one of the king's many wives, most likely Kiya, a wife of Akhenaten who was often referred to as the "Greatly Beloved Wife."

Tutankhamen was only a child when he became king, for although he reigned eight full years, examination of his body has shown that he was little more than eighteen years old at the time of his death. He may have owed his rise to king to his marriage to Ankhnesamun, the third daughter of the fourteenth century Egyptian rulers, Ikhnaton and Nefertiti. The couple would have no children.

Tutankhamen had originally been named Tutankhaten, meaning "gracious life is Aton," but both he and Ankhnesamun (originally Ankhnespaten) dropped from their names all references to the sun god Aten and the cult (a religious following) that was promoted by Akhenaten. He then became known as Tutankhamen, "gracious life is Amon (an Egyptian god)." Soon after, the royal couple abandoned Amarna, the city built by Akhenaten for the sole worship of Aten. Tutankhamen apparently left the city very early in his reign, for, with the exception of a few scarabs (Egyptian beetles that were inscribed and buried alongside mummies), no trace of him has been found at Amarna.

The reign of King Tutankhamen

The addition to Tutankhamen's label as "Ruler of Southern On" shows that he regarded Thebes as his capital city. There can be little doubt that he made every effort to satisfy the supporters of the god Amun; a *stele* (statue) erected near the Third Pylon of the temple of Karnak depicts Tutankhamen offering to gods Amun and Mut. The accompanying text tells of the state of decay into which the temples and shrines of the gods had fallen

Tutankhamen.
Courtesy of the Library of Congress.

fragment Ay bears the title of vizier, or high government official. He had already posed as a coregent (coruler) before the death of Tutankhamen. After Tutankhamen's death, Ay married his widow. The cause of Tutankhamen's death is unknown, although, due to skull damage found in his remains, many believe he was assassinated.

The tomb of Tutankhamen

Tutankhamen is probably the best-known of the pharaohs, owing to the fortunate discovery of his treasure-filled tomb virtually intact. His burial place in the Valley of the Kings had escaped the fate of the tombs of other ancient Egyptian kings. Fortunately, the entrance was hidden from tomb raiders by debris heaped over it during the cutting of the later tomb of the twelfth century B.C.E. King Ramses VI. In 1922 Howard Carter (1873–1939) discovered Tutankhamen's tomb after searching for nearly ten years. Tutankhamen's tomb remains as one of the greatest and most important discoveries in archeology (the study of ancient forms of life). From Carter's discovery, historians were able to piece together the life of King Tutankhamen.

The tomb room contained more than five thousand objects, many of which were covered with gold and beautifully carved. The most famous of these objects is probably the lifelike gold mask that covered the face of Tutankhamen's mummy. Carter also uncovered military items, clothing, jewelry, and many statues of Tutankhamen and Egyptian gods. In fact, there were so many items in the tomb that many are still being examined today and have yet to be displayed in museums—nearly eighty years after their discovery.

during the period of Aten. Tutankhamen had a large hall at Luxor decorated with reliefs illustrating the festival of Amen-Re.

Despite the existence of the standard paintings of the pharaoh slaying his foes, it is doubtful that Tutankhamen engaged in any serious military operations. Tutankhamen was a trained archer and in his tomb were found many trophies from his hunts.

There is some indication that the actual power behind the throne was an elderly official named Ay, who is depicted on a fragment of gold leaf with Tutankhamen. On another

For More Information

Brier, Bob. *The Murder of Tutankhamen: A True Story.* New York: Putnam, 1998.

Carter, Howard, and A. C. Mace. *The Tomb of Tut-ankh-amen.* New York: Cooper Square Publishers, 1963.

Desroches-Noblecourt, Christiane. *Tutankhamen: Life and Death of a Pharaoh.* Garden City, NY: Doubleday, 1965.

El Mahdy, Christine. *Tutankhamen: The Life and Death of the Boy-King.* New York: St. Martin's Press, 2000.

James, T. G. H. *Tutankhamun.* Vercelli, Italy: Friedman/Fairfax Publishers, 2000.

DESMOND
TUTU

Born: October 7, 1931
Klerksdorp, South Africa
South African antiapartheid activist and religious leader

In the 1980s Archbishop Desmond Tutu became South Africa's most well-known opponent of apartheid, that country's system of racial discrimination, or the separation of people by skin color. In 1984, he was awarded the Nobel Peace Prize for his work in South Africa.

Apartheid

South African apartheid allowed white Africans, who made up 20 percent of the population, to reserve for themselves about 87 percent of the land, most natural resources, and all meaningful political power. Black Africans who found themselves in lands reserved for whites were made citizens of one of ten homelands, which the white-controlled government (but virtually no one else) called nations. In order to remove black people from areas reserved for whites, the government kicked out many from their homes, though their families had in some cases occupied them for decades. Black South Africans in the Republic were forced into the lowest-paying jobs, denied access to most public places, and had drastically lower life expectancies than whites. Meanwhile, white South Africans had one of the highest standards of living in the world.

Black opposition to these conditions began in 1912 when the African National Congress (ANC) was formed. Until the 1960s it engaged in various peaceful campaigns of protest that included marches, petitions, and boycotts (refusing to purchase or participate in businesses)—actions which ultimately helped blacks little. In 1960, after police fired on a crowd at Sharpeville, South Africa, killing sixty-nine and wounding many others, and after the ANC leader Nelson Mandela (1918–) was imprisoned for life in 1964, many black Africans decided to abandon the policy of nonviolent resistance. Most ANC members, led by Oliver Tambo, left South Africa and launched a campaign of sabotage (destruction) from exile. The government increased its violence in return. In 1976, five hundred black students were shot during protests, and in 1977 and 1980 black leader Steve Biko (1946–1977) and trade unionist Neil Aggett were killed while in police custody. Beginning in 1984 violence again swept South Africa. By the time the government

Desmond Tutu.
Reproduced by permission of AP/Wide World Photos.

years old. In Johannesburg he first met the Anglican priest Trevor Huddleston who was strongly against apartheid and became Tutu's main role model. At the age of fourteen he contracted tuberculosis, a terrible disease which effects the lungs and bones, and was hospitalized for twenty months. He wanted to become a doctor, but because his family could not afford the schooling, he became a teacher.

When the government instituted a system of racially discriminatory education in 1957, a system that would separate black students from white students, Tutu left teaching and entered the Anglican Church. Ordained (declared a priest) in 1961, he earned a bachelor of arts degree in 1962 from the University of South Africa, and then a master's degree from the University of London. From 1970 to 1974 he lectured at the University of Lesotho, Botswana, and Swaziland. In 1975 he became dean of Johannesburg, a position from which he publicly challenged white rule. He became bishop of Lesotho in 1976, and in 1985 bishop of Johannesburg. A short fourteen months later, in April 1986, he was elected archbishop of Cape Town, South Africa, the first black person to head the Anglican Church in southern Africa.

declared a state of emergency in June 1986, more than two thousand individuals had been killed.

Rise of Tutu

Against this backdrop Desmond Tutu emerged as the leading spokesman for nonviolent resistance to apartheid. Desmond Mpilo Tutu was born on October 7, 1931, to Zachariah and Aletta Tutu, in Klerksdorp, a town in the Transvaal region of South Africa. Tutu was born a Methodist but became an Anglican when his family changed religions. The Tutu family moved to Johannesburg, South Africa, when Desmond was twelve

Begins the fight

By the 1980s clergymen (religious leaders) were among the most passionate opponents of apartheid within South Africa. Allan Boesak, a biracial minister, and Beyers Naude, head of the Christian Institute, were unusually outspoken. Naude was silenced in the late 1970s by being banned, a unique South African punishment by which the victim was placed under virtual house arrest (forced to stay at home by court order) and could not speak or be quoted publicly. Tutu's international recognition as a critic of apartheid came when he became first general secretary of the South African Council of Churches in 1978.

Nobel Prize

The problem faced by antiapartheid clergymen was how to oppose both violent resistance and apartheid, which was itself increasingly violent. Tutu was determined in his opposition, and he spoke out both in South Africa and abroad, often comparing apartheid to Nazism (a radical movement of racial superiority led by Adolf Hitler [1889—1945]) and communism (where a strong-handed government controls goods and services within a country). As a result the government twice revoked his passport, and he was jailed briefly in 1980 after a protest march. Tutu's view on violence reflected the tension in the Christian approach to resistance: "I will never tell anyone to pick up a gun. But I will pray for the man who picks up a gun, pray that he will be less cruel than he might otherwise have been. . . ."

Another issue Tutu faced was whether other nations should be urged to apply economic sanctions (limitations) against South Africa. Many believed that sanctions would hurt the white-controlled economy, therefore forcing apartheid to end. Others believed the sanction would hurt the black community more. Tutu favored sanctions as the only hope for peaceful change. He also opposed the "constructive engagement" policy of U.S. president Ronald Reagan (1911–). When the new wave of violence swept South Africa in the 1980s and the government failed to make fundamental changes in apartheid, Tutu pronounced constructive engagement a failure.

A new era

In 1989 F. W. de Klerk (1936–) was elected the new president of the Republic of South Africa. He had promised to abolish apartheid, and at the end of 1993 he made good on his promise when South Africa's first all-race elections were announced. On April 27, 1994, South Africans elected a new president, Nelson Mandela, and apartheid was finally over. Mandela symbolized South Africa's new freedom, since until 1990 he had spent twenty-seven years as a political prisoner because of his outspoken opposition to apartheid.

In 1997 Tutu received the Robie Award for his work in humanitarianism. The award came in the midst of Tutu's battle with prostate cancer, and shortly after the presentation he announced plans to undergo several months of cancer treatment in the United States. As head of South Africa's Truth and Reconciliation Commission, a group that investigates apartheid crimes, Tutu planned to set up an office in the United States, where he could continue his work throughout the rigorous cancer treatment. It was determined in October 1999 that the cancer had not spread to other parts of Tutu's body. In August 2001, Tutu returned to South Africa after spending two years in the United States undergoing cancer treatment.

Receiving the Robie was certainly not Tutu's first recognition: he was the second South African to earn the Nobel Peace Prize. The first was Albert Luthuli of the ANC, who received it in 1960 for the same sort of opposition to apartheid.

For More Information

Bentley, Judith. *Archbishop Tutu of South Africa.* Hillside, NJ: Enslow, 1988.

Du Boulay, Shirley. *Tutu: Voice of the Voiceless.* Grand Rapids, MI: Eerdmans, 1988.

Lantier, Patricia and David Winner.. *Desmond Tutu: Religious Leader Devoted to Freedom.* Milwaukee: G. Stevens Children's Books, 1991.

Lelyveld, Joseph. *Move Your Shadow.* New York: Time Books, 1985.

Tutu, Desmond. *The Rainbow People of God.* New York: Doubleday, 1994.

MARK TWAIN

Born: November 30, 1835
Florida, Missouri
Died: April 21, 1910
Redding, Connecticut
American writer and humorist

Mark Twain, American humorist (comic writer) and novelist, captured a world audience with stories of boyhood adventure and with commentary on man's faults that is humorous even while it probes, often bitterly, the roots of human behavior.

Childhood along the Mississippi

Mark Twain was born Samuel Langhorne Clemens on November 30, 1835, in the frontier village of Florida, Missouri. He spent his boyhood in nearby Hannibal, on the banks of the Mississippi River, observing its busy life, fascinated by its romance, but chilled by the violence and bloodshed it bred. Clemens was eleven years old when his lawyer father died. In order to help the family earn money, the young Clemens began working as a store clerk and a delivery boy. He also began working as an apprentice (working to learn a trade), then a compositor (a person who sets type), with local printers, contributing occasional small pieces to local newspapers. At seventeen his comic sketch "The Dandy Frightening the Squatter" was published by a sportsmen's magazine in Boston, Massachusetts.

In 1853 Clemens began wandering as a journeyman printer to St. Louis, Missouri; Chicago, Illinois; New York, New York; and Philadelphia, Pennsylvania; settling briefly with his brother, Orion, in Iowa before setting out at twenty-two years old to make his fortune, he hoped, beside the lush banks of the Amazon River in South America. Instead, traveling down the Mississippi River, he became a steamboat river pilot until the outbreak of the Civil War (1861–65), when Northern forces clashed with those of the South over slavery and secession (the South's desire to leave the Union).

Western years

In 1861 Clemens traveled to Nevada, where he invested carelessly in timber and silver mining. He settled down to newspaper work in Virginia City, until his reckless pen and redheaded temper brought him into conflict with local authorities; it seemed profitable to escape to California. Meanwhile he had adopted the pen name of Mark Twain, a riverman's term for water that is just safe enough for navigation.

In 1865, Twain began to write a short story, *The Jumping Frog of Calaveras County,* which first brought him national attention. Most of his western writing was hastily, often carelessly, done and he later did little to preserve it.

Traveling correspondent

In 1865 the *Sacramento Union* commissioned Mark Twain to report on a new excursion service to Hawaii. His accounts as published in the newspaper provided the basis for his first successful lectures and years later were collected in *Letters from the Sandwich Islands* (1938) and *Letters from Honolulu* (1939). His travel accounts were so well received that he was contracted in 1866 to become a traveling correspondent for the *Alta California;* he would circle the globe, writing letters.

In 1870 Twain married Olivia Langdon. After a brief residence in upstate New York as an editor and part owner of the *Buffalo Express,* he moved to Hartford, Connecticut, where he lived for twenty years; there three daughters were born, and prosperity as a writer and lecturer (in England in 1872 and 1873) seemed guaranteed. *Roughing It* (1872) recounted Mark Twain's travels to Nevada and reprinted some of the Sandwich Island letters.

Meanwhile Mark Twain's account of steamboating experiences for the *Atlantic Monthly* (1875; expanded to *Life on the Mississippi,* 1883) captured the beauty, glamor, and danger of the Mississippi River. Boyhood memories of life beside that river were written into *The Adventures of Tom Sawyer* (1875), which immediately attracted young and old

Mark Twain.
Reproduced by permission of AP/Wide World Photos.

alike. With more exotic and foreign settings, *The Prince and the Pauper* (1882) and *A Connecticut Yankee in King Arthur's Court* (1889) attracted readers also, but *The Adventures of Huckleberry Finn* (1885), in which Mark Twain again returned to the river scenes he knew best, was considered unacceptable by many.

"Tom" and "Huck"

Twain's *Tom Sawyer,* better organized than *Huckleberry Finn,* is a narrative of innocent boyhood play that accidentally discovers evil as Tom and Huck witness a murder by Injun Joe in a graveyard at midnight. The boys run away, are thought dead, but turn up at their own funeral. Tom and Huck decide to seek out the murderer and the reward offered for his capture. It is Tom and his sweetheart who, while lost in a cave, discover the hiding place of Injun Joe. Though the townspeople unwittingly seal the murderer in the cave, they close the entrance only to keep adventuresome boys like Tom out of future trouble. In the end, it is innocent play and boyish adventuring which really triumph.

Huckleberry Finn is considered by many to be Mark Twain's finest creation. Huck lacks Tom's imagination; he is a simple boy with little education. One measure of his character is a proneness to deceit, which seems instinctive, a trait shared by other wild things and relating him to nature—in opposition to Tom's tradition-grounded, book-learned, imaginative deceptions. *The Adventures of Huckleberry Finn,* a loosely strung series of adventures, can be viewed as the story of a quest for freedom and an escape from what society requires in exchange for success. Joined in flight by a black companion, Jim, who seeks freedom from slavery, Huck discovers that the Mississippi is peaceful (though he is found to be only partially correct) but that the world along its shores is full of trickery, including his own, and by cruelty and murder. When the raft on which he and Jim are floating down the river is invaded by two criminals, Huck first becomes their assistant in swindles but is finally the agent of their exposure.

Whatever its faults, Twain's *Huckleberry Finn* is a classic. Variously interpreted, it is often thought to suggest more than it reveals, speaking of what man has done to confuse himself about his right relation to nature. It can also be thought of as a treatment of man's failures in dealing with his fellows and of the corruption that man's only escape is in flight, perhaps even from himself. Yet it is also an apparently artless story of adventure and escape so simply and directly told that novelist Ernest Hemingway (c.1899–1961) once said that all American literature begins with this book.

Last writings

After a series of unsuccessful business ventures in Europe, Twain returned to the United States in 1900. His writings grew increasingly bitter, especially after his wife's death in 1905. *The Man That Corrupted Hadleyburg* (1900) exposed corruption in a small, typical American town. *Eve's Diary* (1906), written partly in memory of his wife, showed a man saved from bungling only through the influence of a good woman.

In 1906 Twain began to dictate his autobiography to Albert B. Paine, recording scattered memories without any particular order. Portions from it were published in periodicals later that year. With the income from the excerpts of his autobiography, he built a large house in Redding, Connecticut, which he named Stormfield. There, after several trips to Bermuda to improve his declining health, he died on April 21, 1910.

For More Information

Kaplan, Justin. *Mr. Clemens and Mark Twain: A Biography.* New York: Simon and Schuster, 1966.

Krauth, Leland. *Proper Mark Twain.* Athens: University of Georgia Press, 1999.

Paine, Albert Bigelow. *Mark Twain, A Biography: The Personal and Literary Life of*

Samuel Langhorne Clemens. New York: Harper & Bros., 1912. Reprint, Philadelphia: Chelsea House, 1997.

Twain, Mark. *The Autobiography of Mark Twain.* New York: Harper, 1959. Reprint, New York: Perennial Classics, 2000.

Ward, Geoffrey C., and Dayton Duncan. *Mark Twain.* New York: Knopf, 2001.

Wecter, Dixon. *Sam Clemens of Hannibal.* Boston: Houghton Mifflin, 1952. Reprint, New York: AMS Press, 1979.

JOHN UPDIKE

Born: March 18, 1932
Shillington, Pennsylvania
American author and poet

Author John Updike mirrored his America in poems, short stories, essays, and novels, especially the four-volume "Rabbit" series.

Early life

John Hoyer Updike was born on March 18, 1932, in Shillington, Pennsylvania. His father, Wesley, was a high school mathematics teacher, the model for several sympathetic father figures in Updike's early works. Because Updike's mother, Linda Grace Hoyer Updike, had literary dreams of her own, books were a large part of the boy's early life. A sickly child, Updike turned to reading and art as an escape. In high school, he worked on the school newspaper and excelled in academics and upon graduation was admitted into Harvard University in Cambridge, Massachusetts.

At the age of twenty-two, Updike began his writing career when he published his first story "Friends from Philadelphia," in the *New Yorker* in 1954. Since childhood Updike had admired the *New Yorker* and always dreamed

John Updike.

Reproduced by permission of AP/Wide World Photos.

of becoming a cartoonist for the magazine. He majored in English at Harvard where he developed his skills as a graphic artist and cartoonist for the *Lampoon,* the college's humor magazine. In 1953, his junior year at Harvard, he married Mary Pennington, a Radcliffe art student. Upon graduation the following year, Updike and his bride went to London, England, where he had won a Knox fellowship (scholarship) for study at the Ruskin School of Drawing and Fine Art in Oxford, England.

Updike returned to the United States in 1955 and took a job as a staff writer at the New Yorker at the invitation of famed editor E. B. White (1899–1985), achieving a life-long goal. But after two years and many "Talk of the Town" columns, he left New York City for Ipswich, Massachusetts, to devote himself full time to his own writing.

Twenty years of poetry

Updike began his remarkable career as a poet in 1958 by publishing his first volume, a collection of poems titled *The Carpentered Hen.* It is a book of light, amusing verse in the style of Ogden Nash (1902–1971) and Robert Service (1874–1958). The poetry possesses several styles shared by his fiction: careful attention to the sounds of words and of their meanings, the use of popular culture by identifying objects by familiar brand names, and the imitation of the popular press through advertising language.

Updike's output of light verse diminished with the publication of each succeeding volume of poems. His poetry has been collected in several volumes, among them *Telephone Poles and Other Poems* (1963); *Midpoint* (1969), which is a personal look at the midpoint of his life; and *Tossing and Turning* (1977), which some critics consider his finest collection of verse.

The "Rabbit" series and other novels

Although Updike's reputation rests on his complete body of work, he was first established as a major American writer upon the publication of his novel *Rabbit Run* (1960)—although at that date no one could have predicted the rich series of novels that would follow. It chronicled the life of Harry (Rabbit) Angstrom, creating as memorable an American character as any that appeared in the twentieth century. Harry Angstrom's life peaked in high school where he was admired as a superb basketball player. But by the age of twenty-six he is washed up in a dead-end job, demonstrating gadgets in a dime store, living a disappointed and constricted life. His natural reaction to this problem is to "run" (as would his namesake). And he runs, fleeing his wife and family as though the salvation of his soul depends upon it. The climax of Rabbit's search results in tragedy, but it is to the credit of Updike's skill that great sympathy for a dislikable character is brought forth from readers.

The second novel in the series, *Rabbit Redux* (1971), takes up the story of Harry Angstrom ten years later at the age of thirty-six. Updike continues Rabbit's story against a background of current events. The novel begins on the day of the moon shot, when the first human walked on the moon. It is the late 1960s and the optimism of American technology is countered by the sour feelings towards race riots, antiwar protests, and the drug culture. His family is falling apart, mirroring the problems of the country at large. Rabbit finally overcomes his dismal situation and brings "outsiders" into his home, attempting to recreate his family.

The next book in the series is *Rabbit Is Rich* (1981), which won the 1982 Pulitzer Prize. Rabbit is forty-six and finally successful, selling Japanese fuel-efficient cars during the time of the oil crisis in the 1970s. In this novel Rabbit's son Nelson's failure becomes the counterweight to Rabbit's success.

Rabbit at Rest (1990) brings Rabbit into the 1980s to confront an even grimmer set of problems: acquired immune deficiency syndrome (AIDS; an incurable disease that attacks the immune system), cocaine addiction, and terrorism. Rabbit suffers a heart attack and is haunted by ghosts of his past. Death looms ever larger. In these four novels an insignificant life presses and insists itself upon our consciousness, and we realize that this life has become the story of our common American experience recorded over three decades.

Other works

Updike wrote many other major novels, including *The Centaur* (1963), *Couples* (1965), *A Month of Sundays* (1975), *The Witches of Eastwick* (1984), *Brazil* (1993), and *Bech at Bay* (1998). Updike was also the author of several volumes of short stories, among them *Pigeon Feathers* (1962), *The Music School* (1966), *Bech: A Book* (1970), *Museums and Women* (1972), and *Bech Is Back* (1982).

In 1999 Updike published *More Matter: Essays and Criticism,* a collection of occasional pieces, reviews, speeches, and some personal reflection. On February 27, 2000, his novel *Gertrude and Claudius* was published by Knopf. The book was based on William Shakespeare's (1564–1616) play *Hamlet.*

Updike has been honored throughout his career: twice he received the National Book Critics Circle Award and the Pulitzer Prize. He also received the American Book Award and was elected to the American Academy of Arts and Letters. Updike has been one of the most productive American authors of his time, leading even his most dedicated fans to confess, as Sean French did in *New Statesman and Society,* "Updike can write faster than I can read."

For More Information

Bloom, Harold, ed. *John Updike.* Broomall, PA: Chelsea House, 1987.

De Bellis, Jack. *The John Updike Encyclopedia.* Westport, CT: Greenwood Press, 2000.

Schiff, James A. *John Updike Revisited.* New York: Twayne Publishers, 1998.

Updike, John. *Self-Consciousness: Memoirs.* New York: Knopf, 1989.

VINCENT VAN GOGH

Born: March 30, 1853
Groot-Zundert, Holland
Died: July 29, 1890
Auvers, France
Dutch painter

Vincent Van Gogh was a Dutch painter whose formal distortions and humanistic concerns made him a major pioneer of twentieth-century expressionism, an artistic movement that emphasized expression of the artist's experience.

Childhood

Born on March 30, 1853, at Groot-Zundert in the province of Brabant, Holland, Vincent Willem Van Gogh was the son of a Protestant minister, Theodorus Van Gogh. Exactly a year before his birth, his mother, Cornelia, gave birth to an infant, also named Vincent, who was stillborn, or dead upon birth. His grieving parents buried the child and set up a tombstone to mark the grave. As a result, Vincent Van Gogh grew up near the haunting sight of a grave with his own name upon it. His mother later gave birth to Theo, his younger brother, and three younger sisters. Not much is known about Van Gogh's earlier education, but he did receive some encouragement from his mother to draw and paint. As a teenager he drew and painted regularly.

Van Gogh's uncle was a partner in Goupil and Company, art dealers. Vincent entered the firm at the age of sixteen and remained there for six years. He served the firm first in The Hague, the political seat of the Netherlands, and then in London, England, where he fell in love with his landlady's daughter, who rejected him. Later he worked for Goupil's branch in Paris, France.

Because of Van Gogh's unpleasant attitude, Goupil dismissed him in 1876. That year he returned to England, worked at a small school at Ramsgate, and did some preaching. In early 1877 he clerked in a bookshop in Dordrecht. Then, convinced that the ministry ought to be his calling, he joined a religious seminary in Brussels, Belgium. He left three months later to become an evangelist (a preacher) in a poor mining section of Belgium, the Borinage. Van Gogh exhibited the necessary dedication, even giving away his clothes, but his odd behavior kept the miners at a distance. Once again, in July 1879, he found himself dismissed from a job. This period was a dark one for Van Gogh. He wished to give himself to others but was constantly being rejected.

In 1880, after much soul searching, Van Gogh decided to devote his life to art, a profession he accepted as a spiritual calling. When in London he had visited museums, and he had drawn a little while in the Borinage. In October 1880 he attended an art school in Brussels, where he studied the basics of perspective (representing three-dimensional objects on a two-dimensional surface) and anatomy (the human body). From April to December 1881 he stayed with his parents, who were then in Etten, and continued to work on his art. At this time, too, he studied at the academic art school at The Hague, where his cousin Anton Mauve taught.

Dutch period

During Van Gogh's Dutch period (1880–1886) he created works in which his overriding concerns for his fellow man were growing. His subjects were poor people, miners, peasants, and inhabitants of almshouses, or houses for the poor. Among his favorite painters at this time were Jean François Millet (1814–1875), Rembrandt (1606–1669), and Honoré Daumier (1808–1879). Complementing Van Gogh's dreary subject matter of this time were his colors, dark brownish and greenish shades. The masterpiece of Van Gogh's Dutch period is the *Potato Eaters* (1885), a night scene in which peasants sit at their meal around a table.

Van Gogh decided to go to Paris in early 1886, partially because he was drawn to the simple and artistic life of the French city. His younger brother, Theo, was living in Paris, where he directed a small gallery maintained by Goupil and Company. Theo had supported Vincent financially and emotionally from the time he decided to become a painter, and would continue to do so throughout his life. The letters between the brothers are among the most moving documents in all the history of Western art. Vincent shared Theo's apartment and studied at an art school run by the traditional painter Fernand Cormon, where he met Émile Bernard (1868–1941) and Henri de Toulouse-Lautrec (1864–1901), who became his friends.

By now Van Gogh was largely under the influence of the impressionists, a style of painting where the artist concentrates on the immediate impression of a scene by the use of light and color. Especially influenced by Camille Pissarro (1830–1903), Van Gogh was persuaded to give up the gloomy tones of his Dutch period for bright, high-keyed colors. Also, his subject matter changed from the world of peasants to a typically impressionistic subject matter, such as cafés and cityscapes around Montmartre, an area of northern Paris. He also copied Japanese prints. While subjects and handling were obviously taken from impressionism, there frequently could be detected a certain sad quality, as in a scene of *Montmartre* (1886), where pedestrians are pushed to the outer sides of an open square.

Stay at Arles

Longing for a place of light and warmth, and tired of being entirely financially dependent on Theo, Van Gogh left for Arles in southern France in February 1888. The pleasant country about Arles and the warmth of the place restored Van Gogh to health. In his fifteen months there he painted over two hundred pictures. At this time he applied color in simplified, highly dense masses, his drawing became more energetic and confused than ever before, and objects seemed to radiate a light of their own without giving off shadows. During this period he also turned to painting portraits and executed several self-portraits. Among the masterpieces of his Arles period are the *Fishing Boats on the Beach at Saintes-Maries* (June 1888); the *Night Café* (September); and the *Artist's Bedroom at Arles* (October).

At Arles Van Gogh suffered fainting spells and seizures (involuntary muscle

Vincent Van Gogh.
Courtesy of the Library of Congress.

spasms). The local population began to turn against him as well. Paul Gauguin (1848–1903), responding to his invitation, visited him in October 1888, but the two men quarreled violently. Gauguin left for Paris. Van Gogh, in a fit of remorse and anger, cut off his ear. On May 9, 1889, he asked to be admitted to the asylum at Saint-Rémy-de Provence, a hospital for the mentally ill.

Production at Saint-Rémy

In the year Van Gogh spent at the asylum he worked as much as he had at Arles, producing 150 paintings and hundreds of drawings. Van Gogh suffered several attacks but was completely peaceful in between. At this time he received his first critical praise (a good review), an article by the writer Albert Aurier.

During Van Gogh's stay at Saint-Rémy, his art changed markedly. His colors lost the intensity of the Arles period: yellows became coppers; reds verged toward brownish tones. His lines became restless. He applied the paint more violently with thicker impasto, the application of thick layers. Van Gogh was drawn to objects in nature under stress: whirling suns, twisted cypress trees, and surging mountains. In *Starry Night* (1889) the whole world seems engulfed by circular movements.

Van Gogh went to Paris on May 17, 1890, to visit his brother. On the advice of Pissarro, Theo had Vincent go to Auvers, just outside Paris, to submit to the care of Dr. Paul Gachet, an amateur painter and a friend of Pissarro and Paul Cézanne (1839–1906).

Last year at Auvers

Van Gogh arrived at Auvers on May 21, 1890. He painted a portrait of Dr. Gachet and portraits of his daughters, as well as the *Church of Auvers*. The blue of the Auvers period was not the full blue of Arles but a more mysterious, flickering blue. In his last painting, the *Cornfield with Crows,* Van Gogh showed a topsy-turvy world. The spectator himself becomes the object of perspective, and it is toward him that the crows appear to be flying.

At first Van Gogh felt relieved at Auvers, but toward the end of June he experienced fits of temper and often quarreled with Gachet. On July 27, 1890, he shot himself in a lonely field and died the morning of July 29, 1890.

For More Information

Arnold, Wilfred Niels. *Vincent Van Gogh: Chemicals, Crises, and Creativity.* Boston: Birkhäuser, 1992.

Greenberg, Jan. *Vincent Van Gogh: Portrait of an Artist.* New York: Delacorte Press, 2001.

Hammacher, Abraham M. *Genius and Disaster: The Ten Creative Years of Vincent Van Gogh.* New York: H. N. Abrams, 1968.

Isom, Joan Shaddox. *The First Starry Night.* Dallas: Whispering Coyote Press, 1997.

Lubin, Albert J. *Stranger on the Earth: A Psychological Biography of Vincent Van Gogh.* New York: Da Capo Press, 1996.

Metzger, Rainer, and Ingo F. Walther. *Vincent Van Gogh: 1853–1890.* New York: Taschen, 1998.

Schapiro, Meyer. *Vincent Van Gogh.* Garden City, NY: Doubleday, 1980.

JAN VERMEER

Born: October 30, 1632
Delft, Netherlands
Died: December 15, 1675
Delft, Netherlands
Dutch painter

The Dutch painter Jan Vermeer of Delft transformed traditional Dutch themes into images of fantastic poise and peace, rich with symbolic meaning.

Mysterious childhood

The documented facts about Jan Vermeer's life are few. He was born on October 30 or 31, 1632, in Delft, Netherlands, the second of two children to Digna Baltens and Reynier Jansz. His father was an art dealer and silk weaver who also kept a tavern, and Vermeer probably took over the business after his father's death in 1655. It is presumed that his father, who was actively involved with the local artists and collectors, was an early influence on the young child. Vermeer supposedly began his training as an artist around the mid-1640s.

In 1653 Vermeer married a well-to-do Catholic girl from Gouda; they had eleven children. In the year of his marriage he became a master in the Delft painters' guild (an association), of which he was an officer from 1662 to 1663, and again, from 1669 to 1670. He seems to have painted very little and to have sold only a fraction of his limited production, for the majority of his paintings were still in the hands of his family when he died. His dealings in works by other artists seem to have supported his family reasonably well until he was financially ruined following the French invasion of 1672, when France invaded the Spanish Netherlands. He died in 1675 and was buried on December 15. The following year his wife was forced to declare bankruptcy.

Nothing is known about where Vermeer was educated and trained as a painter. In part because verses written following the death of Carel Fabritius (1622–1654) in 1654 mention Vermeer as his successor as Delft's leading artist, it has been suggested that Fabritius was Vermeer's teacher. Certainly Fabritius helped develop Vermeer's interest in perspective experiments (experiments with depth)

Jan Vermeer.
Reproduced by permision of the Bridgeman Art Library.

and his use of a light-flooded wall as a background for figures. But Fabritius lived in Delft only after 1650, by which time Vermeer would have been well on his way toward the completion of his training.

Early works

The warm colors of *The Procuress* relate it to paintings of the Rembrandt school (styled after the painter Rembrandt [1606–1669]) of the 1650s, but its subject matter and composition reflect influence by paintings of the 1620s by the Utrecht Caravaggists, a group of painters in Utrecht, Netherlands, who stressed a new, international style. Considered to be earlier than *The Procuress* are two pictures that resemble it because of the color scheme, dominated by reds and yellows, and because they are larger in size and scale than Vermeer's later works. *Christ in the House of Martha and Mary* is similar to compositions by Hendrick Terbrugghen (1588–1629) and Gerrit van Honthorst (1590–1656), who spread the Caravaggesque (having to do with the painting style of Italian painter Caravaggio [c. 1571–1610]) style in Holland. *Diana and Her Companions,* Vermeer's only mythological subject, is also suggestive of Italy. It is his only painting of figures in a landscape setting.

After these three diverse experiments, which may have owed something to Vermeer's familiarity with works in his father's stock of art, he painted the *Girl Asleep at a Table,* in which he used the warm range of colors of his other early pictures but in terms of subject matter and composition plunged into the mainstream of current Delft painting.

The Soldier and Laughing Girl, marked the shift between Vermeer's early and mature works in that pointillé (gleaming highlights of thick layers of paint, which brightens the surface) appeared for the first time.

Mature period

Vermeer's style just before 1660 is also well represented by *The Cook.* The rich paint surface with its extraordinary quality, the monumental figure perfectly balanced in space and involved in a humble task, and the intense colors dominated by yellow and blue all show Vermeer at the height of his powers.

Following these works, which are assumed to have immediately followed 1660, come the "pearl pictures." *The Concert* of about 1662 and the *Woman with a Water Jug*

of perhaps a year later display the pleasing charms of this period.

More complicated compositions and especially larger space representations mark the major works of the last decade of Vermeer's life. The *Allegory of the Art of Painting* (c.1670) is large and complex in both composition and meaning. On the whole it is not influenced by the hardness and dryness that weakened his later works, such as the *Allegory of the Catholic Faith.*

The quietness, peacefulness, order, and unchanging world of Vermeer's art provide hints of immortality, or the idea that one cannot be affected by death. Perhaps that is why this painter, whose works appear to be as clear as the light of day, has always been thought to be mysterious.

For More Information

Gowing, Lawrence. *Vermeer.* New York: Harper & Row, 1970.

Larsen, Erik. *Jan Vermeer.* New York: Smithmark, 1998.

Wheelock, Arthur K., Jr. *Jan Vermeer.* New York: Abrams, 1981.

Wheelock, Arthur K. *Vermeer & the Art of Painting.* New Haven, CT: Yale University Press, 1995.

JULES VERNE

Born: February 8, 1828
Nantes, France
Died: March 24, 1905
Amiens, France
French novelist and writer

The French novelist Jules Verne was the first authentic writer of modern science fiction. The best of his works, such as *Twenty Thousand Leagues Under the Sea* and *Journey to the Center of the Earth,* are characterized by his intelligent foresight into the technical achievements that are within man's grasp.

Early life

Jules Gabriel Verne was born on February 8, 1828, in Nantes, France, the eldest son of a prosperous lawyer, Pierre Verne, and his wife Sophie. Raised in a middle-class family, Jules despised his parents' constant drive to achieve middle-class respectability. Always rebellious but unsuccessful, Verne learned to escape into his own world of imagination. These feelings would show up in many of Verne's works as an adult.

An otherwise uneventful childhood was marked by one major event. In his twelfth year, Jules worked as a cabin boy on an ocean-going ship. The ship was intercepted by his father before it went to sea, and Jules is said to have promised his parents that in the future he "would travel only in imagination"—a prediction fulfilled in a manner his parents could not have imagined.

Career as a playwright

In 1847 Verne went to Paris, France, to study law, although privately he was already planning a literary career. Owing to the friendship he made with French author Alexandre Dumas the Elder (1802–1870), Verne's first play, *Broken Straws,* was produced—with some success—in 1850. From 1852 to 1855 he held a steady and low-pay-

Jules Verne.

ing position as secretary of a Paris theater, the Théâtre Lyrique. He continued to write comedies and operettas and began contributing short stories to a popular magazine, *Le Musée des familles.*

During a visit to Amiens, France, in May 1856, Verne met and fell in love with the widowed daughter of an army officer, Madame Morel (née Honorine de Viane), whom he married the following January. The circumstance that his wife's brother was a stockbroker may have influenced Verne in making the unexpected decision to embrace this profession. Membership in the Paris Exchange did not seriously interfere with his literary labors, however, because he adopted a rigorous timetable, rising at five o'clock in order to put in several hours researching and writing before beginning his day's work at the Bourse.

First novels

Verne's first long work of fiction, *Five Weeks in a Balloon,* took the form of an account of a journey by air over central Africa, at that time largely unexplored. The book, published in January 1863, was an immediate success. He then decided to retire from stockbroking and to devote himself full time to writing.

Verne's next few books were immensely successful at the time and are still counted among the best he wrote. *A Journey to the Center of the Earth* (1864) describes the adventures of a party of explorers and scientists who descend the crater of an Icelandic volcano and discover an underground world. *The Adventures of Captain Hatteras* (1866) centers on an expedition to the North Pole (not actually reached by Robert Peary until 1909). In *From the Earth to the Moon* (1865) and its sequel, *Round the Moon* (1870), Verne describes how two adventurous Americans—joined, naturally, by a Frenchman—arrange to be fired in a hollow projectile from a gigantic cannon that lifts them out of Earth's gravity field and takes them close to the moon. Verne not only pictured the state of weightlessness his "astronauts" experienced during their flight, but also he had the vision to locate their launching site in Florida, where nearly all of the National Aeronautics and Space Administration's (NASA) space launches take place today.

Later works

Verne wrote his two masterpieces when he was in his forties. *Twenty Thousand Leagues Under the Sea* (1870) relates the voyages of the submarine *Nautilus,* built and commanded by the mysterious Captain Nemo, one of the literary figures in whom Verne incorporated many of his own character traits. *Around the World in Eighty Days* (1873) is the story of a successful bet made by a typical Englishman, Phineas Fogg, a character said to have been modeled on Verne's father, who had a mania for punctuality, or the art of timeliness.

Other popular novels include *The Mysterious Island* (1875) and *Michael Strogoff* (1876). Verne's total literary output comprised nearly eighty books, but many of them are of little value or interest today. One noteworthy feature of all his work is its moral idealism, which earned him in 1884 the personal congratulations of Pope Leo XIII (1810–1903). "If I am not always what I ought to be," Verne once wrote, "my characters will be what I should like to be." His interest in scientific progress was balanced by his religious faith, and in some of his later novels (such as *The Purchase of the North Pole,* 1889), he showed himself to be aware of the social dangers of uncontrolled technological advance.

Verne the man

Verne's personality was complex. Though capable of bouts of extreme liveliness and given to joking and playing practical jokes, he was basically a shy man, happiest when alone in his study or when sailing the English Channel in a converted fishing boat.

In 1886 Verne was the victim of a shooting accident, which left him disabled. The man that shot him proved to be a nephew who was suffering from mental instability.

This incident served to reinforce Verne's natural tendency toward depression. Although he served on the city council of Amiens two years later, he spent his old age in retirement. In 1902 he became partially blind and he died on March 24, 1905 in Amiens.

For More Information

Costello, Peter. *Jules Verne: Inventor of Science Fiction.* London: Hodder and Stoughton, 1978.

Evans, I. O. *Jules Verne and His Work.* New York: Twayne, 1966. Reprint, Mattituck, NY: Aeonian Press, 1976.

Jules-Verne, Jean. *Jules Verne: A Biography.* New York: Taplinger Publishing Company, 1976.

Lottman, Herbert R. *Jules Verne: An Exploratory Biography* New York: St. Martin's Press, 1996.

Lynch, Lawrence W. *Jules Verne.* New York: Twayne Publishers, 1992.

Teeters, Peggy. *Jules Verne: The Man Who Invented Tomorrow.* New York: Walker and Company, 1993.

AMERIGO VESPUCCI

Born: March 9, 1451
Florence, Italy
Died: February 22, 1512
Seville, Spain
Italian navigator

A Florentine navigator and pilot major of Castile, Spain, Amerigo Vespucci, for whom America is named, played a major part in exploring the New World.

Childhood

The father of Amerigo Vespucci was Nastagio Vespucci, and his uncle was the learned Dominican Giorgio Antonio Vespucci, who had charge of Amerigo's education. The entire family was cultured and friendly with the Medici rulers of Florence, a family that ruled Italy from the 1400s to 1737. Domenico Ghirlandaio (1449–1494) painted Amerigo in a family portrait when the youth was about nineteen. However, the explorer had reached his forties by the time he began his voyage to America, so Ghirlandaio's painting shows only an approximate idea of Vespucci's mature appearance.

It is known that Vespucci visited France, in his uncle's company, when he was about twenty-four years old, and that his father intended for him a business career. He did get involved in business, first in Florence and then in Seville, Spain, in a bank. Later, in Seville, he entered a partnership with a fellow Florentine, Gianetto Berardi, and this lasted until Berardi's death at the end of 1495.

Meanwhile, Christopher Columbus (1451–1506) had made his first two voyages to the West Indies, and he returned from the second in June 1496. At this time, he and Vespucci met and talked, and Amerigo appears to have been doubtful of Columbus's belief that he had already reached the outskirts of Asia. Moreover, Vespucci's curiosity about the new lands had been aroused, together with a determination—though no longer young—to see them himself.

Amerigo Vespucci.
Courtesy of the Library of Congress.

First voyage

According to a controversial letter, Vespucci embarked from Cadiz, Spain, in a Spanish fleet on May 10, 1497. Serious doubts have been raised about the letter's authenticity (based on fact), because dates in the letter do not coordinate with authenticated events, and because the voyage, if made, presents serious geographical problems and seems to have passed unnoticed by the cartographers (mapmakers) and historians of the time.

If the letter is real, the ships passed through the West Indies—sighting no islands—and in thirty-seven days reached the mainland somewhere in Central America. This would predate Columbus's discovery of the mainland of Venezuela by a year. On their return to Spain, Vespucci's men discovered the inhabited island of "Iti," identified by some as Bermuda. However, by 1522 the Bermudas were unpopulated. The expedition returned to Cadiz in October 1498.

Vespucci, in all probability, voyaged to America at the time noted, but he did not have command and as yet had had no practical experience piloting a ship. Inexperience could explain many of the errors in the letter, but the strong likelihood remains that the letter was altered.

In 1499 Vespucci sailed again, and this time there is proof of the expedition besides his own letters. His education had included mathematics, and he had surely learned a great deal from his first crossing. From Cadiz, they first dropped to the Cape Verde Islands and then divided forces in the Atlantic. Vespucci explored to Cape Santo Agostinho, at the shoulder of Brazil, after which he coasted westward past the Maracaibo Gulf. This may have been the first expedition to touch Brazil as well as the first to cross the Equator in New World waters. During these travels, Vespucci probably discovered the mouth of the Amazon River.

A new world

Two years later Amerigo went on his most important voyage, this time for King Manuel I (1469–1521) to Brazil. Vespucci, having already been to the Brazilian shoulder, seemed the person best qualified to go as an observer with the new expedition. Vespucci did not command at the start but ultimately took charge at the request of the Portuguese officers.

This voyage traced the South American coast from a point above Cape Sào Roque to Patagonia. Among the important discoveries were Guanabara Bay (Rio de Janeiro) and the Rio de la Plata, which soon began to appear on maps as Rio Jordán. The expedition returned by way of Sierra Leone and the Azores, and Vespucci, in a letter to Florence, called South America Mundus Novus (New World).

In 1503 Amerigo sailed in Portuguese service again to Brazil, but this expedition failed to make new discoveries. The fleet broke up, the Portuguese commander's ship disappeared, and Vespucci could proceed only a little past Bahia before returning to Lisbon, Portugal, in 1504. He never sailed again.

Vespucci's legacy

In 1507 a group of scholars at St-Dié in Lorraine brought out a book of geography entitled "Cosmographiae introductio." One of the authors, Martin Waldseemüller, suggested the name America, especially for the Brazilian part of the New World, in honor of "the illustrious man who discovered it." After some debate, the name was eventually adopted.

During his last years, Amerigo held the office of pilot major, and it became his duty to train pilots, examine them for ability in their craft, and collect data regarding New World navigation. He remained pilot major until his death on February 22, 1512, a month short of his fifty-eighth birthday.

For More Information

Arciniegas, Germán. *Amerigo and the New World: The Life and Times of Amerigo Vespucci.* New York: Knopf, 1955. Reprint, New York: Octagon Books, 1978.

Baker, Nina Brown. *Amerigo Vespucci.* New York: Knopf, 1956.

Donaldson-Forbes, Jeff. *Amerigo Vespucci.* New York: PowerKids Press, 2002.

Fradin, Dennis Brindell. *Amerigo Vespucci.* New York: Franklin Watts, 1991.

Pohl, Frederick Julius. *Amerigo Vespucci, Pilot Major.* New York: Columbia University Press, 1944, revised edition 1966.

Swan, Barry. *Amerigo Vespucci.* Wembly, Middlesex, England: Valley Press, 1998.

VICTORIA

Born: May 24, 1819
London, England
Died: January 22, 1901
Isle of Wight, England
English queen

Victoria was queen of Great Britain and Ireland from 1837 to 1901 and empress of India from 1876 to 1901. During her reign, England grew into an empire of 4 million square miles and 124 million people. As queen, she saw slavery end in the colonies, saw her country undertake successful wars in the Crimea, Egypt, the Sudan, and South Africa, acquired the Suez Canal, and established constitutions in Australia and Canada.

Victoria.
Courtesy of the Library of Congress.

Early life and the throne

Alexandrina Victoria was born in Kensington Palace, London, on May 24, 1819. She was the only child of Edward, Duke of Kent (1767–1820), by Mary Louis Victoria (1786–1861). Her father died when she was very young and her early years were disrupted by family arguments. She grew up under her mother's care and that of Louisa Lehzen, her German governess. The education Victoria received from Lehzen was limited, and she spoke only German until she was three years old.

From 1832 Victoria's mother took her on extended tours through England. On May 24, 1837, she came of age, and on June 20, after the death of her uncle William IV (1765–1837), she inherited the throne. Her chief advisers at first were Prime Minister Lord Melbourne, a Whig (or a member of the liberal political party), and Baron Stockmar, a German sent to London by her uncle King Leopold of the Belgians as adviser to his eighteen-year-old niece. On June 28, 1838, her coronation (crowning ceremony) took place.

In October her first cousin Albert Edward (1819–1861) of Saxe-Coburg-Gotha, came to London. Victoria fell in love with him instantly, proposed to him, and they were married on February 10, 1840. It was a happy marriage and restored the influence of the Crown, which had weakened during the reigns of those that ruled before her. Prince Albert was granted a thirty-thousand-pound annual income by Parliament, the governing body of Great Britain. He also was named regent (acting ruler) in the event of the queen's death in childbirth, and in 1857 was made Prince Consort by Victoria.

In June 1842 Victoria made her first railway journey from Slough, the station nearest Windsor Castle, to Paddington, and in that same year she first went to Scotland, traveling by sea. In 1843 Victoria and Albert visited King Louis Philippe (1773–c.1850). She was the first English monarch to land in France since Henry VIII (1491–1547) visited Francis I (1494–1547) in 1520. King Louis Philippe's return visit was the first voluntary visit to England of any French ruler. In 1845 Victoria, with Albert, made the first of many trips to Germany, staying at Albert's birthplace, Rosenau.

Queen of England

In 1844 Queen Victoria had Osborne Palace built for her on the Isle of Wight and in 1848 Balmoral Castle in Scotland. Until the end of her life she spent part of each spring and fall in these places. In 1851 she and Prince Albert were much occupied with the Great Exhibition, a world's fair held in London and the first of its kind.

In 1856 Victoria and Albert visited Napoleon III (1808–1873) in Paris, and in 1857 the Indian Mutiny against British rule in India led to Victoria's writing that there now existed in England "a universal feeling that India [should] belong to me." In 1858 the British charter that opened trade with Asia, known as the East India Company, was dismantled. That same year Victoria's eldest child, Victoria, married Prince (later Emperor) Frederick of Prussia (today known as Germany). In March 1861 Victoria's mother died, and her eldest son, Albert Edward, while in camp in the Curragh in Ireland, had an affair with an actress called Nelly Clifden. The affair worried Victoria and Albert, who were planning his marriage to Princess Alexandra of Denmark. Meanwhile, Albert was suffering from typhoid fever, a terrible disease that causes fever and other symptoms and is easily spread, and died on December 14, 1861, at the age of forty-two.

In 1862 Victoria's daughter Alice married Prince Louis of Hesse, and a year later her eldest son, the Prince of Wales, married Princess Alexandra of Denmark. Victoria supported Prussia during its war with Denmark over Schleswig-Holstein (a state in northwest Germany) and she approved Russia's brutal crushing of Poland's national uprising in 1863. In 1865 in the Seven Weeks War between Prussia and Austria, Victoria was again pro-Prussian. In 1867 Victoria entertained the Khedive of Egypt and the Sultan of Turkey.

In the Franco-Prussian War of 1870 between France and Prussia, Victoria was still pro-Prussian, though she welcomed the French empress Eugénie and allowed her and the emperor to live at Chislehurst. In 1873 Prime Minister William Gladstone (1809–1898) resigned, and in 1874, to Victoria's delight, Benjamin Disraeli (1804–1881) became prime minister, the chief advisor to the throne. He called the plump, tiny queen "The Faery" and admitted he loved her. That same year Victoria's son Prince Alfred married Marie, daughter of the Russian czar (king), who insisted she be called "Imperial," not "Royal Highness." This encouraged Victoria to look into officially assuming the title "Empress of India," which she did on May 1, 1876.

In 1875 Disraeli bought the majority of the Suez Canal, a key waterway for trade in the Mediterranean Sea, from the bankrupt Khedive of Egypt. That same year Gladstone roused the country with stories of "Bulgarian atrocities" where twelve thousand Bulgarian Christians had been murdered by the Turks. In 1877 Russia declared war on Turkey; Victoria and Disraeli were pro-Turk, sending a private warning to the czar of Russia that, were he to advance, Britain would join in the fight against Russia. In 1878 at the Congress of Berlin, Disraeli obtained, as he told Victoria, "peace with honour."

Last years

In 1887 Victoria's golden jubilee (fifty years in power) was celebrated, and ten years later, her diamond jubilee (sixty years in power) was magnificently celebrated. In 1899 the Boer War broke out, where British soldiers fought against Dutch forces in South Africa. In 1900 Victoria went to Ireland, where most of the soldiers who fought on the British side were recruited. In August she signed the Australian Commonwealth Bill, bringing Australia in the British Empire, and in October lost a grandson in the war.

On January 22, 1901, Queen Victoria died. At sixty-three years, Queen Victoria enjoyed the longest reign in British history. During her reign the British crown was no longer powerful but remained very influential. The Victorian age witnessed the birth of the modern world through industry, scientific discovery, and the expansion of the British empire. Her reign also witnessed the beginnings of pollution, unemployment, and other problems that would plague the twentieth century.

For More Information

Erickson, Carolly. *Her Little Majesty: The Life of Queen Victoria.* New York: Simon & Schuster, 1997.

Hibbert, Christopher. *Queen Victoria: A Personal History.* New York: Basic Books, 2000.

Rennell, Tony. *Last Days of Glory: The Death of Queen Victoria.* New York: Viking, 2000.

Vallone, Lynne. *Becoming Victoria.* New Haven, CT: Yale University Press, 2001.

Weintraub, Stanley. *Victoria: An Intimate Biography.* New York: Dutton, 1987.

GORE VIDAL

Born: October 3, 1925
West Point, New York
American writer

G ore Vidal is one of America's most important literary figures on the basis of an enormous quantity of work, including novels, essays, plays, and short stories.

Influenced by politics

Eugene Luther Gore Vidal was born into a family long important in American politics on October 3, 1925, in West Point, New York. His maternal grandfather was Thomas P. Gore, senator from Oklahoma; his father, Eugene Luther Vidal, was director of air commerce under President Franklin D. Roosevelt (1882–1945); and he is distantly related to Albert Gore (1948–), vice president of the United States in the administration of President Bill Clinton (1946–). Although Vidal was never close to his mother, Nina, he had to live with her after his parent's divorce in 1935. As a child Vidal spent long hours in his grandfather's vast library. There young Vidal began to develop his love of literature and history.

The importance of politics in Vidal's life is obvious from his statement, "The only thing I've ever really wanted in my life was to be president." But Vidal did more than talk: he was the Democratic Party candidate for Congress from New York's 29th District (Duchess County) in 1960; he served in the President's Advisory Committee on the Arts under John F. Kennedy (1917–1963) from 1961 to 1963; he was a cofounder of the New Party, backing Senator Eugene McCarthy (1916–), from 1968 to 1971; he was cochairman and secretary of state-designate of the People's Party in the period 1970–1972; and he ran unsuccessfully for the nomination as the Democratic Party's senatorial candidate in California in 1982.

Literature wins over politics

Although always involved in politics, Vidal was a central figure in literature after 1946. In that year, while working as an editor at E. P. Dutton, he published his first novel, *Williwaw,* based on his service during the last years of World War II (1939–45; a war fought between the Axis powers: Germany, Japan, and Italy—and the Allies: England, France, the Soviet Union, and the United States).

After the poorly received *In a Yellow Wood* in 1947, Vidal had his first best-seller with *The City and the Pillar,* a successful but scandalous novel about a homosexual (a person sexually attracted to a member of their own sex). Although many critics termed it groundbreaking because the hero is an all-American youth, its tragic ending is rather conventional for its time. It may or may not be coincidence that his next five novels were negatively reviewed and were all commercial failures.

In 1954 Vidal developed what he called his five-year plan—that is, to go to Hollywood, write for films and television, and make enough money to be financially independent for the rest of his life. Between 1956 and 1970 he wrote or collaborated on seven screenplays, including the film version of Tennessee Williams's (1911–1983) *Suddenly Last Summer,* on which he worked with the playwright in 1959. Between 1954 and 1960 he also completed fifteen television plays.

Returns to the novel

After the novel *Washington, D.C.,* in 1967, he wrote another novel, *Myra Brecken-*

Gore Vidal.
Reproduced by permission of the Kobal Collection.

ridge (1968), the saga of a homosexual male converted into a female via a sex change operation, called by Nat Hentoff in the *Village Voice,* "the first popular book of perverse pornography." After a long stay on the best-seller lists, it was made into a movie.

Two Sisters (1970) was followed by ten novels, a number of them about politics. They were *Burr* (1973), *Myron* (1974), *1876* (1976), *Kalki* (1978), *Creation* (1981), *Duluth* (1983), *Lincoln* (1984), *Empire* (1987), *Hollywood* (1990), *The Smithsonian Institution* (1998), and *The American Presidency* (1998), the text of Vidal's three-part British television series.

Fame as a critic

While the general public enjoyed Vidal as a novelist, more sophisticated readers and the critics praised him more for his essays, many of which had appeared first in periodicals, published between 1962 and 1993. *The Second American Revolution* (1982) won the National Book Critics Circle Award for Criticism in 1982 and *United States* won the National Book Award in Nonfiction in 1993.

Continuing with literary nonfiction, Vidal released a critically successful memoir in 1995, *Palimpsest: A Memoir.* In it he reflected upon a life peopled with such interesting friends and acquaintances as his relative Jackie Kennedy (1929–1994), President John F. Kennedy (1917–1963), and many others he mixed with in the literary and political scene. In 2000, Vidal's novel *The Golden Age* was published.

In May 2000, Vidal gained controversy by announcing plans to attend the execution of Timothy McVeigh, who was convicted of masterminding the bombing of a federal office building in Oklahoma City, Oklahoma, in 1995, resulting in the deaths of 169 people. Due to scheduling conflicts, Vidal was unable to attend.

For More Information

Baker, Susan, and Curtis S. Gibson. *Gore Vidal: A Critical Companion.* Westport, CT: Greenwood Press, 1997.

Kaplan, Fred. *Gore Vidal: A Biography.* New York: Doubleday, 1999.

Kiernan, Robert F. *Gore Vidal.* New York: F. Ungar Publishing Company, 1982.

Vidal, Gore. *Palimpsest: A Memoir.* New York: Random House, 1995.

VIRGIL

Born: October 15, 70 B.C.E.
Andes, Italy
Died: September 21, 19 B.C.E.
Brundisium, Italy
Roman poet

Virgil, or Publius Vergilius Maro, is regarded as one of the greatest Roman poets. The Romans regarded his *Aeneid,* published two years after his death, as their national epic (a long poem centered around a legendary hero).

Early years and education

Virgil was born on October 15, 70 B.C.E., at Andes near Mantua in Cisalpine Gaul (modern Mantova, 20 to 25 miles southwest of Verona, Italy) of humble parentage. His father, either a potter or a laborer, worked for a certain Magius, who, attracted by the intelligence and industry of his employee, allowed him to marry his daughter, Magia. Because the marriage improved his position, Virgil's father was able to give his son the education reserved for children of higher status. Virgil began his study in Cremona, continued it in Milan, and then went on to Rome to study rhetoric (the study of writing), medicine, and mathematics before giving himself to philosophy (the study of knowledge) under Siro the Epicurean. His education prepared him for the profession of law (the alternative was a military career), but he spoke only once in court. He was shy, retiring, and of halting speech—no match for the aggressive, well-spoken lawyers of the Roman court.

Virgil returned from Rome to his family's farm near Mantua to spend his days in study and writing and to be near his parents. His father was blind and possibly dying. His mother had lost two other sons, one in infancy, the other at the age of seventeen. When Virgil's father died, she remarried and bore another son, Valerius Proculus, to whom Virgil left half his fortune.

In appearance Virgil was tall and dark, his face reflecting the rural lower-class stock from which he came. His health was never strong. Horace (65–8 B.C.E.) tells us that on a journey to Brundisium in 37 B.C.E., he and Virgil were unable to join their fellow travelers in their games for he had sore eyes and Virgil was suffering from indigestion. Poor health and his shy nature and love of study made him a recluse, or one who withdraws from the world.

The farm of Virgil's father was among the land confiscated (forcefully taken) as payment for the victorious soldiers of the Battle of Philippi (42 B.C.E.). But Augustus (63 B.C.E.–14 C.E.) restored the farm to the family. Virgil then rendered thanks to young Caesar in his first *Eclogue*.

The final phrase of the epitaph (etching on a tombstone) on Virgil's supposed tomb at Naples runs "cecini pascua, rura, duces (I sang of pastures, of sown fields, and of leaders)." This summarizes the progression from *Eclogues* to *Georgics* to *Aeneid* (which appeared in that order) and, as has been said, "proposes a miniature of the evolution of civilization from shepherds to farmers to warriors."

Pastoral poems

The *Eclogues* (this, the more usual title, means "Select Poems"; they are also known as

Virgil.
Reproduced by permission of the
Gamma Liaison Network.

Bucolics, or "Pastorals") were written between 42 B.C.E. and 37 B.C.E. These ten poems, songs of shepherds, all about one hundred lines long, were modeled on the pastoral poems, or *Idylls,* of Theocritus of Syracuse (c. 310–250 B.C.E.).

Eclogue 4, the so-called Messianic Eclogue, is the best known. Written in 40 B.C.E., during the temporary rule of Pollio (76 B.C.E.–4 C.E.), Virgil's benefactor (one who gives financial aid) a year or two previously, it hails the birth of a baby boy who will usher in a golden age of peace and prosperity in which even nature herself will participate. The golden age is the new era of peace for which Augustus was responsible, and the child is thought to be the expected offspring of Augustus and Scribonia (the infant turned out to be a girl).

The *Georgics* ("Points of Farming"), a didactic (intended to instruct) poem in four books, was written from 37 B.C.E. to 30 B.C.E. Book 1 treats the farming of land; Book 2 is about growing trees, especially the vine and the olive; Book 3 concerns cattle raising; and Book 4, beekeeping.

The Aeneid

The *Aeneid* is one of the most complex and subtle works ever written. An epic poem of about ten thousand lines and divided into twelve books, it tells of the efforts of the Trojan hero, Aeneas, to find a new homeland for himself and his small band of followers, from the time he escapes from burning Troy until he founds Lavinium (in Italy), the parent town of Rome.

Shortly after Actium, the final battle of the Roman civil war 31 B.C.E., Augustus, the victor, was looking for a poet who could give to his accomplishments their proper literary enhancement in an epic poem. Maecenas (c. 70–8 B.C.E.) offered the commission to Propertius and to Horace, both of whom declined as graciously as possible. Virgil had been less reluctant than the other two and found, through his imagination, a solution. His epic of Augustan Rome would be cast in mythological form, making use of the legend of the founding of Rome by Aeneas, a Trojan hero mentioned by Homer (ninth or eighth century B.C.E.), who, tradition held, escaped from Troy and went to Italy. Virgil's models were the *Iliad* and the *Odyssey* of Homer.

The *Aeneid* can be divided into two parts of six books each or into three parts of four books each. Books 1 through 4, organized around Aeneas's narration of the destruction of Troy and his wanderings, have Carthage as their dramatic setting; Books 5 through 8 act as entertainment between the drama of 1 through 4 and 9 through 12, the story of the fighting in Italy. Moreover, the even-numbered books are highly dramatic, while the odd-numbered books reflect a lessening of tension and have less dramatic value.

Last years

Virgil worked on the *Aeneid* for the last eleven years of his life. The composition of it, from a prose (writing) outline, was never easy for him. Augustus once wrote asking to see part of the uncompleted work. Virgil replied that he had nothing to send and added, "I have undertaken a task so difficult that I think I must have been mentally ill to have begun it."

In 19 B.C.E. Virgil resolved to spend three more years on his epic after taking a trip to Greece, perhaps to check on some details necessary for his revision. At Megara he contracted a fever and became so ill that he returned to Brundisium, where he died on September 21. He left instructions that the *Aeneid* should be burned, but Augustus refused and ordered Various and Tucca, two friends of the poet, to edit it for publication. It appeared in 17 B.C.E.

For More Information

Gale, Monica. *Virgil on the Nature of Things.* New York: Cambridge University Press, 2000.

Levi, Peter. *Virgil: His Life and Times.* New York: St. Martin's Press, 1999.

Wright, David H. *The Roman Vergil and the Origins of Medieval Book Design.* London: British Library, 2001.

ANTONIO VIVALDI

Born: March 4, 1678
Venice, Italy
Died: July 26, 1741
Vienna, Austria
Italian composer, violinist and priest

Antonio Vivaldi was an Italian violinist and composer whose concertos—pieces for one or more instruments—were widely known and influential throughout Europe.

Childhood and early career

Antonio Vivaldi was born in Venice, Italy, on March 4, 1678. His first music teacher was his father, Giovanni Battista Vivaldi. The elder Vivaldi was a well-respected violinist, employed at the church of St. Mark's. It is possible, though not proved, that as a boy Antonio also studied with the composer Giovanni Legrenzi (1626–1690).

Antonio was trained for a clerical (religious service) as well as a musical life. After going through the various introductory stages, he was ordained (authorized) a priest in March 1703. His active career, however, was devoted to music. In the autumn of 1703 he was appointed as a violin teacher at the Ospitale della Pieta in Venice. A few years later he was made conductor of the orchestra at the same institution. Under Vivaldi's direction, this orchestra gave many brilliant concerts and achieved an international reputation.

Vivaldi remained at the Pietà until 1740. But his long years there were broken by the numerous trips he took, for professional purposes, to Italian and foreign cities. He went, among other places, to Vienna, Italy, from 1729 to 1730 and to Amsterdam, Netherlands, from 1737 to 1738. Within Italy he traveled to various cities to direct performances of his operas. He left Venice for the last time in 1740. He died in Vienna on July 26 or 27, 1741.

Vivaldi's music

Vivaldi was very productive in vocal and instrumental music, sacred and secular (nonreligious). According to the latest research, he composed over seven hundred pieces—ranging from sonatas (instrumental compositions usually with three or four movements) and operas (musical dramas consisting of vocal and instrumental pieces) to concertos (musical compositions for one or two vocal performers set against a full orchestra).

Today the vocal music of Vivaldi is little known. But in his own day he was famous and successful as an opera composer. Most of his operas were written for Venice, but some were performed throughout Italy in Rome, Florence, Verona, Vicenza, Ancona, and Mantua.

Vivaldi was also one of the great eighteenth century violin virtuosos, or musicians with superb ability. This virtuosity is reflected in his music, which made new demands on

Antonio Vivaldi.
Reproduced by permission of Archive Photos, Inc.

violin technique. In his instrumental works he naturally favored the violin. He wrote the majority of his sonatas for one or two violins and thorough-bass. Of his concertos, 221 are for solo violin and orchestra. Other concertos are for a variety of solo instruments, including the flute, the clarinet, the trumpet, and the mandolin. He also wrote concertos for several solo instruments, concerti grossi, and concertos for full orchestra. The concerto grosso features a small group of solo players, set against the full orchestra. The concerto for orchestra features differences of style rather than differences of instruments.

Orchestral music

Vivaldi's concertos are generally in three movements, arranged in the order of fast, slow, fast. The two outer movements are in the same key; the middle movement is in the same key or in a closely related key. Within movements, the music proceeds on the principle of alternation: passages for the solo instrument(s) alternate with passages for the full orchestra. The solo instrument may extend the material played by the orchestra, or it may play quite different material of its own. In either case, the alternation between soloist and orchestra builds up a tension that can be very dramatic.

The orchestra in Vivaldi's time was different, of course, from a modern one in its size and constitution. Although winds were sometimes called for, strings constituted the main body of players. In a Vivaldi concerto, the orchestra is essentially a string orchestra, with one or two harpsichords or organs to play the thorough-bass.

Some of Vivaldi's concertos are pieces of program music, for they give musical descriptions of events or natural scenes. *The Seasons,* for instance, consists of four concertos representing the four seasons. But in his concertos the "program" does not determine the formal structure of the music. Some musical material may imitate the call of a bird or the rustling of leaves; but the formal plan of the concerto is maintained.

Vivaldi's concertos were widely known during and after his lifetime. They were copied and admired by another musician, Johann Sebastian Bach (1685–1750). In musical Europe of the eighteenth century Vivaldi was one of the great names.

For More Information

Heller, Karl. *Antonio Vivaldi: The Red Priest of Venice*. Portland, OR: Amadeus Press, 1997.

Kolneder, Walter. *Antonio Vivaldi: His Life and Work*. Edited by Bill Hopkins. Berkeley: University of California Press, 1970.

Landon, H. C. Robbins. *Vivaldi: Voice of the Baroque*. Chicago: University of Chicago Press, 1996.

Morgenstern, Sheldon. *No Vivaldi in the Garage: A Requiem for Classical Music in North America*. Boston: Northeastern University Press, 2001.

VOLTAIRE

Born: November 21, 1694
Paris, France
Died: May 30, 1778
Paris, France
French poet and philosopher

The French poet, dramatist, historian, and philosopher Voltaire was an outspoken and aggressive enemy of every injustice but especially of religious intolerance (the refusal to accept or respect any differences).

Early years

Voltaire was born as François Marie Arouet, perhaps on November 21, 1694, in Paris, France. He was the youngest of the three surviving children of François Arouet and Marie Marguerite Daumand, although Voltaire claimed to be the "bastard [born out of wedlock] of Rochebrune," a minor poet and songwriter. Voltaire's mother died when he was seven years old, and he developed a close relationship with his godfather, a freethinker. His family belonged to the upper-middle-class, and young Voltaire was able to receive an excellent education. A clever child, Voltaire studied under the Jesuits at the Collège Louis-le-Grand from 1704 to 1711. He displayed an astonishing talent for poetry and developed a love of the theater and literature.

Emerging poet

When Voltaire was drawn into the circle of the seventy-two-year-old poet Abbé de Chaulieu, his father packed him off to Caen, France. Hoping to stop his son's literary ambitions and to turn his mind to pursuing law, Arouet placed the youth as secretary to the French ambassador at The Hague, the seat of government in the Netherlands. Voltaire fell in love with a French refugee, Catherine Olympe Dunoyer, who was pretty but barely educated. Their marriage was stopped. Under the threat of a *lettre de cachet* (an official letter from a government calling for the arrest of a person) obtained by his father, Voltaire returned to Paris in 1713 and was contracted to a lawyer. He continued to write and he renewed his pleasure-loving acquaintances. In 1717 Voltaire was at first exiled (forced to leave) and then imprisoned in the Bastille, an enormous French prison, for writings that were offensive to powerful people.

As early as 1711, Voltaire, eager to test himself against Sophocles (c. 496–406 B.C.E.) and Pierre Corneille (1606–1684), had written a first draft of *Oedipe*. On November 18,

Voltaire.

ing the theater daily, script in hand. He also absorbed English thought, especially that of John Locke (1632–1704) and Sir Isaac Newton (1642–1727), and he saw the relationship between free government and creative business developments. More importantly, England suggested the relationship of wealth to freedom. The only protection, even for a brilliant poet, was wealth.

At Cirey and at court, 1729–1753

Voltaire returned to France in 1729. One product of his English stay was the *Lettres anglaises* (1734), which have been called "the first bomb dropped on the Old Regime." Their explosive potential (something that shows future promise) included such remarks as, "It has taken centuries to do justice to humanity, to feel it was horrible that the many should sow and the few should reap." Written in the style of letters to a friend in France, the twenty-four "letters" were a clever and seductive (desirable) call for political, religious, and philosophic (having to do with knowledge) freedom; for the betterment of earthly life; for employing the method of Sir Francis Bacon (1561–1626), Locke, and Newton; and generally for striving toward social progress.

Prior to 1753 Voltaire did not have a home; but for fifteen years following 1733 he had stayed in Cirey, France, in a château (country house) owned by Madame du Châtelet. While still living with her patient husband and son, Émilie made generous room for Voltaire. They were lovers; and they worked together intensely on physics and metaphysics, a philosophy which investigates the nature of reality.

Honored by a respectful correspondence

1718, the revised (changed for improvement) play opened in Paris to a sensational success. The *Henriade,* begun in the Bastille and published in 1722, was Voltaire's attempt to compete against Virgil (70–19 B.C.E.) and to give France an epic poem (a long poem centered around a legendary hero).

While Voltaire stayed in England (1726–1728) he was greatly honored; Alexander Pope (1688–1744), William Congreve (1670–1729), Horace Walpole (1717–1797), and Henry St. John, Viscount Bolingbroke (1658–1751), praised him; and his works earned Voltaire one thousand pounds. Voltaire learned English by attend-

with Frederick II of Prussia (1712–1786), Voltaire was then sent on diplomatic (having to do with international affairs) missions to Prussia. But Voltaire's new interest was his affair with his widowed niece, Madame Denis. This affair continued its passionate and stormy course to the last years of his life. Émilie, too, found solace in other lovers. The simple and peaceful time of Cirey ended with her death in 1749.

Voltaire then accepted Frederick's repeated invitation to live at court. He arrived at Potsdam (now in Germany) with Madame Denis in July 1750. First flattered by Frederick's hospitality, Voltaire then gradually became anxious, quarrelsome, and finally bored. He left, angry, in March 1753, having written in December 1752: "I am going to write for my instruction a little dictionary used by Kings. 'My friend' means 'my slave.'" Frederick took revenge by delaying permission for Voltaire's return to France, by putting him under a week's house arrest at the German border, and by seizing all his money.

Sage of Ferney, 1753–1778

Voltaire's literary productivity did not slow down, although his concerns shifted as the years passed while at his estate in Ferney, France. He was best known as a poet until in 1751 Le Siècle de Louis XIV marked him also as a historian. Other historical works include Histoire de Charles XII; Histoire de la Russie sous Pierre le Grand; and the universal history, Essai sur l'histoire générale et sur les moeurs et l'esprit des nations, published in 1756 but begun at Cirey. An extremely popular dramatist until 1760, he began to be outdone by competition from the plays of William Shakespeare (1564–1616) that he had introduced to France.

The philosophic conte (a short story about adventure) was a Voltaire invention. In addition to his famous Candide (1759), others of his stories in this style include Micromégas, Vision de Babouc, Memnon, Zadig, and Jeannot et Colin. In addition to the Lettres Philosophiques and the work on Newton (1642–1727), others of Voltaire's works considered philosophic are Philosophie de l'histoire, Le Philosophe ignorant, Tout en Dieu, Dictionnaire philosophique portatif, and Traité de la métaphysique. Voltaire's poetry includes—in addition to the Henriade—the philosophic poems L'Homme, La Loi naturelle, and Le Désastre de Lisbonne, as well as the famous La Pucelle, a delightfully naughty poem about Joan of Arc (1412–1431).

Always the champion of liberty, Voltaire in his later years became actively involved in securing justice for victims of persecution, or intense harassment. He became the "conscience of Europe." His activity in the Calas affair was typical. An unsuccessful and depressed young man had hanged himself in his Protestant father's home in Roman Catholic city of Toulouse, France. For two hundred years Toulouse had celebrated the massacre (cruel killings) of four thousand of its Huguenot inhabitants (French Protestants). When the rumor spread that the dead man had been about to abandon Protestantism, the family was seized and tried for murder. The father was tortured; a son was exiled (forced to leave); and the daughters were forcefully held in a convent (a house for nuns). Investigation assured Voltaire of their innocence, and from 1762 to 1765 he worked in their behalf. He employed "his friends, his purse, his pen, his credit" to move public opinion to the support of the Calas family. In 1765, Parliament declared the Calas family innocent.

Voltaire's influence continued to be felt after his death in Paris on May 30, 1778.

For More Information

Carlson, Marvin. *Voltaire and the Theatre of the Eighteenth Century.* Westport, CT: Greenwood Press, 1998.

Mason, Haydn. *Voltaire: A Biography.* Baltimore: Johns Hopkins University Press, 1981.

McLean, Jack. *Hopeless But Not Serious: The Autobiography of the Urban Voltaire.* Edinburgh, Scotland: Mainstream Pub. Projects, 1996.

WERNHER VON BRAUN

Born: March 23, 1912
Wirsitz, Germany
Died: June 16, 1977
Alexandria, Virginia
German-born American scientist

The German-born American space scientist Wernher von Braun, the "father of space travel," developed the first practical space rockets and launch vehicles. His advancements were instrumental in space exploration and in putting the first men on the moon.

An inspired student

Born on March 23, 1912, in Wirsitz, Germany, Wernher von Braun's father, Baron Magnus von Braun, was a founder of the German Savings Bank, a member of the Weimar Republic Cabinet, and minister of agriculture. His mother, the former Emmy von Quistorp, a musician and amateur astronomer (one who studies the universe), was a strong influence on her son, especially after she gave her son a telescope as a present. Wernher spent his childhood in several German cities, as the family moved wherever Magnus was transferred.

At the French Gymnasium, Wernher excelled in languages but failed physics and mathematics. He then attended the Hermann Lietz School at Ettersburg Castle, where he developed an intense interest in astronomy and overcame his failures in other subjects. Fascination with the theories of space flight then prompted him to study mathematics and physics with renewed interest. Before he graduated, he was teaching mathematics and tutoring other students.

Von Braun enrolled in the Charlottenburg Institute of Technology in Berlin. He became an active member of the Verein für Raumschiffahrt (VfR; Society for Space Travel) and an associate of Hermann Oberth (1894–1989), Willy Ley (1906–1969), and other leading German rocket enthusiasts. In 1930 Oberth and von Braun developed a small rocket engine, which was a technical success.

German army rocket program

Adolf Hitler (1889–1945) rose to power and became chancellor (leader) of Germany on January 30, 1933. Still upset about the restrictions of the Treaty of Versailles that ended World War I (1914–18), the German army looked to rebuild its forces. The treaty severely restricted Germany's production of weapons, such as guns and cannons. But the treaty made no mention of rockets, and German military planners hoped to develop rockets as weapons. They immediately turned to von Braun.

When World War II (1939–45) began, Germany gave rocket development highest priority. While von Braun developed a large rocket named the V-2, the Nazis (Hitler's army) wanted it as a weapon of war. Von Braun had a different vision: space travel.

By 1943 von Braun's rocket complex was the primary target of the Allied forces (America, France, and Great Britain). When Germany was near collapse, von Braun evacuated his staff to an area where the Americans might capture them. He reasoned that the United States was the nation most likely to use his resources for space exploration. The rocket team, which consisted of more than five thousand coworkers and their families, surrendered to U.S. forces on May 2, 1945.

Early U.S. rocket experiments

During questioning by Allied officers, von Braun prepared a report on rocket development and applications in which he predicted trips to the moon, orbiting satellites, and space stations. Recognizing the potential of von Braun's work, the U.S. Army authorized the transfer of von Braun, 112 of his engineers and scientists, 100 V-2 rockets, and the rocket technical data to the United States.

In 1946 the team moved to what is now the White Sands Proving Grounds in New Mexico. In 1950 they relocated to the Redstone Arsenal in Huntsville, Alabama, where von Braun remained for the next twenty years. He used his free time to write about space travel and to correspond with his fam-

Wernher von Braun.
Courtesy of the Library of Congress.

ily and his cousin, Maria von Quistorp. In early 1947 he obtained permission to return to Germany to marry Maria. They had three children. On April 15, 1955, von Braun and forty of his associates became naturalized citizens.

The Russian space program outpaced that of the United States in the 1950s. When the Russians successfully put *Sputnik I* into space and the U.S. Navy's Vanguard program failed, the United States turned to von Braun's group. Within ninety days, on January 31, 1958, the team launched the free world's first satellite, *Explorer Ion,* into orbit.

U.S. space program

After the creation of the National Aeronautics and Space Administration (NASA), von Braun was appointed director of the George C. Marshall Space Flight Center at Huntsville, Alabama, on July 1, 1960. The space agency sought his advice about techniques later used in landing on the moon. Just before Christmas, 1968, a Saturn V launch vehicle, developed under von Braun's direction, launched *Apollo 8,* the world's first spacecraft to travel to the moon. In March 1970 NASA transferred von Braun to its headquarters in Washington, D.C., where he became deputy associate administrator.

Von Braun resigned from NASA in July 1972 to become vice president for engineering and development with Fairchild Industries of Germantown, Maryland. Besides his work for that aerospace firm, he continued his efforts to promote human space flight, helping to found the National Space Institute in 1975 and serving as its first president. On June 16, 1977, he died of cancer at a hospital in Alexandria, Virginia.

For More Information

Bergaust, Erik. *Wernher von Braun: The Authoritative and Definitive Biographical Profile of the Father of Modern Space Flight.* Washington, DC: National Space Institute, 1976.

Lampton, Christopher. *Wernher von Braun.* New York: Watts, 1988.

Piszkiewicz, Dennis. *Wernher von Braun: The Man Who Sold the Moon.* Westport, CT: Praeger, 1998.

Stuhlinger, Ernst, and Frederick I. Ordway III. *Wernher von Braun, Crusader for Space: An Illustrated Memoir.* Malabar, FL: Krieger, 1994.

KURT VONNEGUT

Born: November 11, 1922
Indianapolis, Indiana
American writer, essayist, and dramatist

K urt Vonnegut is acknowledged as a major voice in American literature and applauded for his subtle criticisms and sharp portrayal of modern society.

Early life

Kurt Vonnegut Jr. was born on November 11, 1922, in Indianapolis, Indiana, the son of a successful architect, Kurt Sr., and his wife, Edith Sophia. Vonnegut was raised along with his sister, Alice, and brother Bernard (whom he spoke of frequently in his works). Fourth-generation Germans, the children were never exposed to their heritage because of the anti-German attitudes that had spread throughout the United States after World War I (1914–18; a war in which many European countries, some Middle Eastern nations, Russia, and the United States fought against Germany, Austria-Hungary, and Turkey). Because of the Great Depression (the severe economic downturn in the 1930s), the Vonneguts lost most of their wealth and the household was never the same. Vonnegut's father fell into severe depression and his mother died after overdosing on sleeping pills the night before Mother's Day. This attainment and loss of the "American Dream" would become the theme of many of Vonnegut's writings.

After attending Cornell University, where he majored in chemistry and biology, he enlisted in the United States Army, serving in the World War II (1939–45; a war fought between the Axis powers: Germany, Italy, and Japan—and the Allies: England, France, the Soviet Union, and the United States). This would set the stage for another crucial element for his writings when he was taken prisoner by the German army. Following the war, Vonnegut studied anthropology at the University of Chicago and later moved to Schenectady, New York, to work as a publicist for the General Electric Corporation. During this period, he also began submitting short stories to various journals, and in 1951, he resigned his position at General Electric to devote his time solely to writing.

The novels

Vonnegut published several novels throughout the 1950s and 1960s, beginning with *Player Piano* in 1952. *Player Piano* depicts a fictional city called Ilium in which the people have given control of their lives to a computer humorously named EPICAC, after a substance that causes vomiting. *The Sirens of Titan* (1959) takes place on several different planets, including a thoroughly militarized Mars, where the inhabitants are electronically controlled. The fantastic settings of these works serve primarily as a metaphor (comparison) for modern society, which Vonnegut views as absurd to the point of being surreal (irrational; dreamlike), and as a backdrop for Vonnegut's central focus: the hapless human beings who inhabit these bizarre worlds and struggle with both their environments and themselves.

Vonnegut once again focuses on the role of technology in human society in *Cat's Cradle* (1963), widely considered one of his best

Kurt Vonnegut.
Reproduced by permission of AP/Wide World Photos.

works. The novel recounts the discovery of a form of ice, called *ice-nine,* which is solid at a much lower temperature than normal ice and is capable of solidifying all water on Earth. *Ice-nine* serves as a symbol of the enormous destructive potential of technology, particularly when developed or used without regard for the welfare of humanity.

Slaughterhouse-Five

Vonnegut's reputation was greatly enhanced in 1969 with the publication of *Slaughterhouse-Five,* an antiwar novel that appeared during the peak of protest against

American involvement in the Vietnam War (1955–75; when American forces aided South Vietnam in their fight against North Vietnam).

Vonnegut described *Slaughterhouse-Five* as a novel he was compelled to write, since it is based on one of the most extraordinary and significant events of his life. During World War II when he was a prisoner of the German Army, Vonnegut witnessed the Allied bombing of Dresden, Germany, which destroyed the city and killed more than one hundred thirty-five thousand people. One of the few to survive, Vonnegut was ordered by his captors to aid in the grisly task of digging bodies from the rubble and destroying them in huge bonfires. Because the city of Dresden had little military value, its destruction went nearly unnoticed in the press. *Slaughterhouse-Five* is Vonnegut's attempt to both document and criticize this event.

Like Vonnegut, the main character of *Slaughterhouse-Five,* named Billy Pilgrim, was present at the bombing of Dresden and has been deeply affected by the experience. His feelings develop into spiritual uncertainty that results in a nervous breakdown. In addition, he suffers from a peculiar condition, of being "unstuck in time," meaning that he randomly experiences events from his past, present, and future. The novel is therefore a complex, nonchronological (in no order of time) narrative in which images of suffering and loss prevail.

Breakfast of Champions

After the publication of *Slaughterhouse-Five,* Vonnegut entered a period of depression during which he vowed, at one point, never to write another novel. He concentrated, instead, on lecturing, teaching, and finishing a play, *Happy Birthday, Wanda June,* that he had begun several years earlier. The play, which ran Off-Broadway from October 1970 to March 1971, received mixed reviews. There were several factors which could be interpreted as the cause of Vonnegut's period of depression, including, as he admitted, the approach of his fiftieth birthday and the fact that his children had begun to leave home. Many critics believe that, having at last come to terms with Dresden, he lost the major inspiration for much of his work; others feel that *Slaughterhouse-Five* may have been the single great novel that Vonnegut was capable of writing. Whatever the cause, *Breakfast of Champions* marked the end of his depression and a return to the novel.

In *Breakfast of Champions,* as in most of Vonnegut's work, there are very clear autobiographical tendencies. In this novel however, the author seems to be even more wrapped up in his characters than usual. He appears as Philboyd Sludge, the writer of the book, which stars Dwayne Hoover, a Pontiac dealer (Vonnegut once ran a Saab dealership) who goes berserk after reading a novel by Kilgore Trout, who also represents Vonnegut. Toward the end of the book, Vonnegut arranges a meeting between himself and Trout, whom Robert Merrill calls his "most famous creation," in which he casts the character loose forever; by this time the previously unsuccessful Trout has become rich and famous and is finally able to stand on his own.

Later work

Breakfast of Champions and *Slapstick, or Lonesome No More* (1976) both examine the widespread feelings of despair and loneliness that result from the loss of traditional culture in the United States; *Jailbird* (1979) recounts the story of a fictitious participant in the Watergate scandal of the Richard Nixon (1913–1994) administration, a scandal which ultimately led to the resignation of the president; *Galapagos* (1985) predicts the consequences of environmental pollution; and *Hocus-Pocus; or, What's the Hurry, Son?* (1990) deals with the implications and aftermath of the war in Vietnam.

In the 1990s, he also published *Fates Worse Than Death* (1991) and *Timequake* (1997). Before its release Vonnegut noted that *Timequake* would be his last novel. Although many of these works are highly regarded, critics frequently argue that in his later works Vonnegut tends to reiterate themes presented more compellingly in earlier works. Nevertheless, Vonnegut remains one of the most-loved American writers.

Kurt Vonnegut Jr. is currently teaching advanced writing classes at Smith College, and in November of 2000, he was named the State Author of New York.

For More Information

Bloom, Harold, ed. *Kurt Vonnegut.* Philadelphia: Chelsea House, 2000.

Marvin, Thomas F. *Kurt Vonnegut: A Critical Companion.* Westport, CT: Greenwood Press, 2002.

Morse, Donald E. *Kurt Vonnegut.* San Bernardino, CA: Borgo Press, 1992.

Vonnegut, Kurt. *Fates Worse Than Death: An Autobiographical Collage of the 1980s.* New York: G. P. Putnam's Sons, 1991.

Vonnegut, Kurt. *Palm Sunday: An Autobiographical Collage.* New York: Delacorte Press, 1981.

RICHARD WAGNER

Born: May 22, 1813
Liepzig, Germany
Died: February 13, 1883
Venice, Italy
German composer

The German operatic composer Richard Wagner was one of the most important figures of nineteenth-century music. Wagner was also a crucial figure in nineteenth-century cultural history for both his criticism and polemical writing, or writing that attacks established beliefs.

Early life

Wilhelm Richard Wagner was born on May 22, 1813, in Leipzig, Germany, into a middle-class family. Raised along with eight siblings, his father, Friedrich, died shortly after Richard's birth, and within the year his mother, Johanna, married Ludwig Geyer. There is still some controversy as to whether or not Geyer, a traveling actor, was Wagner's real father. As a child, Wagner showed little talent or interest in anything except for writing poetry.

Wagner's musical training was largely left to chance until he was eighteen, when he studied with Theodor Weinlig in Leipzig, Germany, for a year. He began his career in 1833 as choral director in Würzburg and composed

Richard Wagner.
Courtesy of the Library of Congress.

his early works in imitation of German romantic compositions. Ludwig van Beethoven (1770–1827) was his major idol at this time.

First works

Wagner wrote his first opera, *Die Feen* (The Fairies), in 1833, but it was not produced until after the composer's death. He was music director of the theater in Magdeburg from 1834 to 1836, where his next work, *Das Liebesverbot* (Forbidden Love), loosely based on William Shakespeare's (1564–1616) *Measure for Measure* was performed in 1836. That year he married Minna Planner, a singer-actress active in local theatrical life.

In 1837 Wagner became the first music director of the theater in Riga, Russia (now the capital of Latvia), where he remained until 1839. He then set out for Paris, France, where he hoped to make his fortune. While in Paris, he developed an intense hatred for French musical culture that lasted the remainder of his life, regardless of how often he attempted to have a Parisian success. It was at this time that Wagner, in financial desperation, sold the scenario for *Der fliegende Holländer* (The Flying Dutchman) to the Paris Opéra for use by another composer. Wagner later set to music another version of this tale.

Wagner returned to Germany, settling in Dresden in 1842, where he was in charge of the music for the court chapel. *Rienzi,* a grand opera in imitation of the French style, enjoyed a modest success. In 1845 *Tannhäuser* premiered in Dresden and proved the first undoubted success of Wagner's career. In November of the same year he finished the poem for *Lohengrin* and began composition early in 1846. While at work on *Lohengrin* he also made plans for his tetralogy (a series of four dramas), *Der Ring des Nibelungen* (The Ring of the Nibelungen), being captivated by Norse sagas. In 1845 he prepared the scenario for the first drama of the tetralogy to be written, *Siegfried's Tod* (Siegfried's Death), which later became *Die Göterdämmerung* (The Twilight of the Gods).

Years of exile

Wagner had to flee Dresden in 1849 in the aftermath of the Revolution of 1848, which resulted in an unsuccessful uprising against the German monarchy or king. He settled in Switzerland, first in Zurich and then near Lucerne. He remained in Switzerland for the most part for the next fifteen years without steady employment, banished from Germany and forbidden access to German theatrical life. During this time he worked on the *Ring*—this dominated his creative life over the next two decades.

The first production of *Lohengrin* took place in Weimar under Franz Liszt's (1881–1886) direction in 1850 (Wagner was not to see *Lohengrin* until 1861). The year 1850 also saw publication of one of Wagner's most vulgar tracts, *The Jew in Music,* in which he viciously attacked the very existence of Jewish composers and musicians, particularly in German society.

In 1853 Wagner formally began composition on the *Rheingold;* he completed the scoring the following year and then began serious work on the *Walküre,* which was finished in 1856. At this time he was toying with the notion of writing the drama *Tristan und Isolde.* In 1857 he finished the composition of Act II of *Siegfried* and gave himself over entirely to *Tristan.* This work was completed in 1859, but it was mounted in Munich only in 1865.

Last years

In 1860 Wagner received permission to reenter Germany except for Saxony, an area in eastern Germany. He was granted full amnesty (political freedom) in 1862. That year he began the music for *Die Meistersinger von Nürnberg* (The Mastersingers of Nuremburg), which he had first thought of in 1845. The *Meistersinger* was completed in 1867; the first performance took place in Munich the following year. Only then did he pick up the threads of the *Ring* and resume work on Act III of *Siegfried,* which was finished in September 1869, a month that also saw the first performance of the *Rheingold*. He wrote the music for *Götterdämmerung* from 1869 to 1874.

The first entire *Ring* cycle (*Rheingold, Walküre, Siegfried,* and *Götterdämmerung*) was given at the Festspielhaus, the shrine Wagner built for himself at Bayreuth, in 1876, over thirty years after the idea for it had first come to mind. He finished *Parsifal,* his final drama, in 1882. Wagner died on February 13, 1883, in Venice, Italy, and was buried at Bayreuth.

For More Information

Gutman, Robert W. *Richard Wagner: The Man, His Mind, and His Music.* New York: Harcourt, Brace & World, 1968. Reprint, San Diego: Harcourt Brace Jovanovich, 1990.

Lee, M. Owen. *Wagner: The Terrible Man and His Truthful Art.* Toronto: University of Toronto Press, 1999.

Magee, Bryan. *The Tristan Chord: Wagner and Philosophy.* New York: Metropolitan Books, 2001.

Newman, Ernest. *Wagner as Man and Artist.* New York: Vintage Books, 1960.

ALICE WALKER

Born: February 9, 1944
Eatonton, Georgia
African American novelist

Pulitzer Prize-winning novelist Alice Walker is best known for her stories about African American women who achieve heroic stature within the borders of their ordinary day-to-day lives.

Early life

Alice Malsenior Walker was born on February 9, 1944, in Eatonton, Georgia, to Willie Lee and Minnie Tallulah (Grant) Walker. Like many of Walker's fictional characters, she was the daughter of a sharecropper (a farmer who rents his land), and the youngest of eight children. At age eight, Walker was accidentally injured by a BB gun shot to her eye by her brother. Her partial blindness caused her to withdraw from normal childhood activities and begin writing poetry to ease her loneliness. She found that writing demanded peace and quiet, but these were difficult things to come by when ten people lived in four rooms. She spent a great deal of time working outdoors sitting under a tree.

Walker attended segregated (separated by race) schools which would be described as inferior by current standards, yet she recalled that she had terrific teachers who encouraged her to believe the world she was reaching for actually existed. Although Walker grew up in a poor environment, she was supported by her community and by the knowledge that she could choose her own identity. Moreover, Walker insisted that her mother granted her "permission" to be a writer and gave her the social, spiritual, and moral substance for her stories.

Upon graduating from high school, Walker secured a scholarship to attend Spelman College in Atlanta, Georgia, where she got involved in the growing Civil Rights movement, a movement which called for equal rights among all races. In 1963, Walker received another scholarship and transferred to Sarah Lawrence College in New York, where she completed her studies and graduated in 1965 with a bachelor's degree. While at Sarah Lawrence, she spent her junior year in Africa as an exchange student. After graduation she worked with a voter registration drive in Georgia and the Head Start program (a program to educate poorer children) in Jackson, Mississippi. It was there she met, and in 1967 married, Melvyn Leventhal, a civil rights lawyer. Their marriage produced one child, Rebecca, before ending in divorce in 1976.

Writing and teaching careers begin

In 1968, Walker published her first collection of poetry, *Once.* Walker's teaching and writing careers overlapped during the 1970s. She served as a writer-in-residence and as a teacher in the Black Studies program at Jackson State College in Tennessee (1968–69) and Tougaloo College in Mississippi (1970–71). While teaching she was at work on her first novel, *The Third Life of Grange Copeland* (1970), which was assisted by an award from the National Endowment for the Arts (1969; a government program to provide money to artists). She then moved north and taught at Wellesley College, in Massachusetts, and the University of Massachusetts at Boston (both 1972–73). In 1973 her collection of short stories, *In Love and Trouble: Stories of Black Women,* and a collection of poetry, *Revolutionary Petunias,* appeared. She received a Radcliffe Institute scholarship (1971–73), a Rosenthal Foundation award, and an American Academy and Institute of Arts and Letters award (both in 1974) for *In Love and Trouble.*

In 1976 Walker's second novel, *Meridian,* was published, followed by a Guggenheim award (in 1977–1978). In 1979 another collection of poetry, *Goodnight, Willie Lee, I'll See You in the Morning,* was published, followed the next year by another collection of short stories, *You Can't Keep a Good Woman Down* (1980).

Walker's third novel, *The Color Purple* was published in 1982, and this work won both a Pulitzer Prize and the American Book Award the following year. Walker was also a contributor to several periodicals and in 1983 published many of her essays, a collection titled *In Search of Our Mother's Gardens: A Collection of Womanist Prose* (1983). Walker worked on her fourth novel while living in Mendocino County outside San Francisco, California.

Walker's novels

Walker's first novel, *The Third Life of Grange Copeland,* centers on the life of a young African American girl, Ruth Copeland, and her grandfather, Grange. As an old man, Grange learns that he is free to love, but love does not come without painful responsibility. At the climax of the novel, Grange summons his newly found knowledge to rescue his granddaughter, Ruth, from his brutal son, Brownfield. The rescue demands that Grange murder his son in order to stop the cycle of cruelty.

Walker's third and most famous novel, *The Color Purple,* is about Celie, a woman so down and out that she can only tell God her troubles, which she does in the form of letters. Poor, black, female, alone and uneducated, held down by class and gender, Celie learns to lift herself up from sexual exploitation and brutality with the help of the love of another woman, Shug Avery. Against the backdrop of Celie's letters is another story about African customs. This evolves from her

Alice Walker.
Reproduced by permission of AP/Wide World Photos.

sister Nettie's letters which Celie's husband hid from Celie over the course of twenty years. Here, Walker presented problems of women bound within an African context, encountering many of the same problems that Celie faces. Both Celie and Nettie are restored to one another, and, most important, each is restored to herself.

Walker's writing analyzed

At the time of publication of Walker's first novel (in 1970), she said in a *Library Journal* interview that, for her, "family relationships are sacred." Indeed, much of

Walker's work describes the emotional, spiritual, and physical devastation that occurs when family trust is betrayed. Her focus is on African American women, who live in a larger world and struggle to achieve independent identities beyond male domination. Although her characters are strong, they are, nevertheless, vulnerable. Their strength resides in their acknowledged debt to their mothers, to their sensuality, and to their friendships among women. These strengths are celebrated in Walker's work, along with the problems women encounter in their relationships with men who regard them as less significant than themselves merely because they are women. What comes out of this belief is, of course, violence. Hence Walker's stories focus not so much on the racial violence that occurs among strangers but the violence among friends and family members, a kind of deliberate cruelty, unexpected but always predictable.

Walker began her exploration of the terrors that beset African American women's lives in her first collection of short stories, *In Love and Trouble*. Here she examined the stereotypes about their lives that misshape them and misguide perceptions about them. Her second short story collection, *You Can't Keep a Good Woman Down,* dramatizes the strength of African American women to rebound despite racial, sexual, and economic difficulties.

For More Information

Bloom, Harold, ed. *Alice Walker.* New York: Chelsea House, 1989.

Gentry, Tony. *Alice Walker.* New York: Chelsea, 1993.

Lauret, Maria. *Alice Walker.* New York: St. Martin's Press, 1999.

Walker, Alice. *The Way Forward Is with a Broken Heart.* New York: Random House, 2000.

Winchell, Donna Haisty. *Alice Walker.* New York: Twayne, 1992.

MADAME C. J. WALKER

Born: December 23, 1867
Delta, Louisiana
Died: May 25, 1919
New York, New York
African American businesswoman

As a manufacturer of hair care products for African American women, Madame C. J. Walker, born Sarah Breedlove, became one of the first American women millionaires.

Struggling childhood

Madame C. J. Walker, named Sarah Breedlove at birth, was born December 23, 1867, in Delta, Louisiana, to Owen and Minerva Breedlove, both of whom were emancipated (freed) slaves and worked on a cotton plantation. At the age of six Sarah's parents died after the area was struck by yellow fever, a deadly disease oftentimes spread by mosquitoes. The young girl then moved to Vicksburg to live with her sister Louvinia and to work as a housemaid. She worked hard from the time she was very young, was extremely poor, and had little opportunity to get an education. In order to escape the terrible environment created by Louvinia's husband, Sarah married Moses McWilliams when she was only fourteen years old. At eighteen she gave birth to a daughter she named Lelia. Two years later her husband died.

Sarah then decided to move to St. Louis, Missouri, where she worked as a laundress (a woman who washes people's clothes as a job) and in other domestic positions for eighteen years. She joined St. Paul's African Methodist Episcopal Church and put her daughter through the public schools and Knoxville College. Sarah, who was barely literate (able to read and write), was especially proud of her daughter's educational accomplishments.

Develops hair care products

By the time Sarah was in her late thirties, she was dealing with hair loss because of a combination of stress and damaging hair care products. After experimenting with various methods, she developed a formula of her own that caused her hair to grow again quickly. She often said that after praying about her hair, she was given the formula in a dream. When friends and family members noticed how Sarah's hair grew back, they began to ask her to duplicate her product for them. She began to prepare her formula at home, selling it to friends and family and also selling it door to door.

Sarah began to advertise a growing number of hair care products with the help of her family and her second husband, Charles Joseph Walker, a newspaperman whom she had married in 1906 after she moved to Denver, Colorado. She also adopted her husband's initials and surname as her professional name,

Madame C. J. Walker.
Reproduced by permission of the Granger Collection.

calling herself Madame C. J. Walker for the rest of her life, even after the marriage ended. Her husband helped her develop mail marketing techniques for her products, usually through the African American-owned newspapers. When their small business was successful, with earnings of about ten dollars a day, Walker thought she should continue to expand, but her husband thought otherwise. Rather than allow her husband's wishes to slow her work, the couple separated.

Business booms

Walker's business continued to expand. She not only marketed her hair care products but also tutored African American men and women in their use, recruiting a group called "Walker Agents." Her products were often used with a metal comb that was heated on the stove, then applied to straighten very curly hair. She also began to manufacture a facial skin cream. The hair process was controversial (open to dispute) because many felt that African American women should wear their hair in natural styles rather than attempt to change the texture from curly to straight. In spite of critics, Walker's hair care methods gained increasing popularity among African American women, who enjoyed products designed especially for them. This resulted in growing profits for Walker's business and an increasing number of agents who marketed the products for her door to door.

Walker worked closely with her daughter Lelia and opened a school for "hair culturists" in Pittsburgh, Pennsylvania,—Lelia College—which operated from 1908 to 1910. In 1910 the Walkers moved to Indianapolis, Indiana, where they established a modern factory to produce their products. They also began to hire African American professionals who could direct various aspects of their operation. Among the workers were tutors who helped Walker get a basic education.

Walker traveled throughout the nation demonstrating her products, recruiting salespersons, and encouraging African American entrepreneurs (business investors). Her rounds included conventions of African American organizations, churches, and civic groups. Not content with her domestic achievements, Walker traveled to the Caribbean and Latin America to promote her business and to recruit individuals to teach her hair care methods. Observers estimated

that Walker's company had about three thousand agents for whom Walker held annual conventions where they were tutored in product use, hygienic (cleaning) care techniques, and marketing strategies. She also gave cash awards to those who were most successful in promoting sales.

At Lelia's urging, Walker purchased property in New York City in 1913, with the belief that a base in that city would be important. In 1916 she moved to a luxurious townhouse she had built in Harlem, and a year later to an estate called Villa Lewaro she had constructed at Irvington-on-Hudson, New York.

Charity and legacy

Although Walker and her daughter lived well, they carefully managed each aspect of their business, whose headquarters remained in Indianapolis, and gave to a number of philanthropic (charity) organizations. According to rumor, Walker's first husband was lynched (killed by a group of people acting outside of the law). Perhaps it was partially for this reason that Walker supported antilynching legislation (laws) and gave generously to the National Association for the Advancement of Colored People (NAACP), eventually willing that organization her estate in Irvington-on-Hudson. The Walkers generously supported religious, educational, charitable, and civil rights organizations.

Walker did not listen to her doctors' warnings that her fast-paced life was hurting her health. On May 25, 1919, when she was fifty-one years old, she died of hypertension (high blood pressure). Her funeral service was held in Mother Zion African Methodist Episcopal Zion Church in New York City.

Celebrated African American educator Mary McLeod Bethune (1875–1955) delivered the eulogy (a tribute), and Walker was buried at Woodlawn Cemetery in the Bronx. Her daughter, Lelia, took over her role as president of the Madame C. J. Walker Manufacturing Company.

For More Information

Bundles, A'Lelia Perry. *On Her Own Ground: The Life and Times of Madam C. J. Walker.* New York: Scribner, 2001.

Lasky, Kathryn. *Vision of Beauty: The Story of Sarah Breedlove Walker.* Cambridge, MA: Candlewick Press, 2000.

Lommel, Cookie. *Madam C. J. Walker.* Los Angeles: Melrose Square, 1993.

McKissack, Pat. *Madam C. J. Walker: Self-Made Millionaire.* Hillside, NJ: Enslow, 1992.

Taylor, Marian. *Madam C. J. Walker.* New York: Chelsea Juniors, 1994.

Yannuzzi, Della A. *Madam C. J. Walker: Self-Made Businesswoman.* Berkeley Heights, NJ: Enslow, 2000.

BARBARA WALTERS

Born: September 25, 1931
Boston, Massachusetts
American newscaster and reporter

Drawing the highest pay in the history of television broadcasting at the time, Barbara Walters became the first woman coanchor of a network evening newscast. She developed to a high art the interviewing of public figures.

Early life

Barbara Walters was born to Dena (Selett) and Lou Walters on September 25, 1931, in Boston, Massachusetts. Her only brother, Burton, had died of pneumonia before Barbara was born, and her sister, Jacqueline, was born mentally handicapped. Her father operated a number of nightclubs, resulting in Barbara attending schools in Boston, New York City, and Miami Beach, Florida. Because of this lifestyle, Walters grew up a lonely and shy child and was especially close to her only playmate and sister, Jacqueline.

Walters earned a bachelor's degree in English from Sarah Lawrence College in 1954. After working briefly as a secretary she landed a job with the National Broadcasting Company's (NBC) New York affiliate WRCA-TV where she quickly rose to producer and writer. She also held various writing and public relations jobs, including a stint as a women's program producer at WPIX-TV in New York City.

Walters's abilities and experience in research, writing, filming, and editing earned her a job as news and public affairs producer for Columbia Broadcasting System (CBS) television. There she wrote materials for noted personalities who appeared on the CBS morning show that competed with NBC's *Today* program. She left CBS because she believed further advancement was unlikely.

Moving in front of the camera

In 1961 Walters was hired by NBC as a writer with an occasional on-the-air feature

Barbara Walters.
Reproduced by permission of Archive Photos, Inc.

accepted this bright, on-the-air newswoman, who also continued to write and produce much of her own material. A few months later, Hugh Downs (1921–) said Walters was the best thing that had happened to the *Today* show during his time as host. They would later be teamed on ABC's program *20/20* as competition to CBS's *Sixty Minutes*.

Today featured stories by Walters that included socially significant topics, and frequently she got on-the-spot experience which gave her reports even more credibility. As her reputation grew, NBC made her a radio commentator on *Emphasis* and *Monitor*. She also participated in such NBC specials as "The Pill" and "The Sexual Revolution" (1967), and in 1969 she covered the ceremony which conferred Prince Charles (1948–) as the Prince of Wales.

Finally in 1974 Walters was named cohost of the *Today* show. By then, her status as a broadcaster had risen to such heights that she had twice been named to *Harper's Bazaar's* list of "100 Women of Accomplishment" (1967 and 1971), *Ladies Home Journal's* "75 Most Important Women" (1970), and *Time's* "200 Leaders of the Future" (1974). As the most influential woman on television, others soon competed for her talents.

for the *Today* show. Within three years Walters became an on-camera interviewer and persuaded such notables as Mamie Eisenhower (1896–1979), Anwar Sadat (1918–1981), and H. R. Haldeman (1926–1993) to appear with her.

Meanwhile, a number of different "show business" women held the post as the "*Today* girl," but none had a journalism background. Mainly they engaged in small talk and read commercials. Some at NBC began to think a different kind of woman might help the show. When the spot was unexpectedly opened, Walters was given the "*Today* girl" slot on a trial basis. The public readily

Million-dollar newswoman

In 1976 Walters accepted a million-dollar-a-year contract for five years to move to ABC, where she became television's first network anchorwoman, the most prestigious job in television journalism. She also anchored and produced four prime-time specials and sometimes hosted or appeared on the network's other news and documentary programs. Her contract stirred professional criticism and jealousy. It not only doubled her income from NBC and her syndicated show, *Not For Women Only,* but it also made her the highest paid newscaster in history at that time. Walter Cronkite (1916–), John Chancellor, and Harry Reasoner then received about four hundred thousand dollars.

Executives of other networks cried that their established anchors might demand salary increases, questioned what they perceived as a "show biz" tint to the dry task of news reporting, and questioned whether the public would accept a woman news anchor. (ABC's private polls before they made their record offer indicated only 13 percent preferred a male anchor, and they knew her presence could easily increase advertising revenues far exceeding her salary.)

Despite Walters's sharp, probing interviewing techniques, she seldom seemed to alienate the person she was interviewing. She revealed some of the secrets of her success in her book *How to Talk With Practically Anybody About Practically Anything* (1970). Others attributed her interviewing success to her amazing ability to ask primarily those questions that the public would want answered.

However, Walters still had her critics. Some interview-subjects said her nervousness distracted them. Others claimed she was so eager that disastrous mistakes occurred, citing the instance when she grabbed another network's microphone as she dashed to get a unique interview. Washington press corps members charged that she acted more as a "star" than as a reporter on presidential trips. However, her professional admirers outnumbered those who criticized her. Walter Cronkite noted her special interviewing talents. Sally Quinn, former rival on *CBS Morn-*

ing News, commented how "nice" Walters was to her.

Still on top

Walters's personal life held considerable interest to the public. Her brief marriage to businessman Bob Katz was annulled, or made void; her thirteen-year marriage to Lee Guber, a theatrical producer, ended in divorce. Still they remained friendly, sharing mutual love for their daughter, Jacqueline Dena. In 1985 she married Merv Adelson, who had also previously been wed twice.

Walters has had a reputation for often being the first to interview world leaders. During the 1996 presidential campaign she interviewed the first African American Chair of the Joint Chiefs of Staff, General Colin Powell (1937–), after his retirement from the military. She has also had exclusive interviews with both Christopher Darden and Robert Shapiro of the O. J. Simpson murder trial, noted by the media as one of the most controversial murder trials of the twentieth century. Walters also had exclusive interviews with billionaire David Geffen, then with Christopher Reeve (1952–) following the horseback riding fall that left him paralyzed. In 1999, Walters was the first to be granted a public interview by Monica Lewinsky, the former White House intern whose affair with President Bill Clinton (1946–) led to his impeachment trial by the U.S. House of Representatives.

Walters's elevation to top-paid broadcaster was credited with raising the status of other women journalists. Her own prowess as a broadcaster exploring socially important issues and as top-notch interviewer were undeniable. In addition, she excelled at bringing to the television public subjects that ranged from show business personalities to heads of state.

In September 2000, Walter renewed her contract with ABC. The lucrative deal reportedly pays Walters $12 million per year, making her one of the highest paid news anchors in the world.

For More Information

Malone, Mary. *Barbara Walters: TV Superstar.* Hillside, NJ: Enslow, 1990.

Oppenheimer, Jerry. *Barbara Walters: An Unauthorized Biography.* New York: St. Martin's Press, 1990.

Remstein, Henna. *Barbara Walters.* Philadelphia: Chelsea House, 1999.

AN
WANG

Born: February 7, 1920
Shanghai, China
Died: March 24, 1990
Boston, Massachusetts
Chinese-born American inventor, engineer,
and business executive

An Wang made important inventions relating to computer memories and to electronic calculators. He was the founder and longtime executive officer of Wang Laboratories Incorporated, a leading American manufacturer of computers and word processing systems.

Childhood and education

An Wang was born the oldest of five children on February 7, 1920, in Shanghai, China, to Yin Lu and Zen Wan Wang. His father taught him English at home and Wang began his formal schooling at age six when he entered the third grade. In elementary school, Wang began to excel in science and mathematics. He became interested in radio as a high school student, built his own radio, and went on to study communications engineering at Chiao-Tung University in his native city. After graduation he stayed on at the university for another year as a teaching assistant. With the outbreak of World War II (1939-45; a war in which France, Great Britain, the Soviet Union, the United States, and other European forces fought against those of Germany, Japan, and Italy), Wang moved to inland China, where he spent the war designing radio receivers and transmitters for the Chinese to use in their fight against Japan.

Wang left China in the spring of 1945, receiving a government stipend (financial support) to continue his education at Harvard University in Cambridge, Massachusetts. He completed his master's degree in communications engineering in one year. After graduation, he worked for an American company for some months and then for a Canadian office of the Chinese government. In 1947, he returned to Harvard University and rapidly completed a doctorate degree in engineering and applied physics. Wang married in 1949, and he and his wife had three children. Six years later Wang became an American citizen.

Invention

In the spring of 1948 Howard Aiken (1900–1973) hired Wang to work at the Harvard Computation Laboratory. This institution had built the ASSC Mark I, one of the world's first digital computers, a few years earlier and was developing more advanced machines under a contract from the U.S. Air Force. Aiken asked Wang to develop a way to store and retrieve data in a computer using magnetic devices. Wang studied the magnetic properties of small doughnut-shaped rings of ferromagnetic material, or materials that can become highly magnetized. Wang soon developed a process where one could read the information stored in a ring by passing a current around it. Researchers at the nearby Massachusetts Institute of Technology (MIT) and elsewhere were interested in the idea of magnetic core storage of information and greatly developed it for use in various computers. Wang published an account of his results in a 1950 article coauthored by W.D. Woo, another Shanghai native who worked at Harvard. He also patented his invention and, despite a long court fight, earned substantial royalties (money earned from sales) from International Business Machines (IBM) and other computer manufacturers who used magnetic core memories. These cores remained a basic part of computers into the 1970s.

Wang was not happy with having others develop and sell his inventions. In 1951 he left the Computation Laboratory and used his life savings to start his own electronics company. He first sold custom-built magnetic shift registers for storing and combining electronic signals. His company also sold machines for magnetic tape control and numerical control. In the mid-1960s Wang

An Wang.
Reproduced by permission of the Corbis Corporation.

invented a digital logarithmic converter that made it possible to perform routine arithmetic electronically at high speeds and relatively low cost. Wang desktop calculators were soon available commercially, replacing traditional machines with mechanical parts. Several calculators operated on one processing unit. These early electronic calculators sold for over one thousand dollars per keyboard. They were used in schools, scientific laboratories, and engineering firms. By 1969, Wang Laboratories had begun to produce less expensive calculators for wider business use. However, Wang saw that the introduction of other technology would allow competitors to sell electronic handheld calculators at a much lower price than the machines his company offered.

Time to change

Confronted with the need to find new products, Wang directed his firm toward the manufacture of word processors and small business computers. The first Wang word processing systems sold in 1976. They were designed for easy access by those unfamiliar with computers, for broad data base management, and for routine business calculations. In addition to such computer networks, the company developed personal computers for office use.

Wang began his business in a room above an electrical fixtures store in Boston, Massachusetts, with himself as the only employee. By the mid-1980s the company had expanded to over fifteen thousand employees working in several buildings in the old manufacturing town of Lowell, Massachusetts, and in factories and offices throughout the world. To acquire money to finance this expansion and to reward competent employees, Wang Laboratories sold stock and piled up a considerable debt. The Wang family retained control of the firm by limiting administrative power to a special class of shareholders. In the early 1980s when company growth slowed while debt remained large, Wang made some effort to reduce his personal control of the business and follow regular corporate management practices.

While remaining a company officer and leading stockholder, Wang gave increased responsibilities to his son Frederick and to other managers. Wang intended to devote even more time to educational activities. He served as an adviser to several colleges and as a member of the Board of Regents of the University of Massachusetts. Wang also took a particular interest in the Wang Institute of Graduate Studies which he founded in 1979. This school offers advanced degrees in software engineering. Difficult times in the computer industry soon led Wang to turn his concentration from these projects and resume full-time direction of Wang Laboratories.

Later years and slowing business

In the last decades of the twentieth century, Wang's economic structure faltered. In 1982 the organization generated more than a billion dollars a year, and by 1989 sales were $3 billion a year. But Wang Laboratories fell on hard times as well. In the early 1990s the former minicomputer maker fell into Chapter 11 bankruptcy and Wang died of cancer in March of 1990 at the age of seventy.

On January 30, 1997, the Eastman Kodak Company bought the Wang Software business unit for $260 million in cash. The deal put Kodak into the document imaging and workflow business and took Wang out of software. Wang also began a relationship with Microsoft, and Michael Brown, chief financial officer for Microsoft, sat on Wang's board of directors. The reorganization enabled the company to prosper once again.

Wang's engineering insight and business success made him a fellow (member) of the Institute of Electrical and Electronic Engineers and a fellow of the American Academy of Arts and Sciences. He received an honorary doctoral degree from the Lowell Technological Institute.

For More Information

Hargrove, Jim. *Dr. An Wang, Computer Pioneer.* Chicago: Children's Press, 1993.

Kenney, Charles. *Riding the Runaway Horse: The Rise and Decline of Wang Laboratories.* Boston: Little, Brown, 1992.

Pugh, E. W. *Memories That Shaped an Industry.* Cambridge, MA: MIT Press, 1984.

Wang, An, and Eugene Linden. *Lessons: An Autobiography.* Reading, MA: Addison-Wesley, 1986.

BOOKER T. WASHINGTON

Born: April 5, 1856
Franklin County, Virginia
Died: November 14, 1915
Tuskegee, Alabama
African American educator, author, and leader

B ooker T. Washington, African American educator and leader, founded Tuskegee Institute for black students. His "Atlanta Compromise" speech made him America's major black leader for twenty years.

Born into slavery

Booker Taliaferro (the Washington was added later) was born a slave in Franklin County, Virginia, on April 5, 1856. His mother was the plantation's cook, while his father, a local white man, took no responsibility for him. From a very early age, Washington recalled an intense desire to learn to read and write.

Washington's mother married another slave, who escaped to West Virginia during the Civil War (1861–65; a war in which Northern forces fought against those of the South over, among other things, secession, or the South's desire to leave the Union). She and her three children were liberated (freed) by a Union army in 1865 and, after the war, joined her husband in West Virginia.

Desire to learn

The stepfather put the boys to work in the salt mines in Malden, West Virginia. Booker eagerly asked for education, but his stepfather gave in only when Booker agreed to work in the mines mornings and evenings to make up for earnings lost while in school. He had known only his first name, but when students responded to roll call with two names, Booker desperately added a famous name, becoming Booker Washington. Learning from his mother that he already had a last name, he became Booker T. Washington.

Overhearing talk about an African American college in Hampton, Virginia, Washington longed to attend the school. Meanwhile, as houseboy for the owner of the coal mines and saltworks, he developed sturdy work habits. In 1872 he set out for Hampton Institute. When he ran out of money, he worked at odd jobs. Sleeping under wooden sidewalks, begging rides, and walking, he traveled the remaining eighty miles and, tired and penniless, asked for admission and assistance. After Hampton officials tested him by making him clean a room, he was admitted and given work as a janitor.

Hampton Institute, founded in 1868 by a former Union general, emphasized manual training. The students learned useful trades

Booker T. Washington.
Reproduced by permission of the
Fisk University Library.

and earned their way. Washington studied brickmasonry (laying of bricks) along with other courses. Graduating in 1876, he taught in a school for two years. Studying at Wayland Seminary in Washington, D.C., he became bored with classical education, considering his fellow students to be more interested in making an impression and living off the black masses than in serving mankind. He became convinced that practical, manual training in rural skills and crafts would save his race, not higher learning, which separated the reality of the black man's miserable existence. In 1879 he was invited to teach at Hampton Institute, particularly to supervise one hundred Native Americans admitted experimentally. He proved a great success in his two years as part of the teaching staff.

Tuskegee Institute

In 1881 citizens in Tuskegee, Alabama, asked Hampton's president to recommend a white man to head their new black college. He suggested Washington instead. The school had an annual legislative appropriation (government money) of two thousand dollars for salaries, but no campus, buildings, students, or staff. Washington had to recruit students and teachers and raise money for land, buildings, and equipment. Hostile rural whites who feared education would ruin black laborers accepted his demonstration that his students' practical training would help improve their usefulness. He and his students built a kiln, an oven used for making bricks, and they erected campus buildings brick by brick.

Under Washington's leadership, Tuskegee Institute became an important force in black education. Tuskegee pioneered in agricultural extension, sending out demonstration wagons that brought better methods to farmers and sharecroppers (farmers who work land owned by another and give a portion of the crop in exchange for the use of the land). Graduates founded numerous "little Tuskegees." African Americans immersed in the poverty of cotton sharecropping improved their farming techniques, income, and living conditions. Washington urged them to become capitalists (business investors), founding the National Negro Business League in 1900. Black agricultural scientist George Washington Carver (c. 1864–1943) worked at Tuskegee from 1896 to 1943, developing new products from peanuts and sweet potatoes. By 1915 Tuskegee had fifteen hundred students and a larger endowment (designated funds) than any other black institution.

"Atlanta Compromise"

In 1895 Washington gave his famous "Atlanta Compromise" speech. Although he shared the late Frederick Douglass's (1817–1895) long-range goals of equality (idea that all races are equal) and integration (bringing different races together), Washington criticized disturbing the peace and other protest strategies. He urged black people to drop demands for political and social rights, concentrating instead on improving job skills and usefulness. "The opportunity to earn a dollar in a factory just now is worth infinitely more than the opportunity to spend a dollar in an opera-house," he said. He appealed to white people to rely on loyal, proven black workers, pointing out that the South would advance to the degree that blacks were allowed to secure education and become productive.

Washington's position so pleased whites, North and South, that they made him the new black spokesman. He became powerful, having the deciding voice in federal appointments of African Americans and in philanthropic grants (charitable donations) to black institutions. Through subsidies, or secret partnerships, he controlled black newspapers, therefore silencing critics. Impressed by his power and hoping his tactics would work, many black people went along. However, increasingly during his last years, such black intellectuals as W. E. B. Du Bois (1868–1963), John Hope (1868–1936), and William Monroe Trotter (1872–1934) criticized his surrender of civil rights (the fight for racial equality) and his stressing of training in crafts, some irrelevant, while forgetting liberal education, which stressed social improvements for black people. Opposition centered in the Niagara Movement, founded in 1905, and the National Association for the Advancement of Colored People (NAACP), which succeeded it in 1910.

Although outwardly calm and nonconfrontational, Washington secretly financed and encouraged attempts and lawsuits to block Southern moves to segregate (to separate black and white Americans) black people and stop them from gaining citizenship. He had lost two wives by death and married a third time in 1893. His death on November 14, 1915, cleared the way for black people to return to Douglass's tactics of protesting for equal political, social, and economic rights. Washington won a Harvard honorary degree in 1891. His birthplace in Franklin County, Virginia, is now a national monument.

For More Information

Harlan, Louis R. *Booker T. Washington: The Making of a Black Leader, 1856–1901.* New York: Oxford University Press, 1972.

Harlan, Louis R. *Booker T. Washington: The Wizard of Tuskegee, 1901–1915.* New York: Oxford University Press, 1983.

Neyland, James. *Booker T. Washington.* Los Angeles: Melrose Square, 1992.

Nicholson, Lois P. *Booker T. Washington.* Philadelphia: Chelsea House, 1997.

Scott, Emmett S., and Lyman Beecher Stowe. *Booker T. Washington.* Garden City, NY: Doubleday, 1916.

Washington, Booker T. *My Larger Education.* Miami, FL: Mnemosyne Publishers, 1969.

Washington, Booker T. *Up from Slavery.* New York: Doubleday, Page & Co., 1901. Reprint, New York: New American Library, 2000.

GEORGE WASHINGTON

Born: February 22, 1732
Bridges Creek, Virginia
Died: December 14, 1799
Mount Vernon, Virginia
American president, politician, and military leader

George Washington (1732–1799) was commander in chief of the American and French forces in the American Revolution (1775–83) and became the first president of the United States.

Virginia childhood

George Washington was born at Bridges Creek (later known as Wakefield) in Westmoreland County, Virginia, on February 22, 1732. His father died when he was eleven years old, and the boy spent the next few years living in different households throughout Virginia. He lived with his mother near Fredericksburg, with relatives in Westmoreland, and with his half brother in Mount Vernon.

Not much is known about Washington's childhood. Many American children have heard the story of how the young Washington took a hatchet and cut down a cherry tree, then admitted his deed because his honest character would not allow him to lie. This tale was probably invented by Mason Locke Weems (1759–1825), author of the biography of Washington that appeared the year after his death. At the age of fourteen Washington had planned to join the British navy but then reluctantly stayed home in obedience to his mother's wishes. By the age of sixteen he had obtained a basic education in mathematics, surveying (the process of measuring and plotting land), reading, and the usual subjects of his time. In 1749 Washington was appointed county surveyor, and his experience on the frontier led to his appointment as a major (a military officer who is above a captain) in the Virginia militia (a small military force that is not part of the regular army) in 1752.

French and Indian War

Washington began to advance in the military ranks during the French and Indian War (1754–63), the American portion of a larger conflict between France and Great Britain over control of overseas territory. In America, this conflict involved a struggle between the two countries over a portion of the Ohio River Valley. Before the war began, Virginia governor Robert Dinwiddie (1693–1770) appointed Washington to warn the French moving into the Ohio Valley against invading English territory. Dinwiddie then made Washington a lieutenant colonel (a military officer who is above a major), with orders to dislodge the French at Pennsylvania's Fort Duquesne, but a strong French force beat the Virginia troops. This conflict triggered the beginning of French and Indian War, and

Great Britain dispatched regular troops in 1755 to remove the French by force.

Later in the year, Dinwiddie promoted Washington to colonel (a military officer who is above a lieutenant colonel) and made him commander in chief of all Virginia troops. In 1758 he accompanied British troops on the campaign that forced the French to abandon Ft. Duquesne. With the threat of violence removed, Washington married Martha Custis (1731–1802) and returned to his life at Mount Vernon.

Early political career

Washington had inherited local importance from his family. His grandfather and great-grandfather had been justices of the peace, a powerful county position in eighteenth-century Virginia. His father had served as sheriff, church warden, and justice of the peace. His half-brother Lawrence had been a representative in the Virginia legislature from Fairfax County. George Washington's entry into politics was based on an alliance with the family of Lawrence's father-in-law.

Washington was elected to the Virginia House of Burgesses (an early representative assembly in Virginia) in 1758 as a representative from Frederick County. From 1760 to 1774 he served as a judge of Fairfax County. His experience on the county court and in the colonial legislature molded his views on British taxation of the thirteen American Colonies (which became the first thirteen states of the United States) after 1763. He opposed the Stamp Act (which placed a tax on printed materials) in 1765. In the 1760s he supported the nonimportation of goods (refusal to import goods) as a means of

George Washington.
Courtesy of the Library of Congress.

reversing British policy. In 1774 he joined the call for a meeting of representatives who would define policies for all thirteen colonies, called the Continental Congress, that would take united colonial action against recent laws directed by the British against Massachusetts.

In July 1774 Washington led the county meeting that was held to adopt the Fairfax Resolves, which he had helped write. These resolves (resolutions) influenced the adoption of the Continental Association, a plan devised by the First Continental Congress (1774) for enforcing nonimportation of British goods. They also proposed the creation of a militia company in each county that was not under the control of a British-appointed governor. This idea became the basis of the development of the Continental Army, the united military forces of the American colonies fighting the British.

By May 1775 Washington, who headed the Fairfax militia company, had been chosen to command the companies of six other counties. When the Second Continental Congress (1775) met after the battles of Lexington and Concord (the first battles of the Revolution) in Massachusetts, Washington was elected unanimously as commander in chief of all Continental Army forces. From June 15, 1775, until December 23, 1783, he commanded the Continental Army. After the French joined the war on the American side in 1778, it was Washington who headed the combined forces of the United States and France in the War of Independence against Great Britain.

Revolutionary Years

Throughout the Revolutionary years Washington developed military leadership, administrative skills, and political sharpness. From 1775 to 1783 he functioned, in effect, as the chief executive of the United States. His wartime experiences gave him a sense of the importance of a unified position among the former colonies. His writings suggested that he favored a strong central government.

Washington returned to his estates at Mount Vernon at the end of the Revolution. There was little time for relaxation, as he was kept constantly busy with farming, western land interests, and navigation of the Potomac River. Finally, Washington led the proceedings at the Federal Convention in 1787 that led to ratification, or confirmation, of the new American constitution.

First American president

The position of president of the United States seemed shaped on the generally held belief that Washington would be the first to occupy the office. In a day when executive power was regarded with suspicion, the constitution established an energetic and independent chief executive. Pierce Butler (1744–1822), one of the Founding Fathers, noted that the Federal Convention would not have made the executive powers so great "had not many of the members cast their eyes toward General Washington as President."

After he was unanimously chosen as president in 1789, Washington helped translate the new Constitution into a workable instrument of government. With his support, the Bill of Rights (a written list of basic rights that are guaranteed to all citizens) was added to the Constitution; an energetic executive branch was established in American government; the departments of state, treasury, and war became official parts of the American president's cabinet; the federal court system was begun; and Congress's power to tax was used to raise money to pay the Revolutionary War debt and to establish American credit at home and abroad.

As chief executive, Washington consulted his cabinet on public policy. He presided over their differences, especially those between Thomas Jefferson (1743–1826) and Alexander Hamilton (1755–1804). Jefferson and Hamilton represented two opposing sides of an extremely important debate during this time about the role of a strong federal government in governing the former British colonies. Hamilton advocated a strong, centralized federal government, whereas Jefferson, fearing that the executive leader would have too much power, pressed for strong states' rights. Hamilton's position is known as the Federalist position; Jefferson's is known as the anti-Federalist or, later, the Republican position (not to be confused with the present-day Republican political party).

Washington approved the Federalist financial program and later, the Hamiltonian proposals, such as funding of the national debt, assumption of the state debts, the establishment of a Bank of the United States, the creation of a national coinage system, and an internal tax on goods. He also presided over the expansion of the federal union from eleven states (North Carolina and Rhode Island ratified [approved] the Constitution after Washington was sworn in as president) to sixteen (Vermont, Kentucky, and Tennessee were admitted between 1791 and 1796). Washington's role as presidential leader was of great importance in winning support for the new government's domestic and foreign policies.

Second term

Despite his unanimous election, Washington expected that the measures of his administration would meet opposition—and they did. By the end of his first term the American political party system was developing. When he mentioned the possibility of retirement in 1792, both Hamilton and Jefferson agreed that he was "the only man in the United States who possessed the confidence of the whole" country and urged him to continue with a second term.

Washington's second term was dominated by foreign-policy considerations. Early in 1793 the French Revolution, which had overthrown the French monarchy in 1789, became the central issue in American politics. France had declared war on Great Britain and appointed Edmond Genet (1763–1834) as minister to the United States. Determined to keep America out of the war and free from European influence, Washington issued a neutrality proclamation (a statement that the United States would not take sides or become involved in the conflict), although the word "neutrality" was not used.

Despite the proclamation, Genet supplied French pirates in American ports and organized expeditions against Florida and Louisiana (which were not then part of the United States). For his undiplomatic conduct, the Washington administration requested and obtained his recall to France. In the midst of the Genet affair, Great Britain began a blockade of France and began seizing neutral ships trading with the French West Indies. Besides violating American neutral rights (the territorial rights of a neutral country), the British still held posts in the American Northwest. The Americans claimed that they plotted with the Indians against the United States.

In 1794 Washington sent John Jay (1745–1829) to negotiate a settlement of the differences between the British and the Americans. Although Jay's Treaty was vastly unpopular—the British agreed to leave the Northwest posts but made no concessions on other key issues—Washington finally accepted it. The treaty also paved the way for a new treaty with Spain, which had feared an alliance of American and British interests against Spain in the Western Hemisphere.

Washington's contributions

Nearly all observers agree that Washington's eight years as president demonstrated that executive power was completely consistent with the spirit of republican government. The term "republican" here refers to the principles of a republic, a form of government in which citizens have supreme power through elected representatives and in which there is no monarchy (hereditary king or queen). Washington put his reputation on the line in a new office under a new Constitution. He realized that in a republic the executive leader, like all other elected representatives, would have to measure his public acts against public opinion. As military commander during the Revolution, he had seen the importance of administrative skills as a means of building public support of the army. As president, he used the same skills to win support for the new federal government.

Despite Washington's dislike of fighting among political "sides," his administrations and policies spurred the beginnings of the first political party system. This ultimately identified Washington with the Federalist party, especially after Jefferson's retirement from the cabinet in 1793.

Retirement

Washington's public service did not end with his retirement from the presidency. During the presidency of John Adams (1735–1826), when America seemed on the brink of a war with France, Adams appointed him commander in chief of the American forces. Washington accepted with the understanding that he would not take field command until troops had been recruited and equipped. Since Adams settled the differences with France by diplomatic negotiations, Washington never assumed actual command. He continued to live at Mount Vernon, where he died on December 14, 1799.

At the time of Washington's death, Congress unanimously adopted a resolution to erect a marble monument in the nation's capital in honor of his great military and political accomplishments. The Washington Monument was completed in 1884.

For More Information

Brookhiser, Richard. *Founding Father: Rediscovering George Washington.* New York: Free Press, 1996.

Clark, E. Harrison. *All Cloudless Glory: The Life of George Washington.* Washington, DC: Regnery Publishers, 1995.

Emery, Noemie. *Washington, A Biography.* New York: Putnam, 1976.

Ferling, John E. *Setting the World Ablaze: Washington, Adams, Jefferson, and the American Revolution.* New York: Oxford University Press, 2000.

Osborne, Mary Pope. *George Washington: Leader of a New Nation.* New York: Dial Books for Young Readers, 1991.

Rosenburg, John. *First in War: George Washington in the American Revolution.* Brookfield, CT: Millbrook Press, 1998.

JAMES
WATT

Born: January 19, 1736
Greenock, Scotland

Died: August 25, 1819
Heathfield, England
Scottish engineer, instrument maker, and inventor

The British instrument maker and engineer James Watt developed an efficient steam engine that was a universal (covering everything) source of power and thereby provided one of the most essential technological parts of the early industrial revolution (a period of rapid economic growth that involved increased reliance on machines and large factories).

Watt's early years

James Watt was born on January 19, 1736, in Greenock, Scotland, the son of a shipwright (a carpenter who builds and fixes ships) and merchant of ships' goods. As a child James suffered from ill health. He attended an elementary school where he learned some geometry as well as Latin and Greek, but he was not well enough to attend regularly. For the most part he was educated by his parents at home. His father taught him writing and arithmetic, and his mother taught him reading.

Of much more interest to James was his father's store, where the boy had his own tools and forge (furnace to shape metals), and where he skillfully made models of the ship's gear that surrounded him. His father taught him how to craft things from wood and metal. He also taught James the skill of instrument making. As a youngster he played with a small carpentry set his father gave him, taking his toys apart, putting them back together, and making new ones.

In 1755 Watt was apprenticed (working for someone to learn a craft) to a London,

England, mathematical instrument maker. At that time the trade primarily produced navigational (ship steering) and surveying (land measuring) instruments. Watt found London to be unpleasant, however. A year later he returned to Scotland.

Watt wanted to establish himself in Glasgow, Scotland, as an instrument maker. However, restrictions imposed by the tradesmen's guilds (associations of craftsmen) stood in his way. Friends at the University of Glasgow eventually arranged for him to be appointed as "mathematical instrument maker to the university" in late 1757. About this time Watt met Joseph Black, who had already laid the foundation (base) of modern chemistry and of the study of heat. Their friendship was of some importance in the early development of the steam engine.

Invention of the steam engine

At the University of Glasgow, Watt had become engaged in his first studies on the steam engine. During the winter of 1763–64 he was asked to repair the university's model of an earlier model of the steam engine made by Thomas Newcomen around the year 1711. After a few experiments, Watt recognized that the fault with the model rested not so much in the details of its construction as in its design. He found that a volume (amount of space taken up by an object or substance) of steam three or four times the volume of the piston cylinder (chamber with a moving object inside of it) was required to make the piston move to the end of the cylinder.

The solution Watt provided was to keep the piston at the temperature of the steam (by means of a jacket heated by steam) and to condense (make less dense) the steam in a

James Watt.
Courtesy of the Library of Congress.

separate vessel (chamber) rather than in the piston. Such a separate condenser avoided the large heat losses that resulted from repeatedly heating and cooling the body of the piston, and so engine efficiency was improved.

It took time for Watt to turn a good idea for a commercial invention into reality. A decade passed before Watt solved all the mechanical problems. Black lent him money and introduced him to John Roebuck of the Carron ironworks in Scotland. In 1765 Roebuck and Watt entered into a partnership.

Watt still had to earn his own living but his employment as surveyor of canal construc-

tion left little time for developing his invention. However, Watt did manage to prepare a patent application on his invention, and the patent was granted on January 5, 1769.

By 1773 Roebuck's financial difficulties brought not only Watt's work on the engine to a standstill but also Roebuck's own business. Matthew Boulton, an industrialist (someone who owns and operates a factory) of Birmingham, England, then became Watt's partner. Watt moved to Birmingham. He was now able to work full time on his invention. In 1775 Boulton accepted two orders to build Watt's steam engine. The two engines were set up in 1776 and their success led to many other orders.

Improvements in the steam engine

Between 1781 and 1788 Watt modified and further improved his engine. These changes combined to make as great an advance over his original engine as the latter was over the Newcomen engine. The most important modifications were a more efficient use of the steam, the use of a double-acting piston, the replacement of the flexible chain connection to the beam by the rigid three bar linkage, the provision of another mechanical device to change the reciprocating (back and forth) motion of the beam end to a rotary (circular) motion, and the provision of a device to regulate the speed.

Having devised a new rotary machine, the partners had next to determine the cost of constructing it. These rotary steam engines replaced animal power, and it was only natural that the new engine should be measured in terms of the number of horses it replaced. By using measurements that millwrights (people who build mills), who set up horse gins (animal-driven wheels), had determined, Watt found the value of one "horse power" to be equal to thirty-three thousand pounds lifted one foot high per minute. This value is still used as the standard for American and English horsepower. The charge of building the new type of steam engine was based upon its horsepower from that time forward.

Other inventions

On Watt's many business trips, there was always a good deal of correspondence (letters) that had to be copied. To avoid this tiresome task, he devised letter-press copying. This works by writing the original document with a special ink. Copies are then made by simply placing another sheet of paper on the freshly written sheet and then pressing the two together.

Watt's interests in applied (practical) chemistry led him to introduce chlorine bleaching into Great Britain and to devise a famous iron cement. In theoretical chemistry, he was one of the first to argue that water was not an element (basic substance of matter made up of only one kind of atom) but a compound (substance made up of two or more elements).

In 1794 Watt and Boulton turned over their flourishing business to their sons. Watt maintained a workshop where he continued his inventing activities until he died on August 25, 1819.

Watt's achievements in perfecting the steam engine have been recognized worldwide. The watt, a unit of electrical power, was named after him.

For More Information

Champion, Neil. *James Watt*. Chicago: Heinemann Library, 2001.

Robinson, Eric, and A. E. Musson. *James Watt and the Steam Revolution*. New York: A. M. Kelley, 1969.

Sproule, Anna. *James Watt: Master of the Steam Engine*. Woodbridge, CT: Blackbirch Press, 2001.

JOHN WAYNE

Born: May 26, 1907
Winterset, Iowa
Died: June 11, 1979
Los Angeles, California
American actor

American actor John Wayne played characters that typically showed a heroic American "can do" spirit in over seventy-five films, mostly Westerns and war movies. He is considered an icon in American film.

"The Duke"

John Wayne was born Marion Mitchell Morrison, of Scotch-Irish descent, to Clyde and Mary Morrison on May 26, 1907, in Winterset, Iowa. He had one brother, Robert Emmet Morrison. He received his nickname "Duke" while still a child, because of his love for a dog of that name. His father was a pharmacist whose business ventures did not succeed. In 1914, when Duke was six, the family moved to California where his father was able to open a drugstore. In 1926 his parents were divorced.

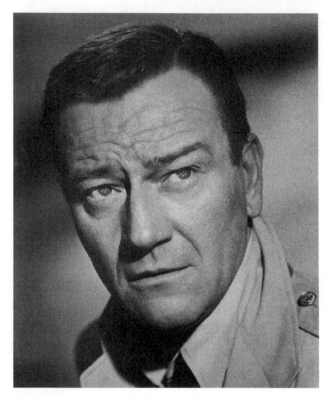

John Wayne.
Courtesy of the Library of Congress.

From the age of twelve Duke helped his father at his drugstore in his spare time. He also supported himself with a variety of odd jobs, including stints as a delivery boy and as a trucker's helper. At first he aspired to attend the Naval Academy and become a naval officer but things did not work out as planned. Fortunately, he was a star football player on the Glendale High School team, and he was accepted at the University of Southern California on a football scholarship. But an accident soon ended his playing career and scholarship. Without funds to support himself, he left the university in 1927 after two years there.

In college Duke worked at the Fox studio lots in Los Angeles, California, as a laborer, prop boy, and extra. While doing so he met director John Ford (1895–1973), who took an interest in him (and would over the years have a major impact on his career). In 1928, after working at various odd jobs for some months, he was again employed at the Fox studios, mostly as a laborer but also as an extra and bit player. His efforts generally went unbilled, but he did receive his first screen credit as Duke Morrison.

Becoming "John Wayne"

Wayne's first real break came in 1929, when through the intervention of Ford he was cast as the lead in a major Fox production, the Western movie *The Big Trail*. According to some biographers, Fox executives found his name inappropriate and changed it to John Wayne, the last name being taken from the American Revolutionary general "Mad Anthony" Wayne.

The Big Trail was not a success and Fox soon dropped Wayne. During the 1930s he worked at various studios, mostly those on what was known as "Poverty Row." Wayne appeared in over fifty feature films and serials, mostly Westerns. He even appeared in some films as "Singing Sandy." Tall, likeable, able to do his own stunts, it appeared that he was doomed to be a leading player in low-budget films.

However, thanks to Ford, with whom Wayne had remained friends, he was cast as the lead in the director's film *Stagecoach,* a 1939 Western that became a hit and a classic. This film was a turning point in Wayne's career. And although it took time for him to develop the mythic-hero image which propelled him to the top of the box office chart, he was voted by movie exhibitors as one of the Top Ten box office attractions of the year—a position he maintained for twenty-three of the next twenty-four years.

Superstar

Wayne appeared in over seventy-five films between 1939 and 1976 when *The Shootist,* his last film, a Western, was released. In the vast majority of these films he was a man of action, be it in the American West or in U.S. wars of the twentieth century. As an actor he had a marvelous sense of timing and of his own persona, but comedy was not his specialty. Action was the essence of his films. Indeed, critics have repeatedly emphasized the manner in which he represented a particular kind of "American Spirit."

As a box-office superstar Wayne had his choice of roles and vehicles, but he chose to remain with the types of films he knew best. As the years passed his only admission to age was from the roles he played. He went from wooing leading ladies, such as Marlene Dietrich (1901–1992) (*Pittsburgh,* 1942), Gail Russell (*Angel and the Badman,* 1947), and Patricia Neal (*Operation Pacific,* 1951) to more mature roles as a rowdy father figure (*McClintock,* 1963), an older brother (*The Sons of Katie Elder,* 1965), and a kind marshal (*Rio Lobo,* 1970).

Wayne's politics were not always right-of-center, but in the latter part of his life he became known for his anticommunism (a political theory where goods and services are owned and distributed by a strong central government) activities. His conservatism began in the mid-1940s. He served as head of the anticommunist Motion Picture Alliance for the Preservation of American Ideals; supported various conservative Republican politicians, including Barry Goldwater and Richard Nixon (1913–1994); and spoke out forcefully on behalf of various causes such as American participation in the Vietnam War (1955–75; when American forces aided South Vietnam with their struggle against North Vietnam).

Later career

Wayne's politics also influenced his activities as a producer and director. Wayne's production companies made all kinds of films, but among them were *Big Jim McClain* (1951), in which he starred as a process server for the House Un-American Activities Committee fighting communists in Hawaii, and *Blood Alley* (1955), in which he played an American who helps a village to escape from the Communist Chinese mainland to Formosa. The two films that Wayne directed also are representative of his politics: *The Alamo* (1960) is an epic film about a heroic last stand by a group of Texans in their fight for independence against Mexico and included some preaching by the Wayne character about democracy as he saw it; and *The Green Berets* (1968), in which Wayne played a colonel leading troops against the North Vietnamese, which was an outspoken vehicle in support of America's role in the war.

Wayne was married three times. He had four daughters and three sons by two of his wives (Josephine Saenez, 1933–1945, and Pilar Palette Weldy, after 1954). His second wife was Esperanza Diaz Ceballos Morrison (1946–1954). Wayne was the recipient of many awards during his career, including an Oscar for his role as the hard-drinking, one-eyed, tough law man in *True Grit* (1969) and an Academy Award nomination for his playing of the career marine in *Sands of Iwo Jima* (1949). Plagued by various illnesses during the last few years of his life, he publicly announced his triumph over lung cancer in 1964. But a form of that disease eventually claimed his life on June 11, 1979.

For More Information

Davis, Ronald L. *Duke: The Life and Image of John Wayne.* Norman: University of Oklahoma Press, 1998.

Levy, Emanuel. *John Wayne: Prophet of the American Way of Life.* Metuchen, NJ: Scarecrow Press, 1988.

McGhee, Richard D. *John Wayne: Actor, Artist, Hero.* Jefferson, NC: McFarland, 1990.

Roberts, Randy, and James S. Olson. *John Wayne: American.* New York: Free Press, 1995.

Shepherd, Donald, and Robert Slatzer with Dave Grayson. *Duke: The Life and Times of John Wayne.* Garden City, NY: Doubleday, 1985.

DANIEL WEBSTER

Born: January 18, 1782
Salisbury, New Hampshire
Died: October 24, 1852
Marshfield, Massachusetts
American orator and lawyer

Daniel Webster, a notable public speaker and leading constitutional lawyer, was a major congressional spokesman for the Northern Whigs during his twenty years in the U.S. Senate.

Childhood

Daniel Webster was born in Salisbury, New Hampshire, on January 18, 1782. His parents were Ebenezer, who worked as a tavern owner and a farmer and was also involved in politics, and his second wife, Abigail. While a child, Daniel earned the nickname "Black Dan" for his dark skin and black hair and eyes. The second youngest of ten children, Daniel developed a passion for reading and learning at a young age. His formal education began in 1796 when he started at Phillips Academy in Exeter. Then when he was fifteen, Daniel went on to Dartmouth College.

After graduating from Dartmouth, Daniel studied law and was admitted to the bar (an organization for lawyers) in 1805. He opened a law office in Portsmouth, New Hampshire, in 1807, where his success was immediate. He became a noted spokesman for the Federalists (a leading political party that believed in a strong federal government) through his addresses on patriotic occasions. In 1808 he married Grace Fletcher.

Early years in politics

Elected to the U.S. House of Representatives in 1813, Webster reenergized the Federalist minority with his attacks on the war policy of the Republicans, the opposing political party. Under his leadership the Federalists often successfully obstructed war measures.

After the War of 1812, when American and British forces clashed over shipping rites, he called for the restructuring of the Bank of the United States, but he voted against the final bill, which he considered defective. As the representative of a region where shipping was basic to the economy, he voted against the protective tariff (tax).

Webster left politics for a while when he moved to Boston, Massachusetts. As a result of his success in pleading before the U.S. Supreme Court, Webster's fame as a lawyer grew, and soon his annual income rose to fifteen thousand dollars a year. In 1819 Webster secured a triumph in defending the Bank of the United States in *McCulloch v. Maryland*. On this occasion Supreme Court Chief Justice John Marshall drew from Webster's brief the belief that the power to tax is the power to destroy. In 1824 Webster was also successful on behalf of his clients in *Gibbons v. Ogden*.

When Webster returned to the U.S. House of Representatives in 1823, his speeches began to attract national attention. From 1825 to 1829 Webster was one of the most faithful backers of President John Quincy Adams (1767–1848), supporting federal internal improvements and supporting Adams in his conflict with Georgia over the removal of the Cherokee Indians.

The Senator

When Webster was elected to the Senate in 1827, he made the first about-face in his career when he became a champion of the protective tariff. This shift reflected the growing importance of manufacturing in Massachusetts and his own close involvement with factory owners both as clients and as friends. It was largely due to his support that the "Tar-

Daniel Webster
Courtesy of the Library of Congress.

iff of Abominations" was passed in 1828. His first wife died shortly after he entered the Senate, and in 1829 he married Catherine Le Roy of New York City.

In January 1830 Webster electrified the nation by his speeches in response to the elaborate explanations of the Southern states' rights doctrines (teachings) made by Senator Robert Y. Hayne of South Carolina. In memorable phrases Webster exposed the weaknesses in Hayne's views and argued that the Constitution (the document that states the principles of the American government) and the Union rested upon the people and not upon the states. These speeches, delivered before crowded Senate galleries, defined the constitutional issues which disturbed the nation for nearly thirty years.

The person

Webster was at the height of his powers in 1830. Regarded by others as one of the greatest orators (public speakers) of the day, he delivered his speeches with tremendous dramatic impact. Yet in spite of his emotional style and the passionate character of his speeches, he rarely sacrificed logic for effect. His striking appearance contributed to the forcefulness of his delivery. Tall, rather thin, and always clad in black, Webster's face was dominated by deep, luminous black eyes under craggy brows and a shock of black hair combed straight back.

In private Webster was more approachable. He was fond of gatherings and was a lively talker, although at times given to silent moods. His taste for luxury often led him to live beyond his means. While his admirers worshiped the "Godlike Daniel," his critics thought his constant need for money deprived him of his independence. During the Panic of 1837, a desperate financial crisis resulting from the expansion into western lands, he was in such desperate circumstances as a result of excessive investments in western lands that only loans from business friends saved him from ruin. Again, in 1844, when it seemed financial pressure might force him to leave the Senate, he permitted his friends to raise a fund to provide him with an income.

Secretary of State

Webster was one of the leaders of the anti-Andrew Jackson (1767–1845) forces that came together in the Whig party, a political party which opposed Jackson's Democrats. Regardless, Webster did endorse President Jackson's stand during the nullification crisis in 1832, where several states threatened to leave the Union unless granted the right to "nullify," or make void, certain federal laws. In 1836 the Massachusetts Whigs named Webster as their presidential candidate, but in a field against other Whig candidates he polled only the electoral votes of Massachusetts. In recognition of his standing in the party and in gratitude for his support during the campaign, President William Henry Harrison (1773–1841) appointed him secretary of state in 1841. He continued in this post under John Tyler (1790–1862), who succeeded to the presidency when Harrison died a month after he was sworn in as president. Among other accomplishments, Webster sent Caleb Cushing (1800–1879) to the Orient (Far East) to establish commercial relations with China, although he was no longer in office when Cushing concluded the agreement. Late in 1843 Webster, feeling that he no longer enjoyed Tyler's confidence, gave in to Whig pressure and retired from office.

Webster, in spite of his disappointment at not receiving the presidential nomination in 1844, actively campaigned for Henry Clay (1777–1852), his rival within the party. On his return to the Senate in 1844, Webster opposed the annexation (acception into the Union) of Texas and as well as the expansionist policies that peaked in the war with Mexico (1846–48), when American forces clashed with Mexico over western lands. After the war he worked to remove slavery from the newly acquired territories which resulted in the Wilmot Proviso.

Although Northern businessmen agreed, the average citizen was outraged over Webster's speech of March 1850 in defense of the new Fugitive Slave Law, a law that provided for the return of escaped slaves. Webster again became secretary of state in July 1850, in Millard Fillmore's Cabinet. In 1852 he lost his last hope for the presidency when the Whigs passed over him in favor of General Winfield Scott (1786–1866), a former Democrat. Deeply outraged, he refused to support the party candidate. He died just before the election on October 24, 1852.

For More Information

Baxter, Maurice G. *One and Inseparable: Daniel Webster and the Union.* Cambridge, MA: Harvard University Press, 1984.

Lodge, Henry Cabot. *Daniel Webster.* Boston: Houghton, Mifflin, 1883. Reprint, New York: Chelsea House, 1981.

Peterson, Merrill D. *The Great Triumvirate: Webster, Clay, and Calhoun.* New York: Oxford University Press, 1987.

Remini, Robert V. *Daniel Webster: The Man and His Time.* New York: W. W. Norton, 1997.

NOAH WEBSTER

Born: October 16, 1758
West Hartford, Connecticut
Died: May 23, 1843
New Haven, Connecticut
American lexicographer

Noah Webster, American lexicographer (one who compiles a dictionary), remembered now almost solely as the compiler of a continuously successful dictionary, was for half a century among the more influential and most active literary men in the United States.

Early life

Noah Webster was born on October 16, 1758, in West Hartford, Connecticut. The fourth son of five children of Noah and Mercy Steele Webster, young Noah showed exceptional scholarly talents as a child, and his father sacrificed much in order that his son would gain the best education available.

In 1774, at age sixteen, Webster entered Yale College, sharing literary ambitions with his classmate Joel Barlow and tutor Timothy Dwight. His college years were interrupted by terms of military service. After his graduation in 1778, Noah began studying law, but because his father could no longer support him, he took a job as a schoolmaster in Hartford, Litchfield, and Sharon, all in Connecticut. Meanwhile, he read widely and studied law. He was admitted to the bar (an association for lawyers) and received his master of arts degree in 1781. Dissatisfied with the British-made textbooks available for teaching, he determined to produce his own. He had, he said, "too much pride to stand indebted to Great Britain for books to learn our children."

Schoolmaster to America

Webster soon developed the first of his long series of American schoolbooks, a speller titled *A Grammatical Institute of the English*

WEBSTER, NOAH

Noah Webster.
Courtesy of the National Archives and Records Administration.

Language, Part I (1783). Known for generations simply as *The Blue-back Speller,* it was in use for more than a century and sold over seventy million copies. His book's effect on students is said to have been unequaled in the history of American elementary education. Part II of the *Grammatical Institute,* a grammar, reprinted often under various titles, appeared in 1784. Part III, a reader, in the original 1785 edition included sections from yet-unpublished poetry by Dwight and Barlow. Though the reader had a shorter life and more vigorous competition than other parts of the *Institute,* it set a patriotic (having to do with the

love for one's country) and moralistic (having to do with right and wrong) pattern followed by rival books, some of which were thought to attract attention because they were more religiously orientated. Webster stressed what he called the "art of reading" in later volumes, including two secularized (nonreligious) versions of *The New England Primer* (1789, 1801), *The Little Reader's Assistant* (1790), *The Elementary Primer* (1831), and *The Little Franklin* (1836).

Webster toured the United States from Maine to Georgia selling his textbooks, convinced that "America must be as independent in *literature* as she is in *politics,* as famous for *arts* as for *arms,*" but that to accomplish this she must protect by copyright (the legal right of artistic work) the literary products of her countrymen. He pleaded so effectively that uniform copyright laws were passed early in most of the states, and it was largely through his continuing effort that Congress in 1831 passed a bill which ensured protection to writers. On his travels he also peddled (sold from door to door) his *Sketches of American Policy* (1785), a vigorous plea on behalf of the Federalists, a then-popular political party that believed in a strong central government. In Philadelphia, Pennsylvania, where he paused briefly to teach school and see new editions of his *Institute* through the press, he published his politically effective *An Examination into the Leading Principles of the Federal Constitution* (1787).

In New York City, Webster established the *American Magazine* (1787–88), which he hoped might become a national periodical (magazine distributed regularly). In it he pled for American intellectual independence, education for women, and the support of Federalist ideas. Though it survived for only twelve monthly issues, it is remembered as one of the most lively, bravely adventuresome of early American periodicals. He continued as a political journalist with such pamphlets as *The Effects of Slavery on Morals and Industry* (1793), *The Revolution in France* (1794), and *The Rights of Neutral Nations* (1802).

Language reform

But Webster's principal interest became language reform, or improvement. As he set forth his ideas in *Dissertations on the English Language* (1789), theatre should be spelled theater; machine, masheen; plough, plow; draught, draft. For a time he put forward claims for such reform in his readers and spellers and in his *Collection of Essays and Fugitiv* [sic] *Writings* (1790), which encouraged "reezoning," "yung" persons, "reeding," and a "zeel" for "lerning"; but he was too careful a Yankee to allow odd behavior to stand in the way of profit. In *The Prompter* (1790) he quietly lectured his countrymen in corrective essays written plainly, in a simple and to-the-point style.

After Webster married in 1789, he practiced law in Hartford for four years before returning to New York City to edit the city's first daily newspaper, the *American Minerva* (1793–98). Tiring of the controversy (open to dispute) brought on by his forthright expression of Federalist opinion, he retired to New Haven, Connecticut, to write *A Brief History of Epidemic and Pestilential Diseases* (1899) and to put together a volume of *Miscellaneous Papers* (1802).

The dictionaries

From this time on, Webster gave most of his attention to preparing more schoolbooks, including *A Philosophical and Practical Grammar of the English Language* (1807). But he was primarily concerned with assembling *A Compendious Dictionary of the English Language* (1806); its shorter version, *A Dictionary . . . Compiled for the Use of Common Schools* (1807, revised 1817); and finally, in two volumes, *An American Dictionary of the English Language* (1828). In range this last surpassed (went beyond) any dictionary of its time. A second edition, "corrected and enlarged" (1841), became known popularly as *Webster's Unabridged*. Conservative contemporaries (people of the same time or period), alarmed at its unorthodoxies (untraditional) in spelling, usage, and pronunciation and its proud inclusion of Americanisms, dubbed the work as "Noah's Ark." However, after Webster's death the rights were sold in 1847 to George and Charles Merriam, printers in Worcester, Massachusetts; and the dictionary has become, through many revisions, the foundation and defender of effective American lexicography.

Webster's other late writings included *A History of the United States* (1832), a version of the Bible (1832) cleansed of all words and phrases dangerous to children or "offensive especially to females," and a final *Collection of Papers on Political, Literary and Moral Subjects* (1843). Tall, redheaded, lanky, humorless, he was the butt of many cruel criticisms in his time. Noah Webster died in New Haven on May 23, 1843.

For More Information

Micklethwait, David. *Noah Webster and the American Dictionary*. Jefferson, NC: McFarland, 2000.

Moss, Richard J. *Noah Webster*. Boston: Twayne Publishers, 1984.

Rollins, Richard M. *The Long Journey of Noah Webster.* Philadelphia: University of Pennsylvania Press, 1980.

Snyder, K. Alan. *Defining Noah Webster.* Lanham, MD: University Press of America, 1990.

Unger, Harlow G. *Noah Webster: The Life and Times of an American Patriot.* New York: John Wiley & Sons, 1998.

ORSON WELLES

Born: May 16, 1915
Kenosha, Wisconsin
Died: October 10, 1985
Los Angeles, California
American actor, writer, and director

Orson Welles was a Broadway and Hollywood actor, radio actor, and film director. His earliest film production, *Citizen Kane,* was his most famous, although most of his other productions were notable as well.

Early life and education

Orson Welles was born George Orson Welles in Kenosha, Wisconsin, on May 6, 1915, the second son of Richard Welles, an inventor, and Beatrice Ives, a concert pianist. The name George was soon dropped. The family moved to Chicago, Illinois, when Welles was four, and two years later his parents separated formally. The comfortable family life in which Orson was born gradu-

ally fell apart. Orson lived with his mother for the next few years and was deeply involved with her artistic lifestyle. Upon her death, his father resumed the task of continuing the eight-year-old Orson's education. An important early influence on his life was Maurice Bernstein, an orthopedist who would eventually be his guardian after his father's suicide in 1928. Upon Dr. Bernstein's suggestion, young Orson was enrolled in the progressive Todd School in Woodstock, Illinois. There, Orson was first introduced to theater and learned a great deal about production and direction. His formal education ended with graduation in 1931.

After a short stay in Ireland, where Welles was involved in the theater as an actor, he returned to Chicago where he briefly served as a drama coach at the Todd School and coedited four volumes of plays by William Shakespeare (1564–1616). He made his Broadway debut with Katharine Cornell's company in December 1934. He and John Houseman (1902–1988) joined forces the next year to manage a unit of the Federal Theatre Project, one of the work-relief arts projects established by the New Deal, a major nationwide social program intended to spark economic recovery during the 1930s. Welles's direction was inspired, injecting new life into various classics, including an all-African American *Macbeth,* the French farce (humorous ridicule) *The Italian Straw Hat,* and the morality (having to do with right and wrong) play *Dr. Faustus.*

The Mercury Theatre

Welles and Houseman broke with the Federal Theatre Project over its attempt to shut down their June 1937 production of

Marc Blitzstein's pro-labor *The Cradle Will Rock.* They organized the Mercury Theatre, which over the next two seasons had a number of extraordinary successes, including a modern dress *Julius Caesar* (with Welles playing Brutus), an Elizabethan working-class comedy *Shoemaker's Holiday* (rewritten by Welles), and George Bernard Shaw's (1856–1950) *Heartbreak House* (with the twenty-four-year-old Welles convincingly playing an elderly man). Welles also found time to play "The Shadow" on radio and to supervise a "Mercury Theatre on the Air," whose most notorious success was an adaptation of H. G. Wells's (1866–1946) *War of the Worlds,* which resulted in panic as many listeners believed that Martians were invading New Jersey.

In 1939 the Mercury Theatre collapsed as a result of economic problems and Welles went to Hollywood, California, to find the cash to resurrect it. Except for a stirring dramatization of Richard Wright's (1908–1960) *Native Son* in 1940, an unhappy attempt to stage Jules Verne's (1828–1905) *Around the World in 80 Days* (music and lyrics by Cole Porter (c.1891–1964) in 1946, and an unsatisfactory *King Lear* in 1956, his Broadway career was over. He did continue theater activity overseas: during the 1950s he successfully staged *Moby Dick* in England, directed Laurence Olivier (1907–1989) in the London production of Eugène Ionesco's *Rhinoceros,* and wrote a script for the Roland Petit ballet.

Citizen Kane *and other films*

Following an early flirtation with movies and after casting around some months for a subject, Welles filmed *Citizen Kane* in 1939

Orson Welles.
Reproduced by permission of AP/Wide World Photos.

and 1940. Since its release in 1941 this film has generally been praised as one of the best movies of all time. It is a fascinating study of a newspaper publisher. Controversy surrounds the production of this film, which Welles is credited with producing, directing, and coscripting. He also played the leading role. However one views the making of this film, there is no doubt about his role as its catalyst (a provider of action or quick change).

Years later Welles declared "I began at the top and have been making my way down ever since." All the films he directed are of interest, but none matched his initial achievement of *Citizen Kane.* Among his other films are *The Magnificent Ambersons* (1942), *The Lady From Shanghai* (1946), *Othello* (1952), *Touch of Evil* (1958), *The Trial* (1962), and *F Is for Fake* (1973). Most of these films have been marked by disputes and Welles often disowned the final version. His critics argue that a self-destructive tendency caused these problems and cite his experiences with the unfinished *It's All True,* which he embarked on in Brazil in 1942 before finishing the final editing of *The Magnificent Ambersons.* But his supporters called it a destroyed masterpiece (in his absence, one hundred thirty-one minutes were edited down to a final release print of eighty-eight minutes).

A somewhat hammy actor with a magnificent voice, Welles appeared in over forty-five films besides his own. In some of these films, such as *The Third Man* (1949) and *Compulsion* (1959), he was superb. But all too many were junk movies such as *Black Magic* (1949) and *The Tarters* (1960). He accepted these so that he might earn the funds necessary to finance films of his own such as *Chimes at Midnight* (released in 1966, a film based on various Shakespeare plays).

Later career

For various reasons Welles left the United States after World War II (1939–45; a war fought between the Axis: Italy, Japan, and Germany—and the Allies: England, France, the Soviet Union, and the United States), and for three decades lived a kind of uprooted existence abroad, with occasional visits back to America for movie assignments or other work. An intelligent individual with many interests, Welles during World War II had put in a stint as a columnist at the liberal *New York Post* and later gave some thought to a political career. During the latter part of his life, despite being dogged by ill health, he earned a comfortable living doing television commercials for companies such as Paul Masson wines, putting much of what he earned into the production of various films, including *The Other Side of the Wind* (which dealt with an old filmmaker and which was unfinished at the time of his death as well as being involved in litigation, or legal matters). A superb storyteller, Welles—after moving back to the United States in the mid-1970s—was much in demand as a guest on television talk shows.

Married three times, Welles had children with each wife: Virginia Nicolson (Christopher), Rita Hayworth (Rebecca), and his widow Paola Mori (Beatrice). He had many friends in his lifetime, including Oja Kodar, a Yugoslav artist who was his companion and assistant from the mid-1960s onward. Welles shared an Academy Award for the script of *Citizen Kane* and in 1975 was honored by the American Film Institute with a Life Achievement Award. His other awards include a 1958 Peabody Award for a TV pilot. Welles died of a heart attack on October 10, 1985.

For More Information

Carringer, Roger. *The Making of Citizen Kane.* Berkeley: University of California Press, 1985.

Higham, Charles. *Orson Welles: The Rise and Fall of an American Genius.* New York: St. Martin's Press, 1985.

Leaming, Barbara. *Orson Welles, a Biography.* New York: Viking, 1985.

Taylor, John Russell. *Orson Welles: A Celebration*. Boston: Little, Brown, 1986.

Thomson, David. *Rosebud: The Story of Orson Welles*. New York: Knopf, 1996.

Welles, Orson, and Peter Bogdanovich. *This Is Orson Welles*. New York: Harper-Collins, 1992.

EUDORA WELTY

Born: April 13, 1909
Jackson, Mississippi
Died: July 22, 2001
Jackson, Mississippi
American writer and editor

E udora Welty is considered one of the most important authors of the twentieth century. Although the majority of her stories are set in the American South and reflect the region's language and culture, critics agree that Welty's treatment of universal (covering or including all) themes and her wide-ranging artistic influences clearly cross all regional boundaries.

Southern childhood

Eudora Alice Welty, the oldest of her family's three children and the only girl, was born on April 13, 1909, in Jackson, Mississippi. That neither of her parents came from the Deep South may have given her some detachment from her culture and helped her become a careful observer of its manners. Her father, Christian Welty, had been raised on a farm in Ohio and had become a country school teacher in West Virginia. Marrying a fellow teacher, Chestina Andrews, he moved to Jackson to improve his fortunes by entering business. From bookkeeper in an insurance company, he eventually advanced to president. Welty described hers as a happy childhood in a close-knit, bookish family. One of her earliest memories was the sound of her parents' voices reading favorite books to one another in the evenings.

Welty's education in the Jackson schools was followed by two years at Mississippi State College for Women between 1925 and 1927, and then by two more years at the University of Wisconsin and a bachelor of arts degree in 1929. Her father, who believed that she could never earn a living by writing stories, encouraged her to study advertising at the Columbia University Graduate School of Business in New York City during 1930 and 1931. The years in Wisconsin and New York broadened Welty's horizons, and the time she spent in New York City was especially meaningful for it was during the peak of The Harlem Renaissance, an artistic awakening that produced many African American artists. Welty and her friends went to dances in Harlem clubs and to musical and theatrical performances all over the city.

Welty returned to Jackson in 1931 after her father's death and worked as a part-time journalist, copywriter, and photographer for the Works Progress Administration (WPA), which was aimed at providing jobs for writers. The latter job took her on assignments throughout Mississippi, and she began using these experiences as material for short stories. In June 1936, her story "Death of a Traveling Salesman" was accepted for publication

Eudora Welty.
Reproduced by permission of AP/Wide World Photos.

in the journal *Manuscript,* and within two years her work had appeared in such respected publications as the *Atlantic* and the *Southern Review.*

Produces fiction

Critical response to Welty's first collection of stories, *A Curtain of Green* (1941), was highly favorable, with many commentators predicting that a first performance so impressive would no doubt lead to even greater achievements. Yet when *The Wide Net, and Other Stories* was published two years later, critics were split as some praised the work and others slammed it.

As Welty continued to develop her vision her fictional techniques gained wider acceptance. Indeed, her most complex and highly symbolic collection of stories, *The Golden Apples,* won critical acclaim, and she received a number of prizes and awards throughout the following decade, including the William Dean Howells Medal of the Academy of Arts and Letters for her novella *The Ponder Heart* (1954).

Occupied primarily with teaching, traveling, and lecturing between 1955 and 1970, Welty produced little fiction. These were years of personal difficulty, as she nursed her mother through a long fatal illness and lost both of her brothers. She was nevertheless at work on long projects, notably *Losing Battles,* which she continued to shape for a decade. Then, in the early 1970s, she published two novels, *Losing Battles* (1970), which received mixed reviews, and the more critically successful *The Optimist's Daughter* (1972), which won a Pulitzer Prize.

Although Welty had published no new volumes of short stories since *The Bride of Innisfallen* in 1955, the release of her *Collected Stories* in 1980 renewed interest in her short fiction and brought all-around praise. In addition, the 1984 publication of Welty's *One Writer's Beginnings,* an autobiographical (having to do with a book written about oneself) work describing her own artistic development, further clarified her work and inspired critics to reinterpret many of her stories. She continued to protect the essential privacy of her daily life, however, by discouraging biographic inquiries, carefully screening interviews, and devoting most of her energies to her work. During the later 1970s this work consisted largely of collecting her nonfiction writings for publication as *The Eye of the Story* and of assembling her short stories as *The Collected Stories of Eudora Welty*. With these two important collections she rounded out the shape of her life's work in literary commentary and fiction.

Later career

An invitation to give a series of lectures at Harvard in 1983 resulted in the three autobiographical pieces published as *One Writer's Beginnings* the next year. Perhaps because she wished to forestall (keep away) potential biographers or because she came to accept public interest in a writer's early experiences in shaping her vision, Welty provided in *One Writer's Beginnings* a recreation of the world that nourished her own imagination. Characteristically, however, she left out family difficulties and other personal matters, focusing instead on the family love of books and storytelling, the values and examples her parents provided, and the physical sensations of life in Jackson that influenced her literary sensitivities.

Welty's fictional chronicle of Mississippi life adds a major comic vision to American literature, a vision that supports the power of community and family life and at the same time explores the need for peace. In his 1944 essay, Robert Penn Warren (1905–1989) identifies these twin themes in Welty's work as love and separateness. While much of modern American fiction has focused on isolation and the failure of love, Welty's stories show how tolerance and generosity allow people to adapt to each other's weaknesses and to painful change. Welty's fiction particularly celebrates the love of men and women, the fleeting joys of childhood, and the many dimensions and stages of women's lives.

With the publication of *The Eye of the Story* and *The Collected Stories,* Eudora Welty achieved the recognition she has long deserved as an important American fiction writer. Her position was confirmed in 1984 when her autobiographical *One Writer's Beginnings* made the best-seller lists with sales over one hundred thousand copies. During the early decades of her career, she was respected by fellow writers but often dismissed by critics as an oversensitive "feminine" writer. The late 1970s and 1980s, however, saw a critical reevaluation (the act of examining the same thing over again) of her work.

In August of 2000, *Country Churchyards,* with photographs by Welty, excerpts from her previous writings, and new essays by other writers, was published. Welty was inducted into the National Women's Hall of Fame in Seneca Falls, New York, on October 7, 2000. Welty died at the age of ninety-two on July 22, 2001, in Jackson, Mississippi.

For More Information

Aevlin, Albert J. *Welty: A Life in Literature.* Jackson: University Press of Mississippi, 1987.

Carson, Barbara Harrell. *Eudora Welty: Two Pictures at Once in Her Frame.* Troy, NY: Whitston, 1992.

MacNeil, Robert. *Eudora Welty: Seeing Black and White.* Jackson: University of Press of Mississippi, 1990.

Welty, Eudora. *One Writer's Beginnings.* Cambridge, MA: Harvard University Press, 1984.

Edith Wharton.
Reproduced by permission of AP/Wide World Photos.

EDITH
WHARTON

Born: January 24, c. 1861
New York, New York
Died: August 11, 1937
Paris, France
American author

Edith Wharton, American author, chronicled the life of upper-class Americans between the late nineteenth to early twentieth century. She is best known for her novels *The House of Mirth* and *The Age of Innocence*.

Childhood

Edith Wharton was born Edith Newbold Jones in New York City, on January 24, probably in 1861. Like many other biographical facts, she kept her birth year secret. Gossip held that the family's English tutor—not George Frederic Jones—was really Edith's father. The truth may never be known, but Edith evidently believed the story. After the Civil War (1861–65), when Northern forces clashed with those of the South, George Jones took his family to Europe, where they could have a better quality of life. In Europe, young Edith began to develop her love of literature and writing.

Back in New York City, by the age of eighteen Edith had published poems in magazines and in a privately printed volume and had experimented with fiction. However, events put off her writing career. The family's second long European trip ended in her father's death. In New York City again, she evidently fell in love with Walter Berry; yet she became engaged to Edward Wharton, eleven years her senior and a wealthy Bostonian. They were married in 1885.

Time to write

Marriage brought Edith Wharton two things she valued most, travel and leisure for writing. In the early 1890s her stories began appearing in magazines, but her first commercial success was a book written with an architect, *The Decoration of Houses* (1897). She sought help on it from Walter Berry, who remained in some uncertain way part of her life until his death in 1927. Soon after this book, Wharton suffered a nervous breakdown. For therapy her physician suggested she write fiction. In 1899 a collection of stories, *The Greater Inclination,* appeared—the first of her thirty-two volumes of fiction.

In 1905, after Wharton began her friendship with writer Henry James (1843–1916), her first masterpiece, *The House of Mirth,* laid bare the cruelties of the New York City society. Her range was apparent in *Tales of Men and Ghosts* (1910), a collection of chillers, and in the celebrated novella *Ethan Frome* (1911). In 1910 the Whartons moved to France, where Edward Wharton suffered a nervous breakdown and was placed in a sanitorium, a hospital for the mentally unstable. After their divorce in 1913, Edith Wharton stayed in France, writing lovingly about it in *French Ways and Their Meanings* (1919) and other books.

The Age of Innocence, a splendid novel of New York, won the Pulitzer Prize (1921), and a dramatization of Wharton's novella *The Old Maid* won the Pulitzer Prize for drama (1935). Edith Wharton died of a heart attack on August 11, 1937, and was buried in Versailles, France, next to Walter Berry.

For More Information

Dwight, Eleanor. *Edith Wharton: An Extraordinary Life.* New York: Abrams, 1994.

Joslin, Katherine. *Edith Wharton.* New York: St. Martin's Press, 1991.

Kellogg, Grace. *The Two Lives of Edith Wharton: The Woman and Her Work.* New York: Appleton-Century, 1965.

Lewis, R. W. B. *Edith Wharton: A Biography.* New York: Harper & Row, 1975.

Wharton, Edith. *Backward Glance.* New York: Scribner, 1934. Reprint, New York: Scribner, 1964.

JAMES WHISTLER

Born: July 10, 1834
Lowell, Massachusetts
Died: July 17, 1903
London, England
American painter and etcher

The American painter, etcher, and lithographer James Whistler created a new set of principles for the fine arts, championed art for art's sake, and introduced a subtle style of painting in which atmosphere and mood were the main focus.

Early life

James Abbott McNeill Whistler was born in Lowell, Massachusetts, on July 10, 1834, the son of Major George Whistler, a railroad engineer, and Anna McNeill. In 1842 Czar Nicholas I (1796–1855) of Russia invited Major Whistler to build a railroad from St. Petersburg to Moscow and offered the princely salary of twelve thousand dollars a year. In St. Petersburg the family lived luxuriously, with several servants, and James and his brother had a governess and a Swedish tutor. Because French was the court language, the boys soon became fluent in it. On one occasion the Whistlers took a trip fifteen miles out of St. Petersburg to Tsarkoe Selo. Here, in the palace built by Catherine the Great (1729–1896), there was a suite of apartments in the Chinese style containing many fine examples of Oriental porcelain. James was fascinated by this collection and later became a collector of blue-and-white porcelain.

Whistler's interest in drawing, which had begun when he was four, greatly increased

James Whistler.
Courtesy of the Library of Congress.

After an unsuccessful apprenticeship (a job acquired to learn a trade) with the Winaas Locomotive Works in Baltimore, Maryland, Whistler obtained a job in Washington, D.C., with the Coast and Geodetic Survey. He was always late, often absent, and was the despair of his employer. However, he had the finest training in etching (the process of producing a design or a picture off a hard surface with the use of chemicals) and learned the basic principles of printmaking.

Departure for Europe

With a three hundred fifty dollar-a-year inheritance from his father, Whistler went abroad to study art. He arrived in Paris, France, in 1855 and at once threw himself into the artistic life of the French students. While copying in the Parisian art museum the Louvre in 1858, Whistler met Henri Fantin-Latour (1836–1904), who in turn introduced him to Alphonse Legros (1837–1911) and other artists, including the great realist painter Gustave Courbet (1819–1877). In 1858 Whistler brought out *Twelve Etchings from Nature,* known as the French Set. The next year his first important painting, *At the Piano,* influenced by Fantin-Latour and Dutch seventeenth-century interiors, was rejected by the Paris Salon (an art gallery), although it was accepted by the Royal Academy in London, England, in 1860.

Whistler's painting *Wapping* (1861) shows the influence of Courbet's realism, an art style that seeks to capture reality. One of the figures in the foreground is the redheaded Irish beauty Joanna Hiffernan, known as Jo, who became both Whistler's model and mistress. He painted her as *The White Girl* (1862), standing in a white dress, against a

during the years in Russia, and in 1845 he was enrolled in a drawing course at the Academy of Fine Arts in St. Petersburg. In 1849 Major Whistler died, and Mrs. Whistler returned to the United States with her sons, settling in Pomfret, Connecticut. James decided he wanted to go to the U.S. Military Academy at West Point, which his father had attended, and obtained an appointment in 1851. At West Point he stood first in the drawing course but did poorly in chemistry. Because he constantly broke the rules, he racked up two hundred eighteen demerits (marks for bad conduct) and as a result was dismissed in 1854.

white background, with her red hair over her shoulder. The figure is medieval (having to do with the Middle Ages) in feeling with a remoteness and deep-thinking gaze that place it close to the Pre-Raphaelite painters, a band of painters that reacted against the unimaginative and traditional historical paintings of their time. Whistler knew their work; he had met Dante Gabriel Rossetti (1828–1882) in 1862 and was decidedly influenced by the Pre-Raphaelites at this time. Although *The White Girl* was rejected by the Royal Academy in 1862 and the Paris Salon of 1863, it was a sensation at the Salon des Refusés, admired by artists though laughed at by the public.

In 1863 Whistler leased a house in the Chelsea section of London, where he set up housekeeping with Jo. His mother arrived late that year and spent the rest of her life in England. Whistler became a collector of blue-and-white porcelain as well as Oriental costumes, in which he posed his models for such pictures as *La Princess du pays de la porcelaine* (1864).

The nocturnes

In 1871 Whistler published the sixteen etchings, *Views of the Thames,* known as the Thames Set. He also did a series of atmospheric paintings which he called nocturnes. He liked to go out on the river at twilight and was fascinated by the foggy or misty effects in the fading light. In putting these impressions on canvas from memory, he made use of the Japanese concept of space as a well-balanced design in which perspective plays no part. In the famous *Arrangement in Grey and Black, the Artist's Mother* (1872) he composed the picture with disarming simplicity, keeping the Japanese concept of space in mind.

During 1877 Whistler exhibited several paintings, including *Falling Rocket,* a nocturne showing the mysterious and elusive (hard to grasp) effects of fireworks at night at Cremorne Gardens. It outraged John Ruskin (1819–1900), considered the country's finest judge of good taste in England, and he wrote an insulting review of the exhibition. Whistler sued him for libel (a written statement that hurts someone's public image) in what was the most sensational art trial of the century and was awarded very little money. The trial ruined Whistler financially, and he had to sell his new house and sell off his porcelain collection.

Fortunately, the Fine Arts Society commissioned Whistler to do twelve etchings of Venice, Italy. He spent fourteen months in Venice doing many etchings as well as small oils, watercolors, and pastels. His etching style was now completely changed. He treated his themes with the utmost delicacy, using a spidery line and lively curves, and he often wiped the plates to give tone. His Venetian work sold well and he was financially reestablished. He took a house in London with Maud Franklin, who had replaced Jo as model and mistress.

On the evening of January 31, 1885, Whistler delivered at Prince's Hall the "Ten O'Clock," his famous lecture summing up his theories on the nature of beauty in polished prose. He mentioned the poetry that evening mists produce when "the tall chimneys become campanili and the warehouses are palaces at night."

Master lithographer

One of Whistler's finest achievements was in the field of lithography (the process of printing on metal), which he concentrated on for a ten-year period beginning in 1887.

Drawing in the most spirited way, he used a stump as well as a pencil and obtained effects never achieved by a lithographer before him. He had great ability with watercolors and small oils which sometimes depicted the seaside or shop fronts in Chelsea. In portraiture he favored full-length standing poses, influenced by Diego Velàzquez (1465–1524), and was more concerned with subtle tones and atmosphere than he was with exact likenesses.

In 1888 Whistler married E. W. Godwin's widow, Beatrix. The Whistlers moved to Paris in 1893 but two years later were back in England. Trixie, as his wife was called, died of cancer in 1896. After her death, Whistler maintained studios in both Paris and London. He died in London on July 17, 1903.

For More Information

Anderson, Ronald K., and Anne Koval *James McNeill Whistler: Beyond the Myth.* New York: Carroll & Graf, 1995.

Berman, Avis. *James McNeill Whistler.* New York: H. N. Abrams, 1993.

Fleming, Gordon H. *James Abbott McNeill Whistler: A Life.* New York: St. Martin's Press, 1991.

Whistler, James M. *The Gentle Art of Making Enemies.* New York: John W. Lovell Company, 1890. Reprint, New York: Dover Publications, 1967.

E. B. WHITE

Born: July 11, 1899
Mount Vernon, New York

Died: October 1, 1985
North Brooklin, Maine
American essayist and author

E. B. White was one of the most influential modern American essayists, largely through his work for the *New Yorker* magazine. He also wrote two children's classics and revised William S. Strunk's *The Elements of Style,* widely used in college English courses.

Becoming a writer

Elwyn Brooks White was born on July 11, 1899, in Mount Vernon, New York, the son of a piano manufacturer, Samuel Tilly White, and Jessie Hart. The family was comfortably well off, but not wealthy. Raised with two brothers and three sisters, White attended local public schools in Mount Vernon. He went on to attend Cornell University, graduating in 1921.

White was offered a teaching position at the University of Minnesota, but turned it down because his goal was to become a writer. He worked for the United Press International and the American Legion News Service in 1921 and 1922 and then became a reporter for the *Seattle Times* in 1922 and 1923. White then worked for two years with the Frank Seaman advertising agency as a production assistant and copywriter. During this time he had poems published in "The Conning Tower" of Franklin P. Adams, the newspaper columnist who helped several talented young people achieve success during the 1920s and 1930s.

New Yorker

In 1925 White published the article "Defense of the Bronx River" in the *New Yorker* magazine, his first piece in this publication. It led to his being named a contributing editor in 1927, an association which continued until his death in 1985.

From the time of its origin, *The New Yorker* was one of the most well-received periodicals in the nation. It featured such celebrities as Alexander Woolcott, Dorothy Parker (1893–1967), Robert Benchley (1889–1945), and George S. Kaufman (1889–1961) as contributors, so White was in the company of the best when he was added to the staff.

At some time White became the principal contributor to the magazine's column "Notes and Comment" and set the tone of informed, intelligent, tolerant, faintly amused city life in observations on the passing scene, a feature that continued after his death.

A name for himself

In 1929 White published a poetry collection, *The Lady Is Cold,* and then joined fellow *New Yorker* writer James Thurber (1894–1961) in *Is Sex Necessary?* Freudian psychology, or the study of the subconscious, had been enormously influential in America in the 1920s, giving rise to many volumes analyzing or presenting advice on the subject. The time was ripe for a parody (a literary or artistic work that copies the style of an existing subject in order to make fun of it) of such books, and these two came up with a witty, low key work featuring passages like this: "The sexual revolution began with Man's discovery that he was not attractive to Woman, as such. . . . His masculine appearance not only failed to excite Woman, but in many cases it only served to bore her. The result was that Man found it necessary to develop attractive personal traits to offset his

E. B. White.
Reproduced by permission of the Corbis Corporation.

dull appearance. He learned to say funny things. He learned to smoke, and blow smoke rings. He learned to earn money. This would have been a solution to his difficulty, but in the course of making himself attractive to Woman by developing himself mentally, he had inadvertently [unintentionally] become so intelligent an animal that he saw how comical the whole situation was."

Also in 1929, White married *New Yorker* editor Katharine Sergeant Angell; the marriage produced one son. He published *Ho Hum* in 1931, *Another Ho Hum* in 1932, *Every Day Is Saturday* in 1934, and in 1936, in the *New Yorker,* under the pseudonym (pen name) Lee Strout White, the essay "Farewell My Lovely!" One of his best-known pieces, it was suggested to him by a manuscript submitted by Richard L. Strout of the *Christian Science Monitor.* It served as the basis for the book *Farewell to the Model T,* published later that same year.

White's next work was a poetry collection, *The Fox of Peapack* (1938), the same year that he began the monthly column "One Man's Meat" for *Harper's* magazine, a column which lasted five years. There followed the essay collection *Quo Vadimus?* in 1939; an editing job with his wife, *The Subtreasury of American Humor,* in 1941; and *One Man's Meat,* a collection of his *Harper's* columns, in 1942.

Children's books

In 1945 White entered a new field with great success, writing *Stuart Little* for children. The story of a mouse born to normal human parents was clearly intended to console young people who thought themselves different or odd, and it carried the message that Stuart's parents never batted an eye when their son turned out to be a mouse and that the hero could build himself a good life.

After *The Wild Flag* in 1946 and *Here Is New York* in 1949, White returned to children's literature with his most popular book in the genre (category), *Charlotte's Web,* in 1952. The story of the bond between the young pig Wilbur and the clever spider who saves his life is a look at the power of friendship and a reminder to young readers that death is a part of life. *The Second Tree from the Corner* came in 1954. Three years later White and his wife gave up their New York City apartment and moved permanently to North Brooklin, Maine.

Elements of Style

While an undergraduate at Cornell, White had taken a course with Professor William S. Strunk Jr. Strunk used a text he had written and published at his own expense, a thin volume titled *The Elements of Style.* White edited it, revised it, and added the chapter "An Approach to Style," offering such advice as "Place yourself in the background; do not explain too much; prefer the standard to the offbeat." The book sold widely and became a college campus fixture for the next twenty years in several editions.

Honors began to pour in for White. He won the Gold Medal for Essays and Criticism from the National Institute of Arts and Letters in 1960, the Presidential Medal of Freedom in 1963, the Laura Ingalls Wilder Medal for his children's books in 1970, and the National Medal for Literature in 1971. In 1973 he was elected to the American Academy of Arts and Letters.

E. B. White's influence was great, particularly in his popular essays, which served as models for two generations of readers. In the 1930s, 1940s, and 1950s, the *New Yorker* was judged by critics to be a model of elegant yet simple style in nonfiction, and White was in no small measure responsible for this reputation. He died on October 1, 1985, in North Brooklin, Maine.

For More Information

Craats, Rennay. *E. B. White.* Mankato, MN: Weigl Publishers, 2002.

Elledge, Scott. *E. B. White: A Biography.* New York: Norton, 1984.

Gherman, Beverly. *E. B. White: Some Writer!* New York: Atheneum, 1992.

Sampson, Edward C. *E. B. White*. New York: Twayne Publishers, 1974.

Tingum, Janice. *E. B. White: The Elements of a Writer*. Minneapolis: Lerner, 1995.

WALT WHITMAN

Born: May 31, 1819
West Hills, New York
Died: March 26, 1892
Camden, New Jersey
American poet

Walt Whitman is generally considered to be the most important American poet of the nineteenth century. He wrote in free verse (not in traditional poetic form), relying heavily on the rhythms of common American speech.

Childhood and early career

Walt Whitman was born on May 31, 1819, in West Hills, Long Island, the second of nine children. His family soon moved to Brooklyn, where he attended school for a few years. Young Whitman took to reading at an early age. By 1830 his formal education was over, and for the next five years he learned the printing trade. For about five years, beginning in 1836, he taught school on Long Island; during this time he also founded the weekly newspaper *Long-Islander*.

By 1841 Whitman was in New York City, where his interests turned to journalism. His short stories and poetry of this period were indistinguishable from the popular work of the day, as was his first novel, *Franklin Evans, or the Inebriate* (1842). For the next few years Whitman edited several newspapers and contributed to others. He was dismissed from the *Brooklyn Eagle* because of political differences with the owner. In 1848 he traveled south and for three months worked for the *New Orleans Crescent*. The sheer physical beauty of the new nation made a vivid impression on him, and he was to draw on this experience in his later poetry.

First edition of Leaves of Grass

Not much is known of Whitman's literary activities that can account for his sudden transformation (change) from journalist and hack writer into revolutionary poet. The first edition of *Leaves of Grass* (1855) opened with a rather casual portrait of Whitman, the self-professed "poet of the people," dressed in workman's clothes. In a lengthy preface Whitman announced that his poetry would celebrate the greatness of the new nation—"The Americans of all nations at any time upon the earth have probably the fullest poetical nature. The United States themselves are essentially the greatest poem"—and of its peoples—"The largeness of nature or the nation were monstrous without a corresponding largeness and generosity of the spirit of the citizen." Of the twelve poems (the titles were added later), "Song of Myself," "The Sleepers," "There Was a Child Went Forth," and "I Sing the Body Electric" are the best known today. In these Whitman turned his back on the literary models of the past. He stressed the rhythms of common American speech, delighting in informal and slang expressions.

Walt Whitman.
Courtesy of the National Archives and Records Administration.

The first edition of *Leaves* sold poorly. Fortunately, Whitman had sent Ralph Waldo Emerson (1803–1892) a free copy, and in his now famous reply, Emerson wrote: "I find it the most extraordinary piece of wit and wisdom that America has yet contributed. . . . I greet you at the beginning of a great career." Emerson's enthusiasm for *Leaves of Grass* was understandable, for he had strongly influenced the younger poet. Whitman echoed much of Emerson's philosophy in his preface and poems. Emerson's letter had a profound impact on Whitman, completely overshadowing the otherwise poor reception the volume received.

Second edition of Leaves of Grass

For the second edition of *Leaves of Grass* (1856), Whitman added twenty new poems to his original twelve. With this edition, he began his lifelong practice of adding new poems to *Leaves of Grass* and revising those previously published in order to bring them into line with his present moods and feelings. Also, over the years he was to drop a number of poems from *Leaves*.

Among the new poems in the 1856 edition were "Crossing Brooklyn Ferry" (one of Whitman's masterpieces), "Salut au Monde!," "A Woman Waits for Me," and "Spontaneous Me." Most of the 1855 preface he reworked to form the nationalistic poem "By Blue Ontario's Shore." Like the first edition, the second sold poorly.

The third edition of *Leaves* (1860) was brought out by a Boston publisher, one of the few times in his career that Whitman did not have to publish *Leaves of Grass* at his own expense. This edition, referred to by Whitman as his "new Bible," contained the earlier poems plus one hundred forty-six new ones. For the first time Whitman arranged many of the poems in special groupings, a practice he continued in all later editions. The most notable of these "groups" were "Children of Adam," a gathering of love poems, and "Calamus," a group of poems celebrating the brotherhood and comradeship of men, or, in Whitman's phrase, "manly love."

Whitman and the Civil War

Soon after the outbreak of the Civil War (1861–65; a war between regions of the United States in which Northern forces clashed with those of the South), Whitman went to Virginia to search for his brother George, reported wounded in action. Here Whitman experienced the war firsthand. He remained in Washington, D.C., working part-time in the Paymaster's Office. He devoted many long hours serving as a volunteer aide in the hospitals in Washington, ministering to the needs of the sick and wounded soldiers. His daily contact with sickness and death took its toll. Whitman himself became ill with "hospital malaria." Within a few months he recovered. In January 1865 he took a clerk's position in the Indian Bureau of the Department of the Interior.

The impact of the war on Whitman was reflected in his separately published *Drum-Taps* (1865). In such poems as "Cavalry Crossing a Ford," "The Wound-Dresser," "Come Up from the Fields Father," "Vigil Strange I Kept on the Field One Night," "Sight in Camp in the Daybreak Gray and Dim," and "Year That Trembled and Reel'd Beneath Me," Whitman caught with beautiful simplicity of statement the horror, loneliness, and anguish caused by the war.

Later career

Following the Civil War and the publication of the fourth edition, Whitman's poetry became increasingly preoccupied with themes relating to the soul, death, and immortality (living forever). He was entering the final phase of his career. Within the span of some dozen years, the poet of the body had given way to the poet of internationalism (not concentrating on a single country) and the cosmic (relating to the universe). Such poems as "Whispers of Heavenly Death,"

"Darest Thou Now O Soul," "The Last Invocation," and "A Noiseless Patient Spider," with their emphasis on the spiritual, paved the way for "Passage to India" (1871), Whitman's most important (and ambitious) poem of the post–Civil War period.

In 1881 Whitman settled on the final arrangement of the poems in *Leaves of Grass,* and thereafter no revisions were made. (All new poems written after 1881 were added as annexes [additions] to *Leaves.*) The seventh edition was published by James Osgood. The Boston district attorney threatened prosecution against Osgood unless certain poems were removed. When Whitman refused, Osgood dropped publication of the book. However, a Philadelphia, Pennsylvania, publisher reissued the book in 1882.

In his last years Whitman received the respect due a great literary figure and personality. He died on March 26, 1892, in Camden, New Jersey. *Leaves of Grass* has been widely translated, and Whitman's reputation is now worldwide.

For More Information

Allen, Gay Wilson. *The Solitary Singer: A Critical Biography of Walt Whitman.* New York: Macmillan, 1955. Reprint, Chicago: University of Chicago Press, 1985.

Loving, Jerome. *Walt Whitman: The Song of Himself.* Berkeley: University of California Press, 1999.

Reef, Catherine. *Walt Whitman.* New York: Clarion Books, 1995.

Reynolds, David S. *Walt Whitman's America: A Cultural Biography.* New York: Knopf, 1995.

ELIE
WIESEL

Born: September 30, 1928
Sighet, Romania
Romanian-born American writer and teacher

Romanian-born American writer, speaker, and teacher Elie Wiesel is a survivor of the Holocaust, the massive killing of Jews by the Nazis, Germany's radical army during World War II (1939–45; a war fought between the Axis powers: Italy, Germany, and Japan—and the Allies: England, France, the Soviet Union, and the United States). Wiesel is currently the chairman of the United States Holocaust Memorial Council.

Childhood

Elie Wiesel was born in Sighet, Romania, on September 30, 1928. He was the third of four children and the only son of Shlomo and Sarah Wiesel. Wiesel was encouraged by his father to learn modern Hebrew literature, and his mother encouraged him to study the sacred Jewish texts. His father instilled in him the ability to reason and from his mother, he learned faith. When he was fifteen, Wiesel and his family were taken to the concentration camps (harsh political prisons) at Birkenau and Auschwitz, Poland, where he remained until January 1945 when, along with thousands of other Jewish prisoners, he was moved to Buchenwald in a forced death march. Buchenwald was freed on April 11, 1945, by the U.S. Army, but neither Wiesel's parents nor his younger sister survived. His two remaining sisters survived, and they were reunited after the war ended in 1945.

After the war Wiesel went to France where he completed secondary school, studied at the Sorbonne in Paris, France, and began working as a journalist for an Israeli newspaper. In 1956 he moved to New York City to cover the United Nations (UN; a multinational organization aimed at world peace) and became a U.S. citizen in 1963. He was the Andrew Mellon Professor of Humanities at Boston (Massachusetts) University in the mid-1980s.

His writings

Wiesel's writings bear witness to his year-long ordeal and to the Jewish tragedy. In 1956 Wiesel's first book, a Yiddish memoir entitled *And the World Was Silent,* was published in Argentina. Two years later a much smaller version of the work was published in France as *La Nuit.* After the 1960 English language publication of *Night,* Wiesel wrote more than thirty-five books: novels, collections of short stories and essays, and plays. His works established him as the most widely known and admired Holocaust writer.

Only in *Night* does Wiesel speak about the Holocaust directly. Throughout his other works, the Holocaust looms as the shadow, the central but unspoken mystery in the life of his protagonists, or main characters. Even pre-Holocaust events are seen as warnings of impending doom. In *Night* he narrates his own experience as a young boy transported to Auschwitz where suffering and death shattered his faith in both God and humanity. *Night* is widely considered a classic of Holocaust literature.

Night was followed in 1961 by *Dawn,* the story of a young Holocaust survivor brought to work for the underground in preindependence Israel. Young Elisha is ordered to execute a British army officer in retaliation for the hanging of a young Jewish fighter. Through Elisha's ordeal, Wiesel describes the transformation of the Jewish people from defenseless victims into potential victimizers. The execution occurs at dawn, but the killing is an act of self-destruction with Elisha its ultimate victim.

The struggle between life and death continues to dominate Wiesel's third work of the trilogy (a set of three), but in *The Accident* (*Le Jour* in French), published in 1962, God is not involved in either life or death. The battle is waged within the protagonist, now a newspaper correspondent covering the United Nations, who is fighting for life after an accident. In these three early works Wiesel moved from a universe greatly influenced by God to a godless one. The titles of his books grow brighter as the presence of God becomes dimmer, yet the transition is never easy.

Other roles

Wiesel, in addition to his literary activities, played an important role as a public orator, or speaker. Each year he gave a series of lectures on Jewish tradition at New York City's 92nd Street Young Men's Christian Association (YMCA). These lectures formed the basis for his retelling of Jewish tales: stories of Hasidism (eighteenth- and nineteenth-century Jewish pietists [people who stress extreme religious studies and practices]) which Wiesel published in *Souls on Fire* (1972), *Somewhere a Master* (1982), and *Four Hasidic Masters* (1978). Biblical legends are covered in *Messengers of God* (1975), *Images from the Bible* (1980), and *Five Biblical Portraits* (1981). Wiesel spun his own tales in

Elie Wiesel.
Reproduced by permission of AP/Wide World Photos.

such works as *Legends of Our Time* (1968), *One Generation After* (1970), and *A Jew Today* (1978). The themes of these stories remained tragedy and joy, madness and hope, the fragility of meaning, and the quest for faith.

As a social activist, Wiesel used his writing to plead for Jews in danger and on behalf of all humanity. From his trips to Russia in 1965 and 1966, he produced *The Jews of Silence* (1966) which describes Wiesel's visits with Soviet Jews, or Jewish people living in the Soviet Union (the former country made up of Russia and several smaller states and run by communism, a political system where goods and services are owned and distributed by a strong central government). Wiesel captured the spiritual reawakening that was to mark the struggle of Soviet Jewry during the 1970s and 1980s. Soviet Jews were not Wiesel's Jews of silence. Western Jews, who dared not speak out on their brothers' behalf, were the silent ones.

Honored

Wiesel was the recipient of numerous awards throughout his career, including the Nobel Peace Prize in 1986. His humanitarian activities were also rewarded with many honors, such as Eleanor Roosevelt Memorial Award (1972) and the International League for Human Rights humanitarian award (1985). Numerous honors have been established in his name, including the Elie Wiesel Chair in Holocaust Studies at Bar-Ilan University and the Elie Wiesel Chair in Judaic Studies at Connecticut College.

Later work

In 1979 President Jimmy Carter (1924–) named Wiesel chair of the President's Commission on the Holocaust, which recommended creation of a memorial museum and educational center in Washington, D.C. In 1980 Wiesel was appointed chairman to the U.S. Holocaust Memorial Council. In 1985 Wiesel led the opposition to President Ronald Reagan's (1911–) trip to a German military cemetery which contained the graves of Adolf Hitler's (1889–1945) elite S.S. Waffen soldiers.

Speaking in 1984 at the White House, where President Reagan presented him with the Congressional Gold Medal, Wiesel summarized his career, "I have learned that suffering confers no privileges: it depends on what one does with it. This is why survivors have tried to teach their contemporaries how to build on ruins; how to invent hope in a world that offers none; how to proclaim faith to a generation that has seen it shamed and mutilated."

For More Information

Brown, Robert McAfee. *Elie Wiesel: Messenger to All Humanity.* South Bend, IN: Notre Dame University Press, 1989.

Cargas, Harry J. *Conversations with Elie Wiesel.* South Bend, IN: Justice Books, 1992.

Greene, Carole. *Elie Wiesel: Messenger from the Holocaust.* Chicago: Children's Press, 1987.

Wiesel, Elie. *All Rivers Run to the Sea: Memoirs.* New York: Knopf, 1995.

Wiesel, Elie. *Night.* New York: Hill and Wang, 1960.

OSCAR WILDE

Born: October 16, 1854
Dublin, Ireland
Died: November 30, 1900
Paris, France
Irish-born English author, dramatist, and poet

The English author Oscar Wilde was part of the "art for art's sake" movement in English literature at the end of the nineteenth century. He is best known for his brilliant, witty comedies including the play *The Importance of Being Earnest* and his classic novel *The Picture of Dorian Gray.*

Outstanding childhood

Oscar Fingall O'Flahertie Wills Wilde was born in Dublin, Ireland, on October 16, 1854. His father, Sir William Wilde, was a well-known surgeon; his mother, Jane Francisca Elgee Wilde, wrote popular poetry and other work under the pseudonym (pen name) Speranza. Because of his mother's literary successes, young Oscar enjoyed a cultured and privileged childhood.

After attending Portora Royal School in Enniskillen, Ireland, Wilde moved on to study the classics at Trinity College, Dublin, from 1871 to 1874. There, he began attracting public attention through the uniqueness of his writing and his lifestyle. Before leaving Trinity College, Wilde was awarded many honors, including the Berkely Gold Medal for Greek.

Begins writing career

At the age of twenty-three Wilde entered Magdalen College, Oxford, England. In 1878 he was awarded the Newdigate Prize for his poem "Ravenna." He attracted a group of followers whose members were purposefully unproductive and artificial. "The first duty in life," Wilde wrote in *Phrases and Philosophies for the Use of the Young* (1894), "is to be as artificial as possible." After leaving Oxford he expanded his cult (a following). His iconoclasm (attacking of established religious institutions) clashed with the holiness that came with the Victorian era of the late nineteenth century, but this contradiction was one that he aimed for. Another of his aims was the glorification of youth.

Wilde published his well-received *Poems* in 1881. The next six years were active ones.

Oscar Wilde.
Courtesy of the Library of Congress.

He spent an entire year lecturing in the United States and then returned to lecture in England. He applied unsuccessfully for a position as a school inspector. In 1884 he married, and his wife bore him children in 1885 and in 1886. He began to publish extensively in the following year. His writing activity became as intense and as inconsistent as his life had been for the previous six years. From 1887 to 1889 Wilde edited the magazine *Woman's World*. His first popular success as a fiction writer was *The Happy Prince and Other Tales* (1888). *The House of Pomegranates* (1892) was another collection of his fairy tales.

Sexuality of Oscar Wilde

In 1886 Wilde became a practicing homosexual, or one who is sexually attracted to a member of their own sex. He believed that his attacks on the Victorian moral code was the inspiration for his writing. He considered himself a criminal who challenged society by creating scandal. Before his conviction (found guilty) for homosexuality in 1895, the scandal was essentially private. Wilde believed in the criminal mentality. "Lord Arthur Savile's Crime," from *Lord Arthur Savile's Crime and Other Stories* (1891), treated murder and its successful cover-up comically. The original version of *The Picture of Dorian Gray* in *Lippincott's Magazine* emphasized the murder of the painter Basil Hallward by Dorian as the turning point in Dorian's downfall. Wilde stressed that criminal tendency became criminal act.

Dorian Gray was published in book form in 1891. The novel was a celebration of youth. Dorian, in a gesture typical of Wilde, is parentless. He does not age, and he is a criminal. Like all of Wilde's work, the novel was a popular success. His only book of formal criticism, *Intentions* (1891), restated many of the views that *Dorian Gray* had emphasized, and it points toward his later plays and stories. *Intentions* emphasized the importance of criticism in an age that Wilde believed was uncritical. For him, criticism was an independent branch of literature, and its function was important.

His dramas

Between 1892 and 1895 Wilde was an active dramatist (writer of plays), writing what he identified as "trivial [unimportant] comedies for serious people." His plays were popular because their dialogue was baffling, clever, and often short and clear, relying on puns and elaborate word games for their effect. *Lady Windermere's Fan* was produced in 1892, *A Woman of No Importance* in 1893, and *An Ideal Husband* and *The Importance of Being Earnest* in 1895.

On March 2, 1895, Wilde initiated a suit for criminal libel (a statement that damages someone's reputation) against the Marquess of Queensberry, who had objected to Wilde's friendship with his son, Lord Alfred Douglas. When his suit failed in April, countercharges followed. After a spectacular court action, Wilde was convicted of homosexual misconduct and sentenced to two years in prison at hard labor.

Prison transformed Wilde's experience as extremely as had his 1886 introduction to homosexuality. In a sense he had prepared himself for prison and its transformation of his art. *De Profundis* is a moving letter to a friend and apologia (a formal defense) that Wilde wrote in prison; it was first published as a whole in 1905. His theme was that he was not unlike other men and was a scapegoat, or one who bears blame for others. *The Ballad of Reading Gaol* (1898) was written after his release. In this poem a man murdered his mistress and was about to be executed, but Wilde considered him only as criminal as the rest of humanity. He wrote: "For each man kills the thing he loves, / Yet each man does not die."

After Wilde was released from prison he lived in Paris, France. He attempted to write a play in his style before his imprisonment, but this effort failed. He died in Paris on November 30, 1900.

For More Information

Bloom, Harold, ed. *Oscar Wilde.* Philadelphia: Chelsea House, 2002.

Ellmann, Richard. *Oscar Wilde.* New York: Knopf, 1988.

Kaufman, Moises. *Gross Indecency: The Three Trials of Oscar Wilde.* New York: Vintage Books, 1998.

Pearce, Joseph. *The Unmasking of Oscar Wilde.* London: HarperCollins, 2000.

Woodcock, George. *Oscar Wilde: The Double Image.* New York: Black Rose Books, 1989.

LAURA INGALLS WILDER

Born: February 7, 1867
Pepin, Wisconsin
Died: February 10, 1957
Mansfield, Missouri
American writer

American author Laura Ingalls Wilder was the creator of the much-loved children's series of "Little House" books that recounted her life as a young girl on the Western frontier during the late 1800s.

Raised on the American prairie

Laura Ingalls Wilder was born Laura Elizabeth Ingalls on February 7, 1867, in Pepin, Wisconsin, the second of four children. She once described her father, Charles Philip Ingalls, as always jolly and sometimes reckless. Her mother, Caroline Lake Quiner, was educated, gentle, and proud, according to her daughter. Her sisters, all of whom would eventually appear in her books, were Mary, Carrie, and Grace. Laura also had a younger brother, Charles, Jr. (nicknamed Freddie), who died at the age of only nine months.

As a young girl, Laura moved with her family from place to place across America's heartland. In 1874, the Ingalls family left Wisconsin for Walnut Grove, Minnesota, where they lived at first in a dugout house. Two years later, the family moved to Burr Oak, Iowa, where Charles became part-owner of a hotel. By the fall of 1877, however, they had all returned to Walnut Grove. In 1879, the Ingalls family moved again, this time to homestead in the Dakota Territory.

The family finally settled in what would become De Smet, South Dakota, which remained Charles and Caroline's home until they died. Their second winter in De Smet was one of the worst on record. Numerous blizzards prevented trains from delivering any supplies, essentially cutting off the town from December until May. Years later, Laura wrote about her experiences as a young teenager trying to survive the cold temperatures and lack of food, firewood, and other necessities.

Laura attended regular school whenever possible. However, because of her family's frequent moves, she was largely self-taught. In 1882, at the age of fifteen, she received her teaching certificate. For three years, Laura taught at a small country school a dozen miles from her home in De Smet and boarded with a family who lived nearby.

Laura Ingalls Wilder.
Reproduced by permission of the Corbis Croporation.

Married a farmer

During this same period, Ingalls came to know Almanzo Manly Wilder, who had settled near De Smet in 1879 with his brother Royal. Almanzo frequently headed out into the country on his sleigh to pick up the young teacher and drop her off at her parents' home for weekend visits. After courting for a little more than two years, they were married on August 25, 1885. Laura Wilder then quit teaching to help her husband on their farm. She later wrote about this time in her life in her book *The First Four Years.*

The couple's only surviving child, Rose, was born on December 5, 1886. Although all homesteaders (those settling new lands) had to endure the hardships and uncertainty of farm life, the Wilders experienced more than their share of tragedy and misfortune. In August 1889, Wilder gave birth to a baby boy who died shortly after, an event that never appeared in any of her books. Her husband then came down with diphtheria, a terrible disease that causes breathing problems, which left him partially paralyzed. Finally, their house, built by Manly himself, burned to the ground.

On July 17, 1894, the Wilders began their journey to Mansfield, Missouri, the place they would call home for the rest of their lives. There they established a farm and named it Rocky Ridge. Wilder kept a journal of their experiences as they traveled. When she reached Lamar, Missouri, she sent her account of their travels through South Dakota, Nebraska, and Kansas to the *De Smet News.* This was her first published writing.

Produced her first autobiographical work

By the mid-1920s Wilder and her husband were doing little of their own farming on Rocky Ridge, which allowed her to spend most of her time writing. Around this same time, Rose returned to Missouri, built a new home for her parents on Rocky Ridge, and moved into the old farmhouse. She also began encouraging her mother to write the story of her childhood.

Wilder completed her first autobiographical work in the late 1920s. Entitled *Pioneer Girl,* it was a first-person account of her childhood on the frontier from the time she was three until she reached the age of eighteen. After Rose edited the book, Wilder submitted it to various publishers under the name Laura Ingalls Wilder. But no one was interested in her chronicle, which contained plenty of historical facts about her childhood but little in the way of character development.

Created the "Little House" books

Refusing to become discouraged, Wilder changed her approach. The "I" in her stories became "Laura," and the focus moved from the story of one little girl to the story of an entire family's experiences on the new frontier. Wilder also decided to direct her writing specifically at children. Although she sometimes streamlined events, created or omitted others entirely (such as the birth and death of her brother), and opted for happier endings, she wrote about real people and things that had actually happened.

In 1932, at the age of sixty-five, Wilder published the first of her eight "Little House" books, *Little House in the Big Woods*. It told the story of her early childhood years in Wisconsin and was a huge hit with readers. *Farmer Boy,* an account of Manly's childhood in New York state, followed in 1933. Two years later, *Little House on the Prairie* appeared on the shelves. Five more books followed that took the reader through Wilder's courtship and marriage to Manly—*On the Banks of Plum Creek* (1937), *By the Shores of Silver Lake* (1939), *The Long Winter* (1940), *Little Town on the Prairie* (1941), and *These Happy Golden Years* (1943). New editions of all of the "Little House" books were reissued by Harper in 1953 with the now-familiar illustrations of Garth Williams (1912–1996).

Wilder was seventy-six years old when she finished the final book in her "Little House" series. By that time, she and her hus-band had sold off the majority of their land and virtually all of their livestock, but they still lived on the remaining seventy acres of Rocky Ridge. It was there that Manly died in 1949 at the age of ninety-two.

Wilder was ninety when she died at Rocky Ridge Farm on February 10, 1957. After her death, her daughter, Rose Wilder Lane, edited the diary her mother had written as she and Manly traveled to Missouri, the one that had first appeared in the De Smet newspaper. The resulting book, *On the Way Home: The Diary of a Trip from South Dakota to Mansfield, Missouri, in 1894,* was published in 1962. Twelve years later, a television series based on Wilder's stories debuted and ran for nine seasons. Through her engaging tales of life on the untamed American frontier, Wilder succeeded beyond her wildest dreams at taking a unique time and place of adventure, hardship, and simple pleasures and making it real to scores of young readers across the world.

For More Information

Anderson, William. *Laura Ingalls Wilder: A Biography.* New York: HarperCollins, 1992.

Miller, John E. *Becoming Laura Ingalls Wilder: The Woman Behind the Legacy.* Columbia: University of Missouri Press, 1998.

Wadsworth, Ginger. *Laura Ingalls Wilder: Storyteller of the Prairie.* Minneapolis: Lerner, 1997.

Wilder, Laura Ingalls. *West from Home: Letters of Laura Ingalls Wilder to Almanzo.* Edited by R. L. MacBride. New York: Harper, 1974.

Zochert, Donald. *Laura: The Life of Laura Ingalls Wilder.* Chicago: Regnery, 1976.

THORNTON WILDER

Born: April 17, 1897
Madison, Wisconsin
Died: December 7, 1975
Hamden, Connecticut
American playwright and novelist

Novelist and playwright Thornton Wilder won two Pulitzer Prizes for his plays *Our Town* and *The Skin of Our Teeth,* written in 1938 and 1942 respectively. His most well-known novel, *The Bridge of San Luis Rey,* also won him a Pulitzer Prize in 1927.

Childhood

Thornton Niven Wilder was born on April 17, 1897, in Madison, Wisconsin, the second son of four children of Amos Parker and Isabella Wilder. In 1906 the family moved to China when his father became the United States Consul-General in Hong Kong. The teenager attended the English China Inland Mission School at Cheefoo but returned with his mother and siblings to California in 1912 because of the unstable political conditions in China at the time. While in high school, Wilder became interested in theater and began regularly attending performances of plays. He also began to demonstrate his unique talents for writing.

Graduating in 1915 from Berkeley High School, Wilder attended Oberlin College before transferring to Yale University in 1917. He served with the First Coast Artillery in Rhode Island in 1918 during World War I (1914–18), when Germany waged war against much of Europe. After the war he returned to his studies at Yale. In 1920 he received his bachelor's degree and saw the first publication of his play *The Trumpet Shall Sound* in *Yale Literary Magazine.*

Writing professionally

Wilder started his novel *The Cabala* at the American Academy in Rome, Italy, in 1921. In New Jersey he taught at the Lawrenceville School while earning a master's degree at Princeton University. He received his degree in 1926, the publication year of *The Cabala.* Its publication came at the same time as the first professional production of *The Trumpet Shall Sound* by the American Laboratory Theater. But it was his breakthrough work, *The Bridge of San Luis Rey* (1927), that thrust him to the forefront of American literature.

A lifelong traveler, Wilder later taught at the University of Chicago, in Illinois, (1930–1936) and the University of Hawaii (1935). He volunteered in World War II (1939–45; the war fought between the Axis: Italy, Germany, and Japan—and the Allies: France, England, the Soviet Union, and the United States). During the war he served in Africa, Italy, and the United States. A lecturer at Harvard in the early 1950s, he received the Gold Medal for Fiction from the Academy of Arts and Letters in 1952. In 1962 he retired to Arizona for almost two years, then renewed his travels. Wilder was awarded the Presidential Medal of Freedom in 1963 and the National Book Committee's National Medal for Literature (first time presented) in 1965.

Career as a playwright

Wilder's first successful dramatic work, which he started at Oberlin, was *The Angel That*

Troubled the Waters (1928). A four-act play, *The Trumpet Shall Sound* (1919–20), was produced unsuccessfully off-Broadway in 1926. *The Long Christmas Dinner and Other Plays in One-Act*, published in 1931, contained three plays that gained popularity with amateur groups: *The Long Christmas Dinner, Pullman Car Hiawatha*, and *The Happy Journey to Trenton and Camden*. This last series marked Wilder's trademark use of a bare stage for the actors.

Wilder's first Broadway shows were translations: André Obey's *Lucrece* (1932) and *A Doll's House* (1937) by Henrik Ibsen (1828–1906). His dramatic reputation soared with *Our Town* (1938). Written for a bare stage, guided throughout by a narrator, his script examines a small town for the "something way down deep that's eternal about every human being."

Wilder's dramatic work that followed, *The Merchant of Yonkers*, failed initially in 1938. But when produced with slight changes as *The Matchmaker* in 1954, it proved a fascinating farce, or a show made ridiculous for effect. (It later re-emerged as the musical play *Hello, Dolly!* in 1963, then an overwhelming success.) Wilder mingled style and forms even more daringly in *The Skin of Our Teeth*. Here, Wilder described the human race as flawed but worth preserving. A complex and difficult play that drew from James Joyce's (1882–1941) *Finnegans Wake*, it became the work that claimed him his final Pulitzer Prize in 1943.

The essentially conservative (having to do with the commonly accepted) thematic material staged in radical styles made Wilder's plays unique. His later work included an unsuccessful tragedy, *A Life in the Sun* (or *The Alcestiad*, 1955) and three short plays of an

Thornton Wilder.
Reproduced by permission of AP/Wide World Photos.

intended fourteen-play cycle: *Someone from Assisi, Infancy,* and *Childhood* (produced as *Plays for Bleecker Street* in 1962).

Career as a novelist

Wilder established his reputation as a novelist with *The Cabala*, a minor work that showed Wilder's moral (having to do with wrong or right) concerns. *The Bridge of San Luis Rey,* set in eighteenth-century Peru, proved immensely popular and led to the Pulitzer Prize in 1928. *The Woman of Andros* (1930), based on Terence's (c. 185–159 B.C.E.) play *Andria* was not well received. Although Wilder's view of life encouraged heavy criticism (negative judgment), *Heaven's My Destination* (1934), set in the American Midwest, grew in favor over the years. In *The Ides of March* (1948) Wilder tried a novel approach to Julius Caesar (100–44 B.C.E.). *The Eighth Day* in 1967 returned Wilder to a twentieth-century American setting that examined the lives of two families. Wilder's last novel, *Theophilus North,* was published in 1973.

In line with Wilder's diverse interests and scholarly (having to do with learned knowledge) bent, Wilder lectured and published extensively. His Harvard lectures "Toward an American Language," "The American Loneliness," and "Emily Dickinson" appeared in the *Atlantic Monthly* (1952). His topics addressed play writing, fiction, and the role of the artist in society. His range spanned from the works of the ancient Greeks to modern dramatists (writers of plays), particularly Joyce and Gertrude Stein (1874–1946). His observations and letters were published in a variety of works, from André Maurois's (1885–1967) *A Private Universe* (1932) to Donald Gallup's *The Flowers of Friendship* (1953). Wilder died of a heart attack December 7, 1975, in Hamden, Connecticut.

For More Information

Bloom, Harold, ed. *Thornton Wilder.* Philadelphia: Chelsea House, 2002.

Bryer, Jackson R. *Conversations with Thornton Wilder.* Jackson: University Press of Mississippi, 1992.

Castronovo, David. *Thornton Wilder.* New York: Ungar, 1986.

Harrison, Gilbert A. *The Enthusiast: A Life of Thornton Wilder.* New Haven, CT: Ticknor & Fields, 1983.

TENNESSEE WILLIAMS

Born: March 26, 1914
Columbus, Mississippi
Died: February 25, 1983
New York, New York
American dramatist, playwright, and writer

Tennessee Williams, dramatist and fiction writer, was one of America's major mid-twentieth-century playwrights. He is best known for his powerful plays, *A Streetcar Named Desire* and *Cat on a Hot Tin Roof.*

Becoming Tennessee

Tennessee Williams was born Thomas Lanier Williams in Columbus, Mississippi, on March 26, 1914, the second of three children of Cornelius and Edwina Williams. His father, a traveling salesman, was rarely home and for many years the family lived with his mother's parents. As a result, the young boy developed a close relationship with his grandfather, and also his older sister, Rose. William's family life was never a happy one. His parents were resentful of each other, his mother once describing her husband as "a man's man" who loved to gamble and drink. When his father obtained a position at a shoe factory, the family moved to a crowded, low-rent apartment in St. Louis, Missouri.

About this time, young Thomas adopted the name Tennessee (presumably because many of his descendants hailed from that state). Williams grew to hate St. Louis. He and his sisters were often ridiculed by other students because of their Southern accent.

He also skipped school regularly and did poorly in his studies, preferring instead to escape into the world of reading and writing.

At the age of sixteen Williams published his first story. The next year he entered the University of Missouri but left before taking a degree. He worked for two years for a shoe company, spent a year at Washington University (where he had his first plays produced), and earned a bachelor of arts degree from the State University of Iowa in 1938, the year he published his first short story under his literary name, Tennessee Williams.

In 1940 the Theatre Guild produced Williams's *Battle of Angels* in Boston, Massachusetts. The play was a total failure and was withdrawn after Boston's Watch and Ward Society banned it. Between 1940 and 1945 he lived on grants (donated money) from the Rockefeller Foundation and the American Academy of Arts and Letters, on income scraped together from an attempt to write film scripts in Hollywood, and on wages as a waiter-entertainer in Greenwich Village in New York City.

Accomplished playwright

With the production of *The Glass Menagerie* Williams's fortunes changed. The play opened in Chicago, Illinois, in December 1944 and in New York City in March; it received the New York Drama Critics Circle Award and the Sidney Howard Memorial Award. *You Touched Me!*, written with Donald Windham, opened on Broadway in 1945. It was followed by publication of eleven one-act plays, *27 Wagons Full of Cotton* (1946), and two California productions. When *A Streetcar Named Desire* opened in 1947, New York audiences knew a major playwright had

Tennessee Williams.
Courtesy of the Library of Congress.

arrived. *A Streetcar Named Desire* won a Pulitzer Prize. The play combines sensuality, melodrama, and lyrical symbolism (a poetic representation of significant things). A film version was directed by Elia Kazan (1909–) and their partnership lasted for more than a decade.

Although the plays that followed *Streetcar* never repeated its overwhelming success, they kept Williams's name on theater marquees and in films. His novel *The Roman Spring of Mrs. Stone* (1950) and three volumes of short stories brought him an even wider audience. Some writers consider *Summer and Smoke* (1948) Williams's most sensitive play. While *The Rose*

Tattoo (1951) played to appreciative audiences, *Camino Real* (1953) played to confused ones. *Cat on a Hot Tin Roof* (1955) was a smashing success and won the New York Drama Critics Circle Award and a Pulitzer Prize.

Baby Doll (an original Williams-Kazan film script, 1956) was followed by the dramas *Orpheus Descending* (1957), *Garden District* (1958; two one-act plays, *Something Unspoken* and *Suddenly Last Summer*), *Sweet Bird of Youth* (1959), *Period of Adjustment* (1960), and *The Night of the Iguana* (1961). With these plays, critics charged Williams with publicly trying to solve personal problems, while including confused symbolism, sexual obsessions, thin characterizations, and violence and corruption for their own sake. *The Milk Train Doesn't Stop Here Anymore* (1963), *The Seven Descents of Myrtle* (1963; also called *Kingdom of Earth*), and *In the Bar of a Tokyo Hotel* (1969) neither helped Williams's standing with the critics nor proved that Williams's remarkable talent had vanished. Published after his death, *Not about Nightingales* (1998) had been written in 1938 and was Williams's first full-length play.

Later career

Through the 1970s and 1980s, Williams continued to write for the theater, though he was unable to repeat the success of most of his early years. One of his last plays was *Clothes for a Summer Hotel* (1980), based on passionate love affair between the American writer F. Scott Fitzgerald (1896–1940) and his wife, Zelda.

Two collections of Williams's many one-act plays were published: *27 Wagons Full of Cotton* (1946) and *American Blues* (1948). Williams also wrote fiction, including two novels, *The Roman Spring of Mrs. Stone* (1950)

and *Moise and the World of Reason* (1975). Four volumes of short stories were also published. *One Arm and Other Stories* (1948), *Hard Candy* (1954), *The Knightly Quest* (1969), and *Eight Mortal Ladies Possessed* (1974). Nine of his plays were made into films, and he wrote one original screenplay, *Baby Doll* (1956). In his 1975 tell-all novel, *Memoirs,* Williams described his own problems with alcohol and drugs and his homosexuality (the attraction to members of the same sex).

Williams died in New York City on February 25, 1983. In 1995, the United States Post Office commemorated Williams by issuing a special edition stamp in his name as part of their Literary Arts Series. For several years, literary enthusiasts have gathered to celebrate the man and his work at the Tennessee Williams Scholars Conference. The annual event, held along with the Tennessee Williams/New Orleans Literary Festival, features educational, theatrical and literary programs.

For More Information

Hayman, Ronald. *Tennessee Williams: Everyone Else Is an Audience.* New Haven, CT: Yale University Press, 1993.

Holditch, W. Kenneth. *Tennessee Williams and the South.* Jackson: University Press of Mississippi, 2002.

Leverich, Lyle. *Tom: The Unknown Tennessee Williams.* New York: Crown Publishers, 1995.

Rasky, Harry. *Tennessee Williams: A Portrait in Laughter and Lamentation.* New York: Dodd, Mead, 1986.

Spoto, Donald. *The Kindness of Strangers: The Life of Tennessee Williams.* Boston: Little, Brown, 1985.

WOODROW WILSON

Born: December 28, 1856
Staunton, Virginia
Died: February 3, 1924
Washington, D.C.
American president, governor, and educator

Woodrow Wilson was admired as a writer, a scholar, and an educator more than two decades before he became president. He spent twenty-four years working in the academic world as a professor, then as a college president, before he was elected governor of New Jersey. Two years later he was elected president of the United States, led the country through World War I (1914–18) and was the primary architect of the League of Nations.

Early years

Stephen Woodrow Wilson was born in Staunton, Virginia, on December 28, 1856, the son of Joseph and Jeanie Wilson. His father was a Presbyterian minister. Wilson briefly attended Davison University in North Carolina, but transferred to Princeton University and graduated there in 1879. He received his doctorate in 1886 from Johns Hopkins University.

In his doctoral thesis Wilson analyzed the American political system, and criticized what he believed was a breakdown of power in Congress, which was caused by the committee system. He believed that the president ought to solely lead the nation, a view that did not change once he was in the White House.

From 1886 to 1910 Wilson was in academic life—as a professor of political science at Bryn Mawr College, Wesleyan University, and Princeton. In 1902, he was named president of Princeton. He strongly favored an educational system that promoted a close relationship between teachers and students.

From academia to politics

By 1910 Wilson had established such a solid reputation as an educator that the Democratic party in New Jersey offered him the nomination for governor. After winning the election, Governor Wilson showed strong leadership, pushing through legislation dealing with such issues as employers' liability and public utilities. His success made him a prominent candidate for the presidency in 1912. He was nominated on the forty-sixth ballot, and went on to soundly defeat former president Theodore Roosevelt (1858–1919) and current president William Howard Taft (1857–1930) in the November election.

First term as president

In the first two years of his presidency Wilson dominated the Democratic-controlled Congress and secured legislation of great historical significance. The tariff (duties or a kind of tax) was revised downward, beginning a policy that was to be of substantial importance later. The Federal Reserve Act created a banking system under governmental control. The Federal Trade Commission Act created a body that has had an important role in preventing monopolies (an overwhelming concentration of power in an industry).

Early on Wilson faced difficult questions of foreign policy. Wilson refused to recognize

Woodrow Wilson.
Courtesy of the Library of Congress.

Mexico's new military dictator president, Victoriano Huerta, and worked for social reform in that country. In 1914 Wilson ordered the occupation of Veracruz to prevent Huerta from receiving arms from abroad. War was averted when the countries of Argentina, Brazil, and Chile mediated. Huerta was soon overthrown.

Beginning of World War I

In August 1914 World War I broke out in Europe. This was a particularly difficult time for Wilson. In addition to the beginning of the war, his wife, Ellen Axson Wilson

(1860–1914) died. The grieving president kept himself busy with his work and confided in his three daughters and a few close friends. His grief lightened early the following year, when he met Edith Bolling Galt (1872–1961). The couple married in December 1915.

Wilson kept the United States out of the war based on a policy of neutrality (taking no side). But there is little doubt that he sympathized with France and Great Britain and feared the victory of imperial Germany. The warring countries soon began interfering with American trade. The British restricted American commerce, but the Germans proclaimed a new kind of warfare, submarine warfare, with the prospect of American ships being sunk and their passengers and crew being lost. Wilson took German policies more seriously, because they involved the potential destruction of human life, whereas the British interfered only with trade. As early as February 1915, in response to a German declaration instituting the U-boat war, the president declared that Germany would be held to "strict accountability" for the loss of American lives.

For a time thereafter Wilson took no action. But on May 7, 1915, the liner *Lusitania* was sunk, with over a hundred American lives lost. The President addressed a stiff note to Germany. After other painful submarine episodes, Wilson convinced Germany to abandon the U-boat war in 1916.

In the meantime the presidential campaign of 1916 was approaching. Wilson was easily renominated and went on to win a close election against the Republican candidate, former Supreme Court justice (and future chief justice) Charles Evans Hughes

(1862–1948). Part of Wilson's success came from the Democratic platform that touted the president's ability to keep the United States at peace. "He kept us out of war" was a successful pro-Wilson slogan, though Wilson never promised anything about the country's future involvement in the war.

Second term as president

Wilson's efforts to bring the warring countries together were not successful. When the German government sought unlimited warfare on the sea, Wilson severed diplomatic relations with that nation but continued to hope that a direct challenge could be avoided. But on April 2, 1917, Wilson asked Congress for a declaration of war against Germany, and Congress overwhelmingly approved.

Wilson believed that the defeat of Germany was necessary, but he held out hope that at the end of the war a League of Nations might be established that would make impossible the recurrence of another bloody struggle. As early as April 1916 the president had begun to formulate his views on this. He was in favor of an association of nations that would act together against any nation that disrupted peace. There was much support for his point of view.

Fourteen Points

Throughout the war Wilson insisted on two things: the defeat of German militarism and the establishment of peace resting on just principles. In January 1918 he proposed the "Fourteen Points" that would need to be met in order to secure an armistice (cease fire) and begin serious peace negotiations. In the negotiations that autumn he made the acceptance of these points the primary condi-tion on the part of his European associates and of the Germans as well. In November 1918 Wilson succeeded; an armistice was signed. Throughout the world Wilson was looked at with great esteem.

But difficulties loomed. The 1918 elections returned a Republican majority to Congress. The president himself stimulated partisanship by his appeal to elect a Democratic legislature. Though he selected able men to accompany him to the forthcoming peace conference in Paris, France, he did not think of accommodating the Republican opposition. By insisting on going to Paris in person and remaining there until the treaty was finished, he cut himself off from American opinion.

Treaty of Versailles and the League of Nations

At the peace conference Wilson strove to realize his ideals. He worked on drafting the Covenant of the League of Nations. This would provide for a League Council of the five great world powers and four elective members and for an assembly in which every member state would have a vote. Disputes would either go to arbitration or be decided amongst council members. If they failed to do this, they would be subjected to economic and possibly to military sanctions. They were also to agree to respect and preserve the territorial integrity and political independence of the members of the League.

At the talks that eventually led to the Treaty of Versailles, Wilson argued successfully for fairness on many issues, but he had to compromise on two vital points: France and England insisted on huge war reparations (payments for damages) against Germany; and Japan, which had joined the Allies late in the war, was allowed to keep control of a province of China it had invaded. Wilson deeply opposed both resolutions, but he compromised to keep alive his vision for the League of Nations.

The Treaty of Versailles was not to stand the test of time. In detaching substantial territories from Germany and in fixing Germany with responsibility for the war, it furnished the basis for that German nationalism which was to strengthen with Adolf Hitler (1889–1945).

Wilson returned to the United States with a political battle ahead. Many disliked the Treaty of Versailles and opposed the "world politics" concept of the League of Nations. He erred in demanding ratification of the treaty without any changes. He made his appeal in an exhausting countrywide tour. He was hailed by large, enthusiastic crowds, but his health gave way, forcing him back to the White House. A stroke temporarily incapacitated him.

The Senate rejected unconditional ratification but adopted the treaty with reservations that Wilson refused to accept. In January 1920 a compromise was attempted. But Wilson spoiled these efforts by including the issue in the 1920 presidential campaign. In the fall election the Republican candidate, U.S. senator Warren G. Harding (1865–1923) of Ohio, easily defeated a fellow Ohioan, Governor James M. Cox (1870–1957). The new chief executive never sought to bring the Treaty of Versailles to the Senate or to bring the United States into the League, which was by now actually in existence. Wilson's presidency ended in a stunning defeat. Despite this disappointing end to Wilson's eight years in the White House, many historians view him as one of the country's great presidents. Wilson died on February 3, 1924.

For More Information

Clements, Kendrick A. *The Presidency of Woodrow Wilson*. Lawrence: University Press of Kansas, 1992.

Clements, Kendrick A. *Woodrow Wilson: World Statesman*. Rev. ed. Chicago: I. R. Dee, 1999.

Ferrell, Robert H. *Woodrow Wilson and World War I: 1917–1921*. New York: Harper, 1986.

Knock, Thomas J. *To End All Wars: Woodrow Wilson and the Quest for a New World Order*. New York: Oxford University Press, 1992.

Levin, Phyllis Lee. *Edith and Woodrow: The Wilson White House*. New York: Scribner, 2001.

OPRAH WINFREY

Born: January 29, 1954
Kosciusko, Mississippi
African American television host and actress

America's first lady of talk shows, Oprah Winfrey is well known for surpassing her competition to become the most watched daytime show host on television. Her natural style with guests and audiences on the *Oprah Winfrey Show* earned her widespread popularity, as well as her own production company, Harpo, Inc.

A difficult childhood

Oprah Gail Winfrey was born to Vernita Lee and Vernon Winfrey on an isolated farm in Kosciusko, Mississippi, on January 29, 1954. Her name was supposed to be Orpah, from the Bible, but because of the difficulty of spelling and pronunciation, she was known as Oprah almost from birth. Winfrey's unmarried parents separated soon after she was born and left her in the care of her maternal grandmother on the farm.

As a child, Winfrey entertained herself by "playacting" in front of an "audience" of farm animals. Under the strict guidance of her grandmother, she learned to read at two and a half years old. She addressed her church congregation about "when Jesus rose on Easter Day" when she was two years old. Then Winfrey skipped kindergarten after writing a note to her teacher on the first day of school saying she belonged in the first grade. She was promoted to third grade after that year.

At six years old Winfrey was sent north to join her mother and two half-brothers in a Milwaukee ghetto, an extremely poor and dangerous neighborhood. At twelve years old she was sent to live with her father in Nashville, Tennessee. Feeling secure and happy for a brief period she began making speeches at social gatherings and churches, and one time earned five hundred dollars for a speech. She knew then that she wanted to be "paid to talk."

Winfrey, again, was called back by her mother, and she had to leave the safety of her father's home. The poor, urban lifestyle had its negative effect on Winfrey as a young teenager, and her problems were compounded by repeated sexual abuse, starting at age nine, by men that others in her family trusted. Her mother worked odd jobs and did not have much time for supervision.

Oprah Winfrey.
Reproduced by permission of Archive Photos, Inc.

After years of bad behavior, Winfrey's mother sent her back to her father in Nashville.

A turning point

Winfrey said her father saved her life. He was very strict and provided her with guidance, structure, rules, and books. He required his daughter to complete weekly book reports, and she went without dinner until she learned five new vocabulary words each day.

Winfrey became an excellent student, participating as well in the drama club, debate club, and student council. In an Elks Club speaking contest, she won a full scholarship to Tennessee State University. The following year she was invited to a White House Conference on Youth. Winfrey was crowned Miss Fire Prevention by WVOL, a local Nashville radio station, and was hired by the station to read afternoon newscasts.

Winfrey became Miss Black Nashville and Miss Tennessee during her freshman year at Tennessee State. The Nashville Columbia Broadcasting System (CBS) affiliate offered her a job; Winfrey turned it down twice, but finally took the advice of a speech teacher, who reminded her that job offers from CBS were "the reason people go to college." The show was seen each evening on WTVF-TV, and Winfrey was Nashville's first African American female coanchor of the evening news. She was nineteen years old and still a sophomore in college.

Professional career

After Winfrey graduated, WJZ-TV in Baltimore, Maryland, scheduled her to do the local news updates, called cut-ins, during *Good Morning, America,* and soon she was moved to the morning talk show *Baltimore Is Talking* with cohost Richard Sher. After seven years on the show, the general manager of WLS-TV, American Broadcasting Company's (ABC) Chicago affiliate, saw Winfrey in an audition tape sent in by her producer, Debra DiMaio. At the time her ratings in Baltimore were better than Phil Donahue's, a national talk-show host, and she and DiMaio were hired.

Winfrey moved to Chicago, Illinois, in January 1984 and took over as anchor on *A.M. Chicago,* a morning talk show that was consistently last in the ratings. She changed the emphasis of the show from traditional women's issues to current and controversial (debatable) topics, and after one month the show was even with Donahue's program. Three months later it had inched ahead. In September 1985 the program, renamed the *Oprah Winfrey Show,* was expanded to one hour. As a result, Donahue moved to New York City.

In 1985 Quincy Jones (1933–) saw Winfrey on television and thought she would make a fine actress in a movie he was coproducing with director Steven Spielberg (1946–). The film was based on the Alice Walker (1944–) novel *The Color Purple.* Her only acting experience until then had been in a one-woman show, *The History of Black Women Through Drama and Song,* which she performed during an African American theater festival in 1978.

Popularity of Oprah

The popularity of Winfrey's show skyrocketed after the success of *The Color Purple,* and in September 1985 the distributor King World bought the syndication rights (the rights to distribute a television program) to air the program in one hundred thirty-eight cities, a record for first-time syndication. That year, although *Donahue* was being aired on two hundred stations, Winfrey won her time slot by 31 percent, drew twice the Chicago audience as Donahue, and carried the top ten markets in the United States.

In 1986 Winfrey received a special award from the Chicago Academy for the Arts for unique contributions to the city's artistic community and was named Woman of Achievement by the National Organization of Women. The *Oprah Winfrey Show* won several Emmys for Best Talk Show, and Winfrey was honored as Best Talk Show Host.

Production

Winfrey formed her own production company, Harpo, Inc., in August 1986 to produce the topics that she wanted to see produced, including the television drama miniseries based on Gloria Naylor's *The Women of Brewster Place,* in which Winfrey was featured along with Cicely Tyson, Robin Givens, Olivia Cole, Jackee, Paula Kelly, and Lynn Whitfield. The miniseries aired in March 1989 and a regular series called *Brewster Place,* also starring Winfrey, debuted on ABC in May 1990. Winfrey also owned the screen rights to *Kaffir Boy,* Mark Mathabane's autobiographical (having to do with a story about oneself) book about growing up under apartheid in South Africa, as well as Toni Morrison's (1931–) novel *Beloved.*

In September 1996 Winfrey started an on-air reading club. On September 17 Winfrey stood up and announced she wanted "to get the country reading." She told her adoring fans to hasten to the stores to buy the book she had chosen. They would then discuss it together on the air the following month.

The initial reaction was astonishing. *The Deep End of the Ocean* had generated significant sales for a first novel; sixty-eight thousand copies had gone into the stores since June. But between the last week in August, when Winfrey told her plans to the publisher, and the September on-air announcement, Viking printed ninety thousand more. By the time the discussion was broadcast on October 18, there were seven hundred fifty thousand copies in print. The book became a number one best-seller, and another one hundred thousand were printed before February 1997.

The club ensured Winfrey as the most powerful book marketer in the United States. She sent more people to bookstores than morning news programs, other daytime shows, evening magazines, radio shows, print reviews, and feature articles combined. But after a six-year run with her book club, Winfrey decided to cut back in the spring of 2002 and no longer have the book club as a monthly feature.

The future

Although one of the wealthiest women in America and the highest paid entertainer in the world, Winfrey has made generous contributions to charitable organizations and institutions such as Morehouse College, the Harold Washington Library, the United Negro College Fund, and Tennessee State University.

Winfrey renewed her contract with King World Productions to continue *The Oprah Winfrey Show* through the 2003–2004 television season. Winfrey and Harpo Production company plan to develop other syndicated television programming with King World.

For More Information

Brooks, Philip. *Oprah Winfrey: A Voice for the People.* New York: Franklin Watts, 1999.

King, Norman. *Everybody Loves Oprah!* New York: Morrow, 1987.

Patterson, Lillie. *Oprah Winfrey: Talk Show Host and Actress.* Hillside, NJ: Enslow, 1988.

Stone, Tanya Lee. *Oprah Winfrey: Success with an Open Heart.* Brookfield, CT: Millbrook Press, 2001.

Waldron, Robert. *Oprah.* New York: St. Martin's Press, 1987.

ANNA MAY WONG

Born: January 3, 1905
Los Angeles, California
Died: February 3, 1961
Santa Monica, California
Asian American actress

Anna May Wong is chiefly remembered as the first actress of Asian descent to achieve stardom as the "Oriental temptress," so much a fixture of melodramas in the late 1920s and 1930s.

Childhood

Born on Flower Street in Los Angeles, California, in 1907, Anna May Wong was named Wong Liu Tsong, which in Cantonese means "frosted yellow willow." Wong was third-generation Chinese American; her father was born in Sacramento, California, and his father had moved to California during the Gold Rush, where thousands flocked to the state in hopes of striking it rich with gold.

Growing up, Wong and her six brothers and sisters lived in an apartment over the family's run-down laundry. Her first memories were of constant steam and the strong odor of hot-ironed linen. As a young child, Wong became fascinated with the brand new world of movies. She began skipping Chinese school in the evenings to watch such movies as *The Perils of Pauline* (1914) at the local theater. By the time she was eleven, Wong decided she was going to be a movie actress. Against all odds, she got her first part at age fourteen when an agent hired three hundred Chinese girls as extras in the 1919 film *The Red Lantern.* Hardly visible in the film, she went on to get a few more minor roles.

Hollywood calls

For two years, Wong worked after school as an extra without telling her parents, who, she knew, would not approve. At age sixteen, her father found her a job as a secretary, but Wong was fired as unqualified one week later. When she returned home, fearing her father's anger, she found a letter from a director's office offering her a role in the film *Bits of Life* (1921). It would bring Wong her first screen credit. Although Wong's father strongly objected to his daughter's chosen career, he eventually gave in on the condition that an adult escort, often he himself, would accompany the young Wong on the film sets at all times. When she was not in front of the cameras, her father locked her into her room on the set.

At age seventeen, Wong had one of the few romantic lead roles she would ever play in *Toll of the Sea* (1923), the first Technicolor (an early color film) feature ever made. As a young village girl who marries an American sailor, Wong captured the media's attention for the first time. Reporters began to appear at the laundry in the hopes of catching Wong for an interview or a photo.

International fame came in 1924 with *The Thief of Bagdad,* in which Wong played an exotic Mongol slave girl opposite star Douglas Fairbanks Sr. (1883–1939). Wong's role embarrassed her family. Although Wong would continue to support her family for many years, she remained close only to her brother, Richard.

The movie star's life

The success of *Bagdad* led to countless new offers. She appeared as an Eskimo in *The Alaskan* and a Native American girl in *Peter Pan*. In addition to film roles, Wong also worked as a model. She made a few more films, but soon became aggravated with the roles and with Hollywood's practice of casting non-Asians in the few leading Asian roles. Wong finally fled to Europe where, in London, she costarred with Charles Laughton (1899–1962) in *Piccadilly*. After the film, director Basil Dean produced a Chinese play, *A Circle of Chalk,* specifically for Wong. She successfully played opposite the rising new talent, Laurence Olivier (1907–1989), in London's New Theater.

Wong remained in Europe for three years, where she was hailed for her film and stage appearances. In Germany and France, she made foreign versions of her British films, including Germany's first sound picture. She spoke both German and French so fluently that critics could hardly believe they were hearing her voice instead of a native actress. During her career, Wong taught herself to speak English, Chinese, French, German, and Italian.

Wong's next screen role, *Daughter of the Dragon,* cast her in yet another stereotypical (having to do with opinions based on generalizations) role as the daughter of the infamous Dr. Fu Manchu. Wong then appeared in the thriller *Shanghai Express,* starring Marlene Dietrich (1901–1992). Wong's portrayal of the bad-girl-turned-good inspired better reviews than Dietrich received. Years later, the star would complain that Wong had upstaged her.

Anna May Wong.
Reproduced by permission of the Corbis Corporation.

An early retirement

In 1942, finally fed up with the Hollywood system, Wong retired from films at the age of thirty-five. Throughout the war, she contributed to the war efforts by working for the United China Relief Fund and touring with the United Service Organizations, Inc. (USO; a group that provided entertainment and other services for the U.S. military). During the 1940s and 1950s, Wong took occasional small parts on television, even starring in her own series, *Mme. Liu Tsong,* in which she played the owner of an international chain of art galleries who was also a sleuth.

Seventeen years after retirement, Wong attempted a film comeback. She returned as Lana Turner's (1920–1995) mysterious housekeeper in the 1950 film, *Portrait in Black*. In 1961, while she was preparing for the role of the mother in *Flower Drum Song,* Wong died of a heart attack in her sleep.

For More Information

"Anna May Wong." In *Notable Asian Americans.* Edited by Helen Zia and Susan B. Gall. Detroit: Gale, 1995.

Parish, James Robert, and William T. Leonard. *Hollywood Players: The Thirties.* New Rochelle, NY: Arlington House, 1976.

TIGER WOODS

Born: December 30, 1975
Cypress, California
African/Asian American golfer

American golfer Tiger Woods is the youngest man ever, and the first man of color, to win the Masters Tournament of golf.

Childhood in golf

Tiger Woods was born Eldrick Woods on December 30, 1975, in Cypress, California. He is the only child of Earl and Kultida Woods. His parents identified their son's talent at an unusually early age. They said that he was playing with a putter before he could walk. The boy was gifted not only with excep-

tional playing abilities, but he also possessed a passion for the sport. Woods first gained national attention on a talk show when he beat the famed comedian and avid golfer Bob Hope (1903–) in a putting contest. The young boy was only three at the time, and he was quickly hailed as a prodigy, or a child with remarkable talent. Not long after that, when he was five years old, Woods was featured on the popular television show *That's Incredible!*

Tiger's father has never denied that he devoted his energies to developing his son's talent and to furthering the boy's career as a golfer. During practice sessions, Tiger learned to maintain his composure and to hold his concentration while his father persistently made extremely loud noises and created other distractions. All the while, Tiger's mother made sure that her son's rare talent and his budding golf career would not interfere with his childhood or his future happiness. His mother was a native of Thailand and passed on to her son the mystical ideals of Buddhism, an eastern religion that seeks to go beyond human suffering and existence.

In many ways Woods grew up as a typical middle-class American boy. He developed a taste for junk food and an affection for playing video games. He also spent a fair share of his time clowning around in front of his father's ever-present video camera. As for playing golf, there is no question that the sport was the focus of his childhood. He spent many hours practicing his swing and playing in youth tournaments. Woods was eight years old when he won his first formal competition. From that point he became virtually unstoppable, winning trophies and breaking amateur records everywhere. Media accounts of the boy prodigy had reached nearly legendary proportions by 1994, when he entered Stanford University as a freshman on a full golf scholarship.

College years

During Woods's first year of college, he won the U.S. Amateur title and qualified to play in the Masters tournament in Augusta, Georgia, in the spring of 1995. Although he played as an amateur—not for prize money—Woods's reputation preceded him. By 1996, Woods had won three U.S. Amateur titles, one after another, an amazing accomplishment in itself. Woods was only twenty years old, and in August of 1996, he decided to quit college in order to play professional golf.

Four months later in December, Woods celebrated his twenty-first birthday. He marked the occasion with a legal name change, from Eldrick to Tiger. Woods had been called Tiger by his father even as a youngster. The nickname stuck, and Woods had always been known to his friends, and to the press, as Tiger. It soon became evident that he was destined for success. *Sports Illustrated* named him 1996 "Sportsman of the Year," and by January of 1997, he had already won three professional tournaments. He was a media sensation.

Tiger the champion

In April of 1997, only eight months into Woods's professional career, he played in the prestigious (important and famous) Masters tournament held at Georgia's Augusta National Golf Club. The Masters title is perhaps the greatest honor in the world of golf. In addition to hefty prize money, first-place winners are awarded a green blazer to symbolize their membership among the top golfers in the world.

Tiger Woods.
Reproduced by permission of AP/Wide World Photos.

When the tournament was over, Woods had made history as the youngest person ever to win the Masters title. His score was an unprecedented 270 strokes. His victory margin set another record—twelve strokes ahead of the runner-up. This feat was enhanced by the fact that Woods was the first man of color ever to win the title. He accepted all of these honors with grace and humility, and gave tribute to the African American golfers who came before him and helped pave the way. He also honored his mother (who is Asian) by reminding the world of his diverse ethnic background; he is African American, Thai, Chinese, Native American, and Caucasian.

Less than three months passed until July 6, 1997, when Woods won the Western Open, another major golf tournament. Critics credited his amazing success to relentless work and an extraordinary desire to win.

Impact of Tiger Woods

Woods is credited too with popularizing the sport of golf, not only among African American people and other minorities, but among children of all backgrounds. His personal sponsorship of programs for children has been reported for years, and at least one corporate sponsor found that in order to secure an endorsement (an official document of agreement) from Tiger Woods the price would include the added cost of a generous donation to the Tiger Woods Foundation for inner city children.

In 1999 Woods achieved the greatest moment in his career when he won the PGA Championship by one shot. He had been in the lead for most of the tournament, but lost his lead on the last day, making his one stroke victory over Sergio Garcia even more memorable for the crowd that had gathered to watch. Woods continued his success in November 1999 when he shot the best total ever in the World Cup, helping to lead the United States to victory in the tournament. He was also named the PGA Tour Player of the Year for the second time on November 30, 1999, earning more that $6.6 million in prize money during the season.

On January 9, 2000, Woods won the Mercedes Championship. It was his fifth consecutive victory and, at the time, golf's longest winning streak in forty-six years. On February 7, 2000, he extended that streak by winning the Pebble Beach National Pro-Am. He became the first player since Ben Hogan (1912–1997) in 1948 to win six straight tour events. He went on to win the Bay Hill Invitational on March 19, 2000. On June 18, 2000, he won the U.S. Open, his third major championship. The next month, on July 23, he won the British Open, thus winning the Grand Slam. He became the youngest player to win all four major championships and just the fifth ever.

On April 8, 2001, Woods won the sixty-fifth Masters Tournament at the Augusta National Golf Club. The win made him the only golfer in history to hold the four major championship titles at the same time. Woods won the sixty-sixth Masters Tournament on April 14, 2002. At the turn of the twenty-first century, Woods was the most dominant figure in all of sports, and his name will surely be decorated throughout the record books before his career is over.

For More Information

Owen, David. *The Chosen One: Tiger Woods and the Dilemma of Greatness.* New York: Simon and Schuster, 2001.

Strege, John. *Tiger: A Biography of Tiger Woods.* New York: Broadway Books, 1997.

Woods, Tiger. *How I Play Golf.* New York: Warner Books, 2001.

VIRGINIA WOOLF

Born: January 25, 1882
London, England

Died: March 28, 1941

Lewes, Sussex, England

English novelist, critic, and essayist

The English novelist, critic, and essayist Virginia Woolf ranks as one of England's most distinguished writers of the middle part of the twentieth century. Her novels can perhaps best be described as impressionistic, a literary style which attempts to inspire impressions rather than recreating reality.

Early years and marriage

Virginia Stephen was born in London on January 25, 1882. She was the daughter of Sir Leslie Stephen, a famous scholar and philosopher (a seeker of knowledge) who, among many literary occupations, was at one time editor of *Cornhill Magazine* and the *Dictionary of National Biography*. James Russell Lowell, the American poet, was her godfather. Her mother, Julia Jackson, died when the child was twelve or thirteen years old. Virginia and her sister were educated at home in their father's library, where Virginia also met his famous friends who included G. E. Moore (1873–1958) and E. M. Forster (1879–1970). Young Virginia soon fell deep into the world of literature.

In 1912, eight years after her father's death, Virginia married Leonard Woolf, a brilliant young writer and critic from Cambridge, England, whose interests in literature as well as in economics and the labor movement were well suited to hers. In 1917, for amusement, they founded the Hogarth Press by setting and handprinting on an old press *Two Stories* by "L. and V. Woolf." The volume was a success, and over the years they published many important books, including *Prelude* by Katherine Mansfield (1888–1923), then an unknown writer; *Poems* by T. S. Eliot (1888–1965); and *Kew Gardens* by Virginia Woolf. The policy of the Hogarth Press was to publish the best and most original work that came to its attention, and the Woolfs as publishers favored young and unknown writers. Virginia's older sister Vanessa, who married the critic Clive Bell, participated in this venture by designing dust jackets for the books issued by the Hogarth Press.

Virginia Woolf's home in Tavistock Square, Bloomsbury, became a literary and art center, attracting such diverse intellectuals as Lytton Strachey (1880–1932), Arthur Waley (1889–1966), Victoria Sackville-West (1892–1962), John Maynard Keynes (1883–1943), and Roger Fry (1866–1934). These artists, critics, and writers became known as the Bloomsbury group. Roger Fry's theory of art may have influenced Virginia's technique as a novelist. Broadly speaking, the Bloomsbury group drew from the philosophic interests of its members (who had been educated at Cambridge) the values of love and beauty as essential to life.

As critic and essayist

Virginia Woolf began writing essays for the *Times Literary Supplement* (London) when she was young, and over the years these and other essays were collected in a two-volume series called *The Common Reader* (1925, 1933). These studies range with affection and understanding through all of English literature. Students of fiction have drawn upon these criticisms as a means of understanding Virginia Woolf's own direction as a novelist.

An essay frequently studied is "Mr. Bennett and Mrs. Brown," written in 1924, in

Virginia Woolf.
Reproduced by permission of AP/Wide World Photos.

which Virginia Woolf described the manner in which the older-generation novelist Arnold Bennett would have portrayed Mrs. Brown, a lady casually met in a railway carriage, by giving her a house and furniture and a position in the world. She then contrasted this method with another: one that exhibits a new interest in Mrs. Brown, the mysteries of her person, her consciousness (awareness), and the consciousness of the observer responding to her.

Achievement as novelist

Two of Virginia Woolf's novels in particular, *Mrs. Dalloway* (1925) and *To the Light-* house (1927), successfully follow the latter approach. The first novel covers a day in the life of Mrs. Dalloway in postwar London; it achieves its vision of reality through the reception by Mrs. Dalloway's mind of what Virginia Woolf called those "myriad impressions—trivial, fantastic, evanescent [vanishing], or engraved with the sharpness of steel."

To the Lighthouse is, in a sense, a family portrait and history rendered in subjective (characterized by personal views) depth through selected points in time. Part I deals with the time between six o'clock in the evening and dinner. Primarily through the consciousness of Mrs. Ramsay, it presents the clash of the male and female sensibilities in the family; Mrs. Ramsay functions as a means of balance and settling disputes. Part II is a moving section of loss during the interval between Mrs. Ramsay's death and the family's revisit to the house. Part III moves toward completion of this complex portrait through the adding of a last detail to a painting by an artist guest, Lily Briscoe, and through the final completion of a plan, rejected by the father in Part I, for him and the children to sail out to the lighthouse.

Last years and other books

Virginia Woolf was the author of about fifteen books, the last, *A Writer's Diary,* posthumously (after death) published in 1953. Her death by drowning in Lewes, Sussex, England, on March 28, 1941, has often been regarded as a suicide brought on by the unbearable strains of life during World War II (1939–45; a war fought between the Axis powers: Japan, Italy, and Germany—and the Allies: France, England, the Soviet Union, and the United States). The true explanation seems to be that she had regularly felt symptoms of a mental breakdown and feared it would be permanent.

Mrs. Dalloway, To the Lighthouse, and *Jacob's Room* (1922) represent Virginia Woolf's major achievements. *The Voyage Out* (1915) first brought her critical attention. *Night and Day* (1919) is traditional in method. The short stories of *Monday or Tuesday* (1921) brought critical praise. In *The Waves* (1931) she masterfully employed the stream-of-consciousness technique which stresses "free writing." Other experimental novels include *Orlando* (1928), *The Years* (1937), and *Between the Acts* (1941). Virginia Woolf's championship of women's rights is reflected in the essays in *A Room of One's Own* (1929) and in *Three Guineas* (1938).

For More Information

Bell, Quentin. *Virginia Woolf: A Biography.* New York: Harcourt Brace Jovanovich, 1972.

Bond, Alma Halbert. *Who Killed Virginia Woolf?: A Psychobiography.* New York: Human Sciences Press, 1989.

Caws, Mary Anne. *Virginia Woolf.* Woodstock, NY: Overlook Books, 2002.

Lee, Hermione. *Virginia Woolf.* New York: A. A. Knopf, 1997.

WILLIAM WORDSWORTH

Born: April 7, 1770
Cookermouth, Cumberland, England

Died: April 23, 1850
Rydal Mount, Westmorland, England
English poet

William Wordsworth was an early leader of romanticism (a literary movement that celebrated nature and concentrated on human emotions) in English poetry and ranks as one of the greatest lyric poets in the history of English literature.

His early years

William Wordsworth was born on April 7, 1770, in Cookermouth, Cumberland, England, the second child of an attorney. Unlike the other major English romantic poets, he enjoyed a happy childhood under the loving care of his mother and was very close to his sister Dorothy. As a child he wandered happily through the lovely natural scenery of Cumberland. In grammar school, Wordsworth showed a keen interest in poetry. He was fascinated by the epic poet John Milton (1608–1674).

From 1787 to 1790 Wordsworth attended St. John's College at Cambridge University. He always returned to his home and to nature during his summer vacations. Before graduating from Cambridge, he took a walking tour through France, Switzerland, and Italy in 1790. The Alps made an impression on him that he did not recognize until fourteen years later.

Stay in France

Revolutionary passion in France made a powerful impact on Wordsworth, who returned there in November 1791. He wanted to improve his knowledge of the

William Wordsworth.
Reproduced by permission of the Granger Collection.

French language. His experience in France just after the French Revolution (1789; the French overthrew the ruling monarchy) reinforced his sympathy for common people and his belief in political freedom.

Wordsworth fell passionately in love with a French girl, Annette Vallon. She gave birth to their daughter in December 1792. However, Wordsworth had spent his limited funds and was forced to return home. The separation left him with a sense of guilt that deepened his poetic inspiration and resulted in an important theme in his work of abandoned women.

Publication of first poems

Wordsworth's first poems, *Descriptive Sketches* and *An Evening Walk,* were printed in 1793. He wrote several pieces over the next several years. The year 1797 marked the beginning of Wordsworth's long friendship with Samuel Taylor Coleridge (1772–1834). Together they published *Lyrical Ballads* in 1798. Wordsworth wanted to challenge "the gaudiness [unnecessarily flashy] and inane [foolish] phraseology [wording] of many modern writers." Most of his poems in this collection centered on the simple yet deeply human feelings of ordinary people, phrased in their own language. His views on this new kind of poetry were more fully described in the important "Preface" that he wrote for the second edition (1800).

"Tintern Abbey"

Wordsworth's most memorable contribution to this volume was "Lines Composed a Few Miles Above Tintern Abbey," which he wrote just in time to include it. This poem is the first major piece to illustrate his original talent at its best. It skillfully combines matter-of-factness in natural description with a genuinely mystical (magical) sense of infinity, joining self-exploration to philosophical speculation (questioning). The poem closes on a subdued but confident reassertion of nature's healing power, even though mystical insight may be obtained from the poet.

In its successful blending of inner and outer experience, of sense perception, feeling, and thought, "Tintern Abbey" is a poem in which the writer becomes a symbol of mankind. The poem leads to imaginative thoughts about man and the universe. This cosmic outlook rooted in the self is a central feature of romanticism. Wordsworth's poetry is undoubtedly the most impressive example of this view in English literature.

Poems of the middle period

Wordsworth, even while writing his contributions to the *Lyrical Ballads,* had been feeling his way toward more ambitious schemes. He had embarked on a long poem in unrhymed verse, "The Ruined Cottage," later referred to as "The Peddlar." It was intended to form part of a vast philosophical poem with the title "The Recluse, or Views of Man, Nature and Society." This grand project never materialized as originally planned.

Abstract, impersonal speculation was not comfortable for Wordsworth. He could handle experiences in the philosophical-lyrical manner only if they were closely related to himself and could arouse his creative feelings and imagination. During the winter months he spent in Germany, he started work on his magnum opus (greatest work), *The Prelude, or Growth of a Poet's Mind.* It was published after his death.

However, such a large achievement was still beyond Wordsworth's scope (area of capabilities) at this time. It was back to the shorter poetic forms that he turned during the most productive season of his long literary life, the spring of 1802. The output of these fertile (creative) months mostly came from his earlier inspirations: nature and the common people. During this time he wrote "To a Butterfly," "I Wandered Lonely as a Cloud," "To the Cuckoo," "The Rainbow," and other poems.

Changes in philosophy

The crucial event of this period was Wordsworth's loss of the sense of mystical oneness, which had sustained (lasted throughout) his highest imaginative flights. Indeed, a mood of despondency (depression) descended over Wordsworth, who was then thirty-two years old.

In the summer of 1802 Wordsworth spent a few weeks in Calais, France, with his sister Dorothy. Wordsworth's renewed contact with France only confirmed his disillusionment (disappointment) with the French Revolution and its aftermath.

During this period Wordsworth had become increasingly concerned with Coleridge, who by now was almost totally dependent upon opium (a highly addictive drug) for relief from his physical sufferings. Both friends came to believe that the realities of life were in stark contradiction (disagreement) to the visionary expectations of their youth. Wordsworth characteristically sought to redefine his own identity in ways that would allow him a measure of meaning. The new turn his life took in 1802 resulted in an inner change that set the new course his poetry followed from then on.

Poems about England and Scotland began pouring forth from Wordsworth's pen, while France and Napoleon (1769–1821) soon became Wordsworth's favorite symbols of cruelty and oppression. His nationalistic (intense pride in one's own country) inspiration led him to produce the two "Memorials of a Tour in Scotland" (1803, 1814) and the group entitled "Poems Dedicated to National Independence and Liberty."

Poems of 1802

The best poems of 1802, however, deal with a deeper level of inner change. In Wordsworth's poem "Intimations of Immortality" (March–April), he plainly recognized that "The things which I have seen I now can see no more"; yet he emphasized that although the "visionary gleam" had fled, the memory remained, and although the "celestial light" had vanished, the "common sight" of "meadow, grove and stream" was still a potent (strong) source of delight and solace (comfort).

Thus Wordsworth shed his earlier tendency to idealize nature and turned to a more sedate (calm) doctrine (set of beliefs) of orthodox Christianity. Younger poets and critics soon blamed him for this "recantation" (renouncing), which they equated with his change of mind about the French Revolution. His *Ecclesiastical Sonnets* (1822) are clear evidence of the way in which love of freedom, nature, and the Church came to coincide (come together at the same time) in his mind.

The Prelude

Nevertheless, it was the direction suggested in "Intimations of Immortality" that, in the view of later criticism, enabled Wordsworth to produce perhaps the most outstanding achievement of English romanticism: *The Prelude*. He worked on it, on and off, for several years and completed the first version in May 1805. *The Prelude* can claim to be the only true romantic epic (long, often heroic work) because it deals in narrative terms with the spiritual growth of the only true romantic hero, the poet. The inward odyssey (journey) of the poet was described not for its own sake but as a sample and as an adequate image of man at his most sensitive.

Wordsworth shared the general romantic notion that personal experience is the only way to gain living knowledge. The purpose of *The Prelude* was to recapture and interpret, with detailed thoroughness, the whole range of experiences that had contributed to the shaping of his own mind. Wordsworth refrained from publishing the poem in his lifetime, revising it continuously. Most important and, perhaps, most to be regretted, the poet also tried to give a more orthodox tinge to his early mystical faith in nature.

Later years

Wordsworth's estrangement (growing apart) from Coleridge in 1810 deprived him of a powerful incentive to imaginative and intellectual alertness. Wordsworth's appointment to a government position in 1813 relieved him of financial care.

Wordsworth's undiminished love for nature made him view the emergent (just appearing) industrial society with undisguised reserve. He opposed the Reform Bill of 1832, which, in his view, merely transferred political power from the land owners to the manufacturing class, but he never stopped pleading in favor of the victims of the factory system.

In 1843 Wordsworth was appointed poet laureate (official poet of a country). He died on April 23, 1850.

For More Information

Davies, Hunter. *William Wordsworth: A Biography.* New York: Atheneum, 1980.

Gill, Stephen. *William Wordsworth: A Life.* New York: Oxford University Press, 1989.

Johnston, Kenneth R. *The Hidden Wordsworth: Poet, Lover, Rebel, Spy.* New York: W. W. Norton, 1998.

Negrotta, Rosanna. *William Wordsworth: A Biography with Selected Poems.* London: Brockhampton, 1999.

WRIGHT BROTHERS

ORVILLE WRIGHT

Born: August 19, 1871
Dayton, Ohio
Died: January 30, 1948
Dayton, Ohio

WILBUR WRIGHT

Born: April 16, 1867
Millville, Indiana
Died: May 30, 1912
Dayton, Ohio
American aviators

The American aviation pioneers Wilbur and Orville Wright were the first to accomplish manned, powered flight in a heavier-than-air machine.

Their early years

Wilbur and Orville Wright were the sons of Milton Wright, a bishop of the United Brethren in Christ. Wilbur was born on April 16, 1867, in Millville, Indiana. Orville was born on August 19, 1871, in Dayton, Ohio. Until the death of Wilbur in 1912, the two were inseparable. Their personalities were perfectly complementary (each provided what the other lacked). Orville was full of ideas and enthusiasms. Wilbur was more steady in his habits, more mature in his judgments, and more likely to see a project through.

While in high school, Wilbur intended to go to Yale and study to be a clergyman. However, he suffered a facial injury while playing hockey, which prevented him from continuing his education. For the next three years he continued his education informally through reading in his father's large library.

In their early years the two boys helped their father, who edited a journal called the *Religious Telescope.* Later, they began a paper of their own, *West Side News.* They went into business together as printers producing everything from religious handouts to commercial fliers. In 1892 they opened the Wright Cycle Shop in Dayton. This was the perfect occupation for the Wright brothers because it involved one of the exciting mechanical devices of the time: the bicycle. When the brothers took up the problems of flight, they had a solid grounding in practical mechanics (knowledge of how to build machines).

The exploits of one of the great glider pilots of the late nineteenth century, Otto Lilienthal, had attracted the attention of the Wright brothers as early as 1891, but it was not until the death of this famous aeronautical (having to do with the study of flying and the design of flying machines) engineer in 1896 that the two became interested in gliding experiments. They then decided to educate themselves in the theory and state of the art of flying.

Wilbur Wright (left) and his brother Orville.
Reproduced by permission of AP/Wide World Photos.

Their beginnings in flight

The Wrights took up the problem of flight at a favorable time, for some of the fundamental, or basic, theories of aerodynamics were already known; a body of experimental data existed; and, most importantly, the recent development of the internal combustion engine made available a sufficient source of power for manned flight.

The Wright brothers began by accumulating and mastering all the important information on the subject, designed and tested their own models and gliders, built their own engine, and, when the experimental data they had inherited appeared to be inadequate or wrong, they conducted new and more thorough experiments. The Wrights decided that earlier attempts at flight were not successful because the plans for early airplanes required pilots to shift their bodies to control the plane. The brothers decided that it would be better to control a plane by moving its wings.

First trip to Kitty Hawk

The Wright brothers proceeded to fly double-winged kites and gliders in order to gain experience and to test the data they had. After consulting the U.S. Weather Bureau, they chose an area of sand dunes near the small town of Kitty Hawk, North Carolina, as the site of their experiments. In September 1900 they set up camp there.

The Wrights's first device failed to fly as a kite because it was unable to develop sufficient lift (upward force). Instead, they flew it as a free glider. They kept careful records of their failures as well as of their successes. Their own data showed conclusively that previous tables of information they had were greatly inaccurate.

Returning to Dayton in 1901, the Wright brothers built a wind tunnel (a tunnel wherein one can control the flow of wind in order to determine its effect on an object)—the first in the United States. This is where they tested over two hundred models of wing surfaces in order to measure lift and drag (resistance) factors and to discover the most suitable design. They also discovered that although screw propellers had been used on ships for more than half a century, there was no reliable body of data on the subject and no theory that would allow them to design the proper propellers for their airship. They had to work the problem out for themselves mathematically.

The Wrights, by this time, not only had mastered the existing body of aeronautical science but also had added to it. They now built their third glider, incorporating their findings, and in the fall of 1902 they returned to Kitty Hawk. They made over one thousand gliding flights and were able to confirm their previous data and to demonstrate their ability to control motions of the glider. Having learned to build and to control an adequate air frame, they now determined to apply power to their machine.

Powered flight

The Wright brothers soon discovered, however, that no manufacturer would undertake to build an engine that would meet their specifications, so they had to build their own. They produced one that had four cylinders and developed 12 horsepower (a unit that describes the strength of an engine). When it was installed in the air frame, the entire machine weighed just 750 pounds and proved to be capable of traveling 31 miles per hour. They took this new airplane to Kitty Hawk in the fall of 1903 and on December 17 made the world's first manned, powered flight in a heavier-than-air craft.

The first flight was made by Orville and lasted only 12 seconds, during which the airplane flew 120 feet. That same day, however, on its fourth flight, with Wilbur at the controls, the plane stayed in the air for 59 seconds and traveled 852 feet. Then a gust of wind severely damaged the craft. The brothers returned to Dayton convinced of their success and determined to build another machine. In 1905 they abandoned their other activities and concentrated on the development of aviation. On May 22, 1906, they received a patent for their flying machine.

The next step

The brothers looked to the federal government for encouragement in their venture, and gradually interest was aroused in Washington, D.C. In 1907 the government asked for bids for an airplane that would meet certain requirements. Twenty-two bids were received, three were accepted, but only the Wright brothers finished their contract.

The brothers continued their experiments at Kitty Hawk, and in September 1908, while Wilbur was in France attempting to interest foreign backers in their machine, Orville successfully demonstrated their contract airplane. It was accepted by the government. The event was marred by a crash a week later in which Orville was injured and a passenger was killed.

Wilbur's trip to France proved to be a success. In 1909 the Wright brothers formed the American Wright Company, with Wilbur taking the lead in setting up and directing the business. His death in Dayton on May 30, 1912, left Orville feeling depressed and alone. In 1915 he sold his rights to the firm and gave up his interest in manufacturing in order to turn to experimental work. He had little taste for the busy activity of commercial life.

After his retirement, Orville lived quietly in Dayton, conducting experiments on mechanical problems of interest to him, none of which proved to be of major importance. His chief public activity was service on the National Advisory Committee for Aeronautics (the government agency that came before the National Aeronautics and Space Administration, or NASA), of which he was a member from its organization by President Woodrow Wilson in 1915 until his death in Dayton on January 30, 1948.

The Wright Brothers helped found modern aviation through their curiosity, their inventiveness, and their unwillingness to give up their vision.

For More Information

Culick, Fred E. C., and Spencer Dunmore. *On Great White Wings: The Wright Brothers and the Race for Flight.* Shrewsbury, England: Airlife, 2001.

Freedman, Russell. *The Wright Brothers: How They Invented the Airplane.* New York: Holiday House, 1991.

Howard, Fred. *Wilbur and Orville: A Biography of the Wright Brothers.* New York: Knopf, 1987.

Kelly, Fred C. *The Wright Brothers: A Biography Authorized by Orville Wright.* New York: Farrar, Straus, and Young, 1951. Reprint, New York: Dover Publications, 1989.

Walsh, John Evangelist. *One Day at Kitty Hawk: The Untold Story of the Wright Brothers and the Airplane.* New York: Crowell, 1975.

FRANK LLOYD WRIGHT

Born: June 8, 1869
Richland Center, Wisconsin
Died: April 9, 1959
Phoenix, Arizona
American architect

The American architect Frank Lloyd Wright designed dramatically creative buildings during a career of almost seventy years. His work established the imagery for much of the modern architectural environment.

Early life and education

Frank Lloyd Wright was born on June 8, 1869, in Richland Center, Wisconsin, the first of three children to William, a preacher, and Anna Wright. When he was twelve years old his family settled in Madison, Wisconsin, and Wright worked on his uncle's farm at Spring Green during the summers. After the couple divorced in 1885, Frank lived with his mother, and the two shared a lasting relationship. It was from her that he developed an early love for pure geometric forms and designs, which later influenced his architecture.

Wright developed a passion for the farmland that never left him. He attended Madison High School and left in 1885, apparently without graduating. He went to work as a draftsman, and the following year, while still working, took a few courses in civil engineering at the University of Wisconsin.

In 1887 Wright moved to Chicago, Illinois, worked briefly for an architect, and then joined the firm of Dankmar Adler (1844–1900) and Louis Sullivan (1856–1924). Wright was very much influenced by Sullivan, and, although their relationship ended when Sullivan found out that Wright was designing houses on his own, he always acknowledged Sullivan's influence and referred to him as "lieber meister." In 1893 Wright opened his own office.

Master of domestic architecture

The houses Wright built in Buffalo, New York, and in Chicago and its suburbs before World War I (1914–18), when German-led forces pushed for European domination, gained international fame wherever there were avant-garde (having to do with new ideas and techniques) movements in the arts. Similarly, in the United States, Wright's clients were exceptional individuals and small, adventurous institutions, not governments or national corporations. A small progressive private school (Hillside Home School, Spring Green, 1902) and an occasional private, commercial firm (Larkin Company in Buffalo) came to him, but chiefly, his clients were Midwestern businessmen, practical, unscholarly, independent, and moderately successful, such as the Chicago building contractor Frederick C. Robie, for whom Wright designed houses.

Early, Wright insisted upon declaring the presence of pure cubic mass, the color and texture of raw stone and brick and copper, and the sharp-etched punctures made by unornamented windows and doors in sheer walls (Charnley House, Chicago, 1891). He made of the house a compact block, which might be enclosed handsomely by a hipped roof (Winslow House, River Forest, Illinois, 1893). Soon, the delight in the simplicity of a single mass gave way to his passion for passages of continuous, flowing spaces and he burst the enclosed, separated spaces of classical architecture, removed the containment, the sense of walls and ceilings, and created single, continuously modified spaces, which he shaped by screens, piers, and different planes and masses.

Philosophy of architecture

Wright's philosophy of architecture was composed of several radical (extreme in differ-

Frank Lloyd Wright.
Reproduced by permission of Archive Photos, Inc.

ence) and traditional ideas. There was, first, the romantic idea of honest expression: that a building should be faithful in revealing its materials and structure, as Eugène Emmanuel Viollet-le-Duc (1814–1879) had argued, without any classical ornament or fake surface or structure. There was, second, the idea that a building's form should reflect its plan, its functional arrangement of interior spaces, as Henry Latrobe and Horatio Greenough had proposed. There was, third, the belief that each building should express something new and distinctive in the times (G. W. F. Hegel [1770–1831], Gottfried Semper [1803–1879]) and specifically the new technical resources, such as steel skeletons and electric light and elevators, which suggested skyscrapers and new forms of building (John Wellborn Root). There was, fourth, the ambition, even pride, to achieve an art appropriate to a new nation, an American art, without Continental or English or colonial dependencies. Finally, there was the theory derived by Sullivan from Charles Darwin (1809–1882) and Herbert Spencer (1820–1903) that a building should be similar to a biological organism, a unified work of art, rooted to its soil, organized to serve specified functions, and, as a form, evolved as an organism evolves, fitted to its environment, expressive of its purpose.

If the handsome Taliesin East, whose roofs are rhythmical accents on the edge of a bluff overlooking two valleys, were all that Wright left, he would be remembered as the finest architect who worked in the nineteenth-century tradition of romantic domestic design. But, early, he prepared an idea and an imagery for modern design. He achieved in the Larkin Building, Buffalo (1904; destroyed) an integration of circulation, structure, ventilation, plumbing, furniture, office equipment, and lighting.

Constant search for form

Always distinctive and independent, Wright's style changed often. For about ten years after 1915 he drew upon Mayan (an ancient Indian tribe in Mexico) ornament (Barndall House, Hollywood, California, 1920). Even then Wright avoided the barrenness and abstraction of his designs, he insisted upon having the multiple form of buildings reflect the movement of unique sites: the Kaufmann House, "Falling Water," at Bear Run, Pennsylvania (1936–37), where

interlocked, reinforced-concrete terraces are poised over the waterfall; the low-cost houses (Herbert Jacobs House, Madison, 1937); and the "prairie houses" (Lloyd Lewis House, Libertyville, Illinois, 1940). No architect was more skillful in fitting form to its terrain: the Pauson House in Phoenix, Arizona (1940) rose from the desert, like a Mayan pyramid, its battered wooden walls reflecting the mountains and desert.

Those brilliant rural houses did not reveal how Wright would respond to an urban setting or to the program of a corporate client. But in the Administration Building for the Johnson Wax Company, Racine, Wisconsin (1936–39, with a research tower added in 1950), he astonished architects with his second great commercial building (after the Larkin Building). A continuous, windowless red-brick wall encloses a high, window-lighted interior space; that space, which contains tall columns, is one of the most peaceful and graceful interior spaces in the world. At Florida Southern College he set side-by-side circle and fragmented rhombus (a four-sided plane), recalling Hadrian's Villa at Tivoli, Italy; he set a helix (spiral form structure) inside the Morris Gift Shop in San Francisco, California (1948–49). Ultimately, he conceived of having the helix surround a tall central space: the six-story Guggenheim Museum in New York City (1946–59), which paid in significant functional defects to gain a memorable experience in viewing art, especially where the helix affords views into a side gallery below.

The architectural drawings Wright left behind are magical and lyrical. No one might ever build accordingly, but Wright was never content with the commonplace or ordinary to the conventional or the practical. He imagined the wonderful where others were content with the probable. Wright's drawings suggest how far his talent surpassed any client's capacity fully to realize his dream: a world of sanctuaries and gardens, of earth and machines, of rivers, seas, mountains, and prairies, where grand architecture enables men to dwell nobly.

Wright died at Taliesin West on April 9, 1959. His widow, Olgivanna, directed the Taliesin Fellowship.

For More Information

Gill, Brendan. *Many Masks: A Life of Frank Lloyd Wright.* New York: Putnam, 1987.

Secrest, Meryle. *Frank Lloyd Wright: A Biography.* Chicago: University of Chicago Press, 1998.

Smith, Kathryn. *Frank Lloyd Wright: America's Master Architect.* New York: Abbeville Press Publishers, 1998.

Thomson, Iain. *Frank Lloyd Wright.* San Diego: Thunder Bay Press, 1997.

Thorne-Thomsen, Kathleen. *Frank Lloyd Wright for Kids.* Chicago: Chicago Review Press, 1994.

RICHARD WRIGHT

Born: September 4, 1908
Natchez, Mississippi
Died: November 25, 1960
Paris, France
African American writer

The works of Richard Wright, a politically sophisticated and socially involved African American author, are notable for their passionate sincerity. He was perceptive about the universal problems that had the ability to destroy mankind.

Southern upbringing

Richard Nathaniel Wright was born in Natchez, Mississippi, on September 4, 1908. His mother was a country school teacher and his father an illiterate (a person who is unable to read or write) sharecropper, a poor farmer who shares land with other farmers. The family moved to Memphis, Tennessee, in 1914, and soon the father abandoned them. From then on Richard's education was inconsistent, but he had attained experience beyond his years. He bounced from school to school and desperately tried to make friends and fit in with his fellow classmates.

Wright knew what it was to be a victim of racial hatred before he learned to read, for he was living with an aunt when her husband was lynched (brutally attacked or killed because of one's race). Richard's formal education ended after the ninth grade in Jackson, Mississippi. The fact that his "The Voodoo of Hell's Half-acre" had been published in the local black paper set him apart from his classmates. He was a youth upon whom a dark spirit had already settled.

Becoming a writer

At nineteen Wright decided he wanted to be a writer. He moved to Chicago, Illinois, where he had access to public libraries. He read all he could of Feodor Dostoevsky (1821–1881), Theodore Dreiser (1871–1945), Henry

Richard Wright.
Reproduced by permission of Fisk University Library.

James (1843–1916), and William James (1842–1910). His interest in social problems led to a friendship with the sociologist (a person who studies the interactions of a society) Louis Wirth. When Richard's mother, brother, and an aunt came to Chicago, he supported them as a postal clerk until the job ended in 1929. After months of living on public welfare, he got a job in the Federal Negro Theater Project in the Works Progress Administration, a government relief agency. Later he became a writer for the Illinois Writers' Project.

Meantime, Wright had joined the John Reed Club, beginning an association with the Communist Party, a political party that believes goods and services should be owned and distributed by a strong central government. His essays, reviews, short stories, and poems appeared regularly in communist papers, and by 1937, when he became Harlem editor of the *Daily Worker,* he enjoyed a considerable reputation in left-wing circles. Four novellas (short novels), published as *Uncle Tom's Children* (1938), introduced him to a large general audience.

Native Son

Wright's first novel, *Native Son* (1940), a brutally honest depiction of black, urban, ghetto life, was an immediate success. The story's protagonist, or main character, represents all the fear, rage, rebellion, spiritual hunger and the undisciplined drive to satisfy it, that social psychologists (people who are trained to study the mental and behavioral characteristics of people) were just beginning to recognize as common elements in the personality of the poor people of all races.

Wright's intention was to make the particular truth universal (all around) and to project his native son as a symbol of the poorly treated in all lands. Critics, however, unimpressed by the universal symbol, were interested instead in Wright's passionate criticisms of white racism (belief that one race is superior to another) and the lifestyle it imposed upon African Americans. Wright believed that there was a better way of social organization different from democracy (government by the people), and that Communism could be the better way. These ideas were toned down in the stage version. In 1941 Wright also published *Twelve Million Black Voices: A Folk History of the Negro of the United States.*

By 1940 Wright had married and divorced; and a few months after his second marriage, he broke with the Communist Party. (His "I Tried To Be a Communist," published in the *Atlantic* in 1944, was reprinted in 1949 in *The God That Failed,* edited by Richard Crossman.) The break freed him from social commitments that were beginning to seem troublesome. In *Black Boy,* a fictionalized autobiography (book written about oneself), his only commitment is to truth. The book was published in January 1945, and sales reached four hundred thousand copies by March. Wright accepted an invitation from the French government to visit France, and the three-month experience, in sharp contrast to his experience in his own country, "exhilarated" (excited and refreshed) him with a "sense of freedom." People of the highest intellectual and artistic circles met him "as an equal."

Years overseas

Wright, his wife, and daughter moved permanently to Paris, France. Within a year and a half Wright was off to Argentina, where he "starred" in the film version of *Native Son.* *The Outsider,* the first of three novels written in France, was deeply influenced by existentialism, a philosophy that stresses the individual experience in the universe, whose most famous spokespersons, Jean Paul Sartre (1905–1980) and Simone de Beauvoir (1908–1986), were Wright's close friends. Following *Savage Holiday* (1954), a potboiler (a book, that is usually of poorer quality, written to make money), *The Long Dream* (1958) proved that Wright had been too long out of touch with the American reality to deal with it effectively. None of the novels written in France succeeded. His experiments with poetry did not produce enough for a book.

Nonfiction works

In 1953 Wright visited Africa, where he hoped to "discover his roots" as a black man. *Black Power* (1954) combines the elements of a travel book with a passionate political treatise, or formal writing, on the "completely different order of life" in Africa. In 1955 he attended the Afro-Asian Conference in Bandung, Indonesia, and published his impressions in *The Color Curtain* (1956). *Pagan Spain* (1956), based on two months in Spain, is the best of his nonfiction works. *White Man, Listen* (1957) is a collection of four long essays on "White-colored, East-West relations."

In 1960, following an unhappy attempt to settle in England, and in the midst of a rugged lecture schedule, Wright fell ill. He entered a hospital in Paris on November 25 and died three days later. *Eight Men* (1961), a collection of short stories, and *Lawd Today* (1963), a novel, were published after his death.

For More Information

Fabre, Michel. *Richard Wright: Books and Writers.* Jackson: University Press of Mississippi, 1990.

Rowley, Hazel. *Richard Wright: The Life and Times.* New York: Henry Holt, 2001.

Walker, Margaret. *Richard Wright, Daemonic Genius: A Portrait of the Man, a Critical Look at His Work.* New York: Warner Books, 1988.

Webb, Constance. *Richard Wright; a Biography.* New York: Putnam, 1968.

WILLIAM BUTLER YEATS

Born: June 13, 1865
Dublin, Ireland
Died: January 28, 1939
Roquebrune, France
Irish poet and dramatist

William Butler Yeats was an Irish poet and dramatist (playwright). Some think he was the greatest poet of the twentieth century. He won the Nobel Prize for literature in 1923. The works of William Butler Yeats form a bridge between the romantic poetry of the nineteenth century and the hard clear language of modern poetry.

Early years

William Butler Yeats was born on June 13, 1865, in Dublin, Ireland. He was the oldest of four children of John Butler Yeats, a portrait artist. His father added to William's formal schooling with lessons at home that gave him an enduring taste for the classics. John Yeats had a forceful personality. His personal philosophy was a blend of aestheticism (a belief that art and beauty are important for everything) and atheism (a belief that there is no God). William felt its influence much later as it showed up in his interest in magic and the occult (supernatural)

William Butler Yeats.
Reproduced by permission of the Corbis Corporation.

sciences and in his highly original system of aesthetics (beauty).

At the age of nineteen Yeats enrolled in the Metropolitan School of Art in Dublin, intending to become a painter. In 1887 he became a literary correspondent for two American newspapers. Among his acquaintances at this time were his father's artist and writer friends, including William Morris (1834–1896), George Bernard Shaw (1856–1950), and Oscar Wilde (1856–1900).

Important friendships

In 1889 Yeats met the woman who became the greatest single influence on his life

and poetry, Maud Gonne. She was Yeats's first and deepest love. She admired his poetry but rejected his repeated offers of marriage, choosing instead to marry Major John MacBride. Gonne came to represent for Yeats the ideal of feminine beauty—she appears as Helen of Troy in several of his poems—but a beauty disfigured and wasted by what Yeats considered an unsuitable marriage and her involvement in a hopeless political cause, Irish independence.

Yeats became a founding member of literary clubs in London, England, and Dublin. During this period he became friends with the dramatist John Millington Synge (1871–1909). He was introduced to Synge in 1896, and later directed the Abbey Theatre in Dublin with him.

The American poet Ezra Pound (1885–1972) came to London for the specific purpose of meeting Yeats in 1909. Pound served as Yeats's secretary off and on between 1912 and 1916. Pound introduced Yeats to the Japanese *No* drama (a form of Japanese theater similar in many ways to Greek tragedy). Yeats's verse dramas (plays in the form of poetry) reflect the ceremonial formality and symbolism of *No*.

The death of Maud Gonne's husband seemed to offer promise that she might now accept Yeats's proposal of marriage. She turned him down in 1917. He proposed to her daughter, Iseult MacBride, only to be rejected by her too. That same year he married Miss George Hyde-Less.

Soon after their wedding, Yeats's new wife developed the power of automatic writing (writing as though coming from an outside source) and began to utter strange phrases in her sleep that she thought were dictated by spirits from another world. Yeats copied down these fragments and incorporated them into his occult aesthetic system, published as *A Vision* in 1925. A daughter, Anne Butler Yeats, was born in 1919, and a son, William Michael, two years later.

Poet and dramatist

Yeats's first book of poems, The *Wanderings of Oisin and Other Poems,* was published in 1889. In the long title poem he began his celebration of the ancient Irish heroes Oisin, Finn, Aengus, and St. Patrick. This interest was evident also in his collection of Irish folklore, *Fairy and Folk Tales* (1888). His long verse drama, *The Countess Cathleen* (1892), was a combination of modern dramatic forms with ancient beliefs and modern Irish history. He followed this with his collection of romantic tales and mood sketches, *The Celtic Twilight* (1893). Yeats's *Secret Rose* (1897) includes poems that he called personal, occult, and Irish. More figures from ancient Irish history and legend appeared in this volume.*The Wind among the Reeds* (1899) won the Royal Academy Prize as the best book of poems published that year.

The Abbey Theater

An important milestone in the history of the modern theater occurred in 1902, when Yeats, Maud Gonne, Douglas Hyde, and George Russell founded the Irish National Theatre Society, out of which grew the Abbey Theatre Company in 1904. Yeats's experience with the theater gave to his volume of poems *In the Seven Woods* (1907) a new style—less elaborate, less romantic, and more straight forward in language and imagery.

Some of Yeats's plays show his great interest in ancient royalty and "half-forgotten things," but his poetry was unmistakably new. Yeats's play *At the Hawk's Well,* written and produced in 1915, showed the influence of Japanese *No* drama in its use of masks and in its dances by a Japanese choreographer.

From 1918 to 1923 Yeats and his wife lived in a restored tower at Ballylee (Galway), Ireland. The tower became a prominent symbol in his best poems, notably in those that make up *The Tower* (1928).

Yeats was elected an Irish senator in 1922, a post he filled until his retirement in 1928. He received the Nobel Prize in Literature in 1923. His acceptance of the role and its responsibilities had been foreshadowed (predicted) in his poems *Responsibilities* (1914). The outbreak of civil war in Ireland in 1922 had heightened his conviction that the artist must lead the way through art, rather than through politics, to a harmonious (in tune) ordering of chaos.

Aesthetic theories and systems

Yeats devised his doctrine of the mask as a means of presenting very personal thoughts and experiences to the world without danger of sentimentality (excessive emotions). By discovering the kind of man who would be his exact opposite, Yeats believed he could then put on the mask of this ideal "antiself" and thus produce art from the synthesis (combination) of opposing natures. For this reason his poetry is often structured on paired opposites, as in "Sailing to Byzantium."

Yeats turned to magic for the illogical system that would oppose and complete his art. He drew upon Buddhism (an ancient Eastern religion), as well as upon Jewish and Christian mystic (spiritual) books to try and capture what he thought was a harmony of the opposite elements of life

Yeats believed that history was cyclical (circular) and that every two thousand years a new cycle, which is the opposite of the cycle that has preceded it, begins. In his poem "The Second Coming," the birth of Christ begins one cycle, which ends, as the poem ends, with a "rough beast," mysterious and menacing, who "slouches towards Bethlehem to be born."

Last works

Yeats's last plays were *Purgatory* (1938) and *The Death of Cuchulain* (1938). He died in Roquebrune, France, on January 28, 1929. He had retired there because of ill health. He had the lines of one of his poems engraved on his tombstone in Ireland: "Cast a cold eye / On life, on death. / Horseman, pass by!" Yeats was not only one of the greatest poets and a major figure in the Irish literary renaissance (rebirth), but also wrote some of the greatest of all twentieth-century literature.

For More Information

Jeffares, A. Norman. *W. B. Yeats, a New Biography.* New York: Farrar Straus Giroux, 1989.

Larrissey, Edward. *Yeats the Poet: The Measures of Difference.* New York: Harvester Wheatsheaf, 1994.

Macrae, Alistair D. F. *W. B. Yeats: A Literary Life.* New York: St. Martin's Press, 1994.

BORIS YELTSIN

Born: February 1, 1931
Butko, Siberia, Russia
Russian president, politician, and
government official

B oris Yeltsin, who became president of Russia in 1991, was one of the most complex political leaders of his time. A longtime Communist Party leader, he was an important leader in the reform (social improvement) movements of the late 1980s and 1990s. Yeltsin was perceived at varying times as a folk hero, as a symbol of Russia's struggle to establish a democracy, and as a dictatorial figure (an all-powerful ruler).

Early life

Boris Nikolaevich Yeltsin was born into a Russian working-class family on February 1, 1931, in the small Siberian village of Butko. His parents were Nikolai and Klavdia Yeltsin. He grew up with a younger brother, Mikhail, and a younger sister, Valya. The Yeltsin family lived in communal, or group, situations, first on a farm and later at a construction site where his father worked. His family was in close contact with many other families and their privacy was extremely limited. Yeltsin lived and worked in Siberia for most of his life. His early life, like most of his countrymen in the 1930s and 1940s, was marked by hardship, and as the oldest child Boris had numerous responsibilities at home.

A strong-willed child, Boris twice stood up to the educational system. At his elementary school graduation he criticized his homeroom teacher's abusive behavior, which resulted in him being kicked out of school. He appealed the decision and, after an investigation, the teacher was dismissed. During his last year in high school Yeltsin was stricken with typhoid fever, a terrible disease that causes fever and other symptoms and is easily spread, and forced to study at home. Denied the right to take final examinations because he had not attended school, he appealed and won. His actions were extraordinary considering this happened during the rule of Joseph Stalin (1879–1953), a period when the government had an intense stronghold on its citizens.

Trained as an engineer, Yeltsin graduated from the Ural Polytechnic Institute. He married his wife Naina at a young age and they had two daughters. The family is believed to be closely knit.

Yeltsin initially worked as an engineer in the construction industry in Sverdlovsk, moved into management of the industry, and later began a career in the Communist Party, eventually becoming first secretary of the party in Sverdlovsk. Yeltsin joined the Communist Party at age thirty, relatively late for a man with political dreams.

A party leader in Moscow

In 1985 Mikhail S. Gorbachev (1931–), the new general secretary of the Communist Party of the Soviet Union (CPSU), brought Yeltsin to Moscow to serve as secretary for the construction industry. Within a year he was appointed head of the Communist Party of Moscow. The eighteen months that followed were a time of achievement and frustration, ending in his dismissal as a candidate member of the Politburo (the top members of the Communist Party) and first secretary of the Moscow Party.

Yeltsin disliked Moscow at first and criticized the privileges of the city's political elite (highest social class). As a political leader, Yeltsin often traveled to work on public transportation and mingled with ordinary people, unusual behavior among the Soviet

Boris Yeltsin.
Reproduced by permission of Archive Photos, Inc.

elite, who usually traveled in curtained limousines. Yeltsin criticized the pace of the reforms known as *perestroika* and the behavior of some Politburo members. Yeltsin was removed as secretary of the Moscow Party, and he resigned from the Politburo. Yeltsin remained a party member, and Gorbachev appointed him a deputy minister in the construction industry, an area in which he had decades of experience.

In the late 1980s, after Yeltsin criticized perestroika, his personal relationship with Gorbachev fell apart. In the 1989 elections Yeltsin surprised the party by receiving 90 percent of the vote and, with great difficulty, was elected to the small, but important, parliamentary (governing) body, the Supreme Soviet. Gorbachev was elected (chairman) president of the Soviet Union by the new parliament.

During 1989 and 1990 Yeltsin's views made him a folk hero in Moscow, where crowds chanting "Yeltsin, Yeltsin" were a frequent sight. Yeltsin was also elected to the Russian parliament, which in May 1990 selected him as chairman (president) of the Russian Republic. Later that year, Yeltsin formally resigned from the Communist Party.

President of the Republic of Russia

In June 1991 the Russian Republic held its first election for president, and Yeltsin defeated six opponents to win the presidency. As president he declared the Russian Republic independent of the Soviet Union.

Yeltsin as president of the Russian Republic (RSFSR) and Gorbachev as president of the Soviet Union agreed to cooperate on economic reform, a reversal since their relationship fell apart in 1987. However, on August 19, 1991, eight conservative party and government leaders led a coup (takeover) against the vacationing Gorbachev. Yeltsin led the dramatic opposition to the coup and secured Gorbachev's return to Moscow.

In the aftermath of Gorbachev's rescue, Yeltsin consolidated (unified) his own power. Yeltsin led the movement to dissolve the Russian parliament and outlaw the Communist Party on Russian soil. These acts further weakened Gorbachev's power base. In the fall of 1991 Yeltsin and other republic leaders declared the independence of their respective republics, and in December the presidents of Russia, Ukraine, and Belarus (Belorussia) formed the Commonwealth of Independent States (CIS), declaring they would no longer recognize the Soviet Union as of January 1, 1992. Eight other republics joined the CIS, while four republics became completely independent. Gorbachev resigned before year's end, and as of January 1, 1992, the Soviet Union no longer existed. Yeltsin, who in 1987 had been dismissed from the Soviet leadership, became the head of post-Soviet Russia, the largest of the Soviet successor states.

A new era

Yeltsin began a new chapter in 1992 as president of independent Russia. He undertook an ambitious program of economic reform with mixed results. Businesses were returned to the private sector but the economy began to crumble. Yeltsin's policies were frequently challenged during 1992, ending in a major showdown with the Russian parliament in December 1992. Yeltsin dissolved parliament in September 1993 and a sit-in (peaceful protest) began. In early October 1993, a confrontation occurred, resulting in hundreds of deaths and injuries as well as considerable damage to several Moscow landmarks. The sit-in was eventually stopped.

Yeltsin survived the political crisis, but his reputation suffered. The democratic Yeltsin who protested in the streets of Moscow in the late 1980s was forgotten and a dictatorial (harsh leadership by one) image of Yeltsin emerged. Yeltsin remained at the helm of Russian politics, but as a less heroic figure than the Yeltsin of 1991. Although reelected in 1996, Yeltsin's future was clouded by Russia's economic crisis and the failure of his reform program, combined with the bitter aftertaste of Yeltsin's confrontation with parliament.

Losing power

After the 1996 elections it became clear that Yeltsin had deceived the Russian people about his health. In fact, he had suffered a heart attack prior to elections, and was not well. Although he continued as president, there was talk within the international and Russian community about who would take his place as president.

In 1997 Yeltsin continued to face domestic problems in his new term. The Russian financial picture continued to grow grim, industrial production slowed, and even Russian life expectancy dropped drastically, by six years. Indeed, in 1997, employees frequently waited as long as three months for payment.

Yeltsin had his political stability tested again in May of 1999 when a Communist-led attempt to impeach (to charge with misconduct) him failed. Yeltsin faced five charges—one of the most significant being the accusation that he started the war in Chechnya in 1994—but eventually the charges were dropped. Yeltsin continued to suffer from health problems during his second term, spending large amounts of time out of the public eye as a result. Despite his ill health, Yeltsin remained a dominate political force, dismissing four prime ministers during 1998 and 1999.

Stepping down

Citing the need for new leadership in Russia, Yeltsin suddenly resigned as president on December 31, 1999. Many believed that Yeltsin's declining popularity and failing health contributed to the decision that ended the leader's second term six months early. "I am stepping down ahead of term. I under-stand that I must do it and Russia must enter a new millennium with new politicians, with new faces, with new intelligent, strong, energetic people, and we who have been in power for many years must go," Yeltsin said during a public address on Russian national television.

Though Yeltsin received praise from then-President Bill Clinton (1946–), most Russians would likely disagree with the glowing review of the leader's eight years in office. Yeltsin's attempts to create a better economy were often crippled by corruption and incompetence, and he became increasingly disliked by the Russian people as a result. Yeltsin appointed Russian Prime Minister Vladimir Putin (1952–) as acting president until a March 2000 election. Putin, a former KGB (the Soviet Union secret police) officer and popular politician, served as both acting president and prime minister. Yeltsin planned to start a political foundation and travel Europe in his retirement.

In 2001 Yeltsin was given Russia's highest award known as "Order of Service to the Fatherland, First Degree." President Putin honored Yeltsin with this award for his part in changing the future of Russia by helping to end the Soviet Union.

For More Information

Aron, Leon. *Yeltsin: A Revolutionary Life*. New York: St. Martin's Press, 2000.

Ayer, Eleanor H. *Boris Yeltsin: Man of the People*. New York: Dillon Press, 1992.

Daniels, Robert. *The End of the Communist Revolution*. New York: Routledge, 1993.

Miller, Calvin Craig. *Boris Yeltsin: First President of Russia*. Greensboro, NC: Morgan Reynolds, 1994.

Morrison, John. *Boris Yeltsin: From Bolshevik to Democrat.* New York: Dutton, 1991.

Yeltsin, Boris. *Against the Grain: An Autobiography.* New York: Summit Books, 1990.

PAUL ZINDEL

Born: May 15, 1936
Staten Island, New York
American playwright, screenwriter, and author

From Pulitzer prize-winning playwright to young adult fiction writer, American author Paul Zindel turned his real-life turbulent (marked by disturbance and unrest) teens into fictional stories to show teenagers that their lives and feelings do matter.

Early adventures

Paul Zindel was born on May 15, 1936, in Staten Island, New York. His father, also named Paul, left Zindel, his older sister Betty, and his mother, Betty, for a girlfriend when young Paul was just two years old. This event began Zindel's early adventures. After his father left, Zindel's mother started moving from town to town and from job to job. From shipyard worker to dog breeder, Betty Zindel seemed unable to keep any job. Yet Zindel offered a sort of compliment to his mother: "what mother lacked in money, she made up for being able to talk a mile a minute." Zindel's mother, however, also constantly threatened suicide. Zindel described his home as a "house of fear." He coped not only by creating a fantasy life, but also by wishing he would be abducted by aliens.

In 1951, when Zindel was fifteen, his wish to escape from his home was granted—

Paul Zindel.
Reproduced by permission of AP/Wide World Photos.

although not by aliens, but by doctors. He was diagnosed with tuberculosis. Since tuberculosis is a highly contagious disease of the lungs, he was confined to the hospital for eighteen months—it was here that Zindel wrote his first play.

After recovering, Zindel graduated from high school and left home once again, this time to attend Wagner College in Staten Island. Zindel did not receive a degree in English, literature, or writing, but in 1958, received his bachelor's degree in chemistry and education. In 1959 he also completed a masters of science degree in chemistry. Following college, Zindel found work as a tech-

nical writer for a chemical company. After six months, he quit and became a chemistry teacher at Tottenville High School in Staten Island. In his free time, he continued to write plays such as *Dimensions of Peacocks* and *A Dream of Swallows*. In the early 1960s, both plays ran on stage in New York City.

Success in two genres

In the mid-1960s, Zindel wrote *The Effect of Gamma Rays on Man-in-the-Moon Marigolds. Gamma Rays* tells the story of Tillie, a teenager who feels smothered by her critical mother and a sister who suffers from epilepsy, a severe disorder that effects motor skills. However, Tillie finds hope for her life when the marigolds she exposed to radiation for a science project, bloom. Zindel won many awards for *Gamma Rays,* including the 1971 Pulitzer Prize in drama. Zindel, as stated in the forward to the Bantam Edition, said of this often-awarded play, "I suspect it is autobiographical, because whenever I see a production of it I laugh and cry harder than anyone else in the audience."

After viewing a televised version of *Gamma Rays,* Charlotte Zolotow, an editor at Harper & Row publishers, suggested to Zindel that he write a young adult fiction book. Zindel published *The Pigman* in 1968. *The Pigman* told the story of a betrayed friendship between two high school sophomores, John and Lorraine, and a widower named Mr. Angelo Pignati. After an illness forces Mr. Pignati, the "Pigman," out of his home, he entrusts John and Lorraine with its care and his cherished ceramic pig collection. John and Lorraine betray this trust and the Pigman's friendship, however, by throwing a party where his collection is accidentally smashed. With this book, Zindel not only continued collecting awards, including the American Library Association's Best Young Adult Book citation, but also praise.

Writing for teenagers

Throughout the 1970s and 1980s, Zindel continued writing books for teenagers. *My Darling, My Hamburger* (1969) probed the questions about lust, sex, contraception (birth control), and abortion (a woman's right to end a pregnancy); true love was the subject in *I Never Loved Your Mind* (1970); parental pressure and friendship came under discussion in *Pardon Me, You're Stepping on My Eyeball!* (1976); and truth and the perception (the concept) of truth in *The Undertaker's Gone Bananas* (1978). A collaboration (the work of two or more people) with his wife, Bonnie Hildebrand, whom he had married in 1973, produced *A Star for the Latecomer* in 1980. In that same year, Zindel published a sequel (the next part of a story) to his most popular book *The Pigman. The Pigman's Legacy* returned readers to Mr. Pignati's house where John and Lorraine have a second chance to do the right thing and help another elderly man, Gus, live out his final days. However, this was not Zindel's final tale about a "Pigman."

Zindel's works in the 1990s have stretched his talents even more. In 1993 he published several children's books, including *Fright Party, David and Della,* and *Attack of the Killer.* That same year, he also released *The Fifth-Grade Safari.* Returning to his young adult audience, Zindel published *Loch* in 1994 and *The Doom Stone* the following year.

Over the past thirty years, Zindel has followed his Pigman's advice. From stage and screen plays to young adult fiction books, he has used his imagination and shared his real-life adventures. In 2002 Zindel was awarded the Margaret A. Edwards Award for his lifetime contribution in writing for young adults.

For More Information

Forman, Jack Jacob. *Presenting Paul Zindel.* Boston: Twayne Publishers, 1988.

Zindel, Paul. *The Effect of Gamma Rays on Man-in-the-Moon Marigolds.* New York: Harper, 1971.

Zindel, Paul. *The Pigman.* New York: Bantam Books, 1968.

Zindel, Paul. *The Pigman & Me.* New York: HarperCollins, 1992.

index

Volume numbers are in *italic*; page numbers for main entries are in **boldface**; "(ill.)" following a page number indicates an illustration on the page.

George magazine, 6: 1071

Georgia
   Bond, Julian, 2: 245–46
   Carter, Jimmy, 3: 381
The Georgics (Virgil), 10: 1876

Germ theory
   Lister, Joseph, 6: 1160
   Pasteur, Louis, 1: 1450–53

German art songs (lieder), 9: 1684–87

German language, 5: 838

German Requiem (Brahms), 2: 272

German Workers' Party, 7: 1248

Germany, 1: 170–73; 5: 909–12; 6: 1051;
   7: 1246–49; 9: 1678–81

Germany Workers Party. *See* Nazi Party

Get on the Bus (film), 6: 1128

Getty, J. Paul, 5: **786–87,** 787 (ill.)

Gettysburg Address (Lincoln), 6: 1153

Ghost (film), 5: 799

Giant (film), 4: 568, 569

Gibran, Kahlil, 5: **788–90,** 789 (ill.)

Gibson, Althea, 5: **790–91,** 791 (ill.)

"The Gift Outright" (Frost), 4: 744

Gigi (musical), 5: 887

Gilbert, Humphrey, 8: 1548

Gillespie, Dizzy, 5: **792–94,** 793 (ill.); 8: 1446

Gimpel, the Fool, and Other Stories (Singer), 9: 1725

Ginsburg, Ruth Bader, 5: **794–96,** 795 (ill.)

Giovanni da Fiesole, Fra. *See* Angelico, Fra

Girl Asleep at a Table (Vermeer), 10: 1864

Girondins, 9: 1600

"Give me liberty or give me death!," 5: 884

Gladiators, 4: 749

Gladstone, William, 10: 1871

Glass family (literary characters), 9: 1664–65

The Glass Menagerie (Williams), 10: 1949

Glengarry Glen Ross (Mamet), 7: 1215

"Gloomy Sunday" (song), 5: 919

Gnosticism, 6: 1045

Go Quietly or Else (Agnew), 1: 33

Go Tell It on the Mountain (Baldwin), 1: 158

God. *See also* Religious leaders
   Aristotle, 1: 100
   Calvin, John, 2: 345
   Garvey, Marcus, 4: 769
   Luther, Martin, 6: 1182–83
   Moses, 7: 1343–45
   Muhammad, 7: 1357
   Truth, Sojourner, 10: 1842

The Godfather (film), 3: 517

God's Grace (Malamud), 7: 1210

Godwin, William, 9: 1709

Goeth, Amon, 9: 1680

Goethe, Johann Wolfgang von, 9: 1685

Gold, 5: 820

Goldberg, Whoopi, 5: **797–99,** 798 (ill.)

The Golden Apples (Welty), 10: 1926

Golden Hind (ship), 4: 633

Golding, William, 5: 800 (ill.), **800–801**

Goldman, Charley, 7: 1231

Golfers
   Palmer, Arnold, 8: 1441–43
   Woods, Tiger, 10: 1960–62

Gombe National Park, 5: 805

Gompers, Samuel, 5: **801–4,** 803 (ill.)

Gone with the Wind, 7: 1267–70

Gonne, Maud, 10: 1980–81

Gonzalez, Elian, 3: 396; 8: 1571

The Good Earth (Buck), 2: 309

Good manners, 8: 1509–11

Good Master of the Name of God.
   See Baal Shem Tov

Goodall, Jane, 5: **804–7,** 805 (ill.)

Goodman, Benny, 5: **807–9,** 808 (ill.)

Goodwin, Hannibal, 4: 647

Gorbachev, Mikhail, 5: **809–12,** 810 (ill.);
   10: 1983–84

Gordian Knot, 1: 45

Gordy, Berry, Jr., 5: **813–15,** 814 (ill.); 6: 987;
   9: 1632

Gore, Al, 2: 328–29; 5: **816–18,** 817 (ill.)

The Gospel According to the Son (Mailer), 7: 1208

Gospel music, 6: 1086–87

Gospel of Life *(Evangelism Vitaeor)* (John Paul II),
   6: 1015

Gospels, 6: 1000–1001

Gothic vampire story, 9: 1760

Gould, Jay, 5: **818–21,** 819 (ill.)

Gould, Stephen Jay, 5: **821–24,** 822 (ill.)

Government officials and agents
   Bennett, William, 2: 204–6
   Boone, Daniel, 2: 248
   Cervantes, Miguel de, 3: 410
   Cheney, Dick, 3: 452–53
   Defoe, Daniel, 4: 574–76
   Dole, Elizabeth, 4: 613–16
   Elders, Joycelyn, 4: 663–65
   Franklin, Benjamin, 4: 731–35
   Galbraith, John Kenneth, 4: 746
   Kissinger, Henry, 6: 1104–7
   Newton, Isaac, 7: 1385
   Powell, Colin, 8: 1512–13
   Rice, Condoleezza, 9: 1580–83
   Rousseau, Jean Jacques, 9: 1636–37
   Rowan, Carl, 9: 1639–40
   Yeltsin, Boris, 10: 1982–85

I

J

Pediatric medicine
    Elders, Joycelyn, 4: 663
    Spock, Benjamin, 9: 1740–43
Pedrarias (Arias de Avila, Pedro), 4: 592
Pei, I. M., 8: **1464–67,** 1465 (ill.)
Pelé, 8: **1467–69,** 1468 (ill.)
Pelléas et Mélisande (opera), 4: 570–71
Peloponnesian Wars, 1: 97; 8: 1486
Pendennis (Thackeray), 10: 1803
Pender, Bob, 5: 830
Penicillin, 2: 298
Peninsular War, 7: 1378
Penn, William, 8: **1469–72,** 1470 (ill.)
Pennsylvania
    Penn, William, 8: 1471
Pennsylvania Assembly, 4: 732–33
Penrose, Roger, 5: 862
The Pensées (Pascal), 8: 1449
"Pentagon Papers," 5: 825
Pentecostal Church, 1: 157, 158
People's Republic of China, 4: 587–89; 6: 1106;
    7: 1226–29; 8: 1395; 9: 1779–83. *See also* China;
    Republic of China (Taiwan)
People's Republic of Kampuchea, 8: 1498, 1516
Pepin, King of the Franks, 3: 425
Peptides, 8: 1455
"Percussive movements" (modern dance), 5: 827
Performing Work (*Laborem Exercens*) (John Paul II),
    6: 1015
Perfume, 6: 1108–9
Pergamon (Asia Minor), 4: 748–49
Pericles, 8: 1472–74, **1473 (ill.)**
Perinatology, 1: 81–84
Peripatetic School (Lyceum), 1: 99
Perkins Institute for the Blind (Boston,
    Massachusetts), 6: 1057
Perón, Eva, 8: **1474–77,** 1475 (ill.)
Persia, 1: 45–46; 8: 1500, 1555–57
Persian Communist Party, 8: 1440
Persian Gulf War
    Bush, George, 2: 325
    Cheney, Dick, 3: 453
    Hussein, Saddam, 5: 965
    Powell, Colin, 8: 1513–14
The Persian Letters (Montesquieu), 7: 1330–31
The Persians (Aeschylus), 1: 29
Personal computers, 6: 1009
Personalities, 6: 1044–45
Perspective, 6: 1136–39
Persuasion (Austen), 1: 135
Peru, 4: 592–93; 5: 896
Pesticides, 3: 379; 7: 1374
Petain, Henri Philippe, 4: 579–80

Peter, Emperor of Russia, 3: 401–2
Petrashevsky Circle, 4: 624–25
Phaedo (Plato), 8: 1486–87
The Phantom Menace (film), 6: 1178
Pharoah, Tutankhamen, 10: 1845–47
Phenomenology, 9: 1750
Philadelphia, Pennsylvania, 1: 107
    Franklin, Benjamin, 4: 732
    Philadelphia Centennial Exposition, 2: 198
Philadelphia 76ers, 3: 418
The Philadelphia Story (film), 5: 889–90
Philadelphia Warriors, 3: 417
Philanthropists. *See also* Humanitarians
    Carnegie, Andrew, 3: 367–69
    Charles, Ray, 3: 433
    Cobb, Ty, 3: 492
    Eastman, George, 4: 648
    Ford, Henry, 4: 728
    Gates, Bill, 4: 772
    Lauren, Ralph, 6: 1119
    Rockefeller, John, 9: 1604–6
    Roosevelt, Eleanor, 9: 1621–24
    Walker, Madame C. J., 10: 1896
    Winfrey, Oprah, 10: 1957
Philip II, King of Macedon, 1: 43, 44, 98
Philip IV, King of Spain, 9: 1615
Philippines, 1: 84–86; 7: 1187, 1233–35
Philoctetes (Sophocles), 9: 1736–37
Philosophers
    Arendt, Hannah, 1: 91–93
    Aristotle, 1: 98–100
    Bacon, Roger, 1: 145–47
    Bennett, William, 2: 204
    Buddha, 2: 310–12
    Camus, Albert, 2: 349–51
    Cicero, 3: 475–78
    Confucius, 3: 503–6
    Descartes, René, 4: 590–92
    Dewey, John, 4: 594–97
    Diderot, Denis, 4: 606–8
    Emerson, Ralph Waldo, 4: 680–83
    Galen, 4: 748–50
    Hobbes, Thomas, 5: 915–18
    Jefferson, Thomas, 6: 994–97
    Kant, Immanuel, 6: 1052–54
    Lao Tzu, 6: 1115–17
    Locke, Alain, 6: 1163–66
    Locke, John, 6: 1166–68
    Marcus Aurelius Antoninus, 7: 1236–38
    Marx, Karl, 7: 1246–49
    Mill, John Stuart, 7: 1301–3
    Montesquieu, 7: 1329–31
    Nietzsche, Friedrich, 8: 1387–90

Shakespeare, William, *8:* 1422–23; *9:* **1702–6,** 1704 (ill.), 1597
Shame (Rushdie), *9:* 1649
Sharif, Nawaz, *2:* 219
Sharpville, South Africa, *7:* 1217
Shaw, George Bernard, *9:* **1706–8,** 1707 (ill.)
Shelley, Mary Wollstonecraft, *9:* **1708–11,** 1710 (ill.), 1712
Shelley, Percy, *2:* 333; *9:* 1709–10, **1711–14,** 1712 (ill.)
Shelley, Timothy, *9:* 1709, 1710, 1711
Sheppard, Samuel H., *1:* 151
Sherman, Allen, *3:* 519
Sherpas, *5:* 898, 900
She's Gotta Have It (film), *6:* 1127
Shia Islamic tradition, *6:* 1081. *See also* Islam
Ship of Fools (Porter), *8:* 1508–9
The Shipping News (Proulx), *8:* 1526
Shirley (Brontë), *2:* 284
The Shootist (film), *10:* 1915
Short story writers
    Atwood, Margaret, *1:* 122
    Bradbury, Ray, *2:* 264
    Capote, Truman, *2:* 355
    Cheever, John, *3:* 447–49
    Chekhov, Anton, *3:* 449–51
    Dunbar, Paul Laurence, *4:* 636–37
    Faulkner, William, *4:* 703
    Fitzgerald, F. Scott, *4:* 720
    García Márquez, Gabriel, *4:* 762
    Hawthorne, Nathaniel, *5:* 862–65
    Irving, Washington, *5:* 975–77
    Joyce, James, *6:* 1038
    Kafka, Franz, *6:* 1047–49
    Kipling, Rudyard, *6:* 1101–3
    London, Jack, *6:* 1169–70
    Malamud, Bernard, *7:* 1208–10
    McMillan, Terry, *7:* 1273–75
    Oates, Joyce Carol, *8:* 1413–16
    Poe, Edgar Allan, *8:* 1490–92
    Porter, Katherine Anne, *8:* 1507–9
    Proulx, E. Annie, *8:* 1525–26
    Salinger, J. D., *9:* 1666–67
    Singer, Isaac Bashevis, *9:* 1724–26
    Stoker, Bram, *9:* 1760–61
    Thackeray, William Makepeace, *10:* 1801–4
    Updike, John, *10:* 1857
    Walker, Alice, *10:* 1894
    Welty, Eudora, *10:* 1926–27
Showa Tenno. *See* Hirohito, Emperor of Japan
Showboat (musical), *5:* 850
"Shuttle" diplomacy, *6:* 1106–7
Shuttle, space. *See* National Aeronautics and Space

Administration (NASA)
Shutzstaffel (SS—Nazi security squad)
    Barbie, Klaus, *1:* 170–73
    Schindler, Oskar, *9:* 1679–80
Sicherheitsdienst (SD—Nazi intelligence and security), *1:* 171
Sick Child (Munch), *7:* 1363
Sickle cell anemia, *8:* 1455
Siddal, Elizabeth, *9:* 1634–35
Siddhartha Gautama. *See* Buddha
Sikhs (India), *4:* 757
Silas Marner (Eliot), *4:* 667
The Silence of the Lambs (film), *5:* 939
Silent Spring (Carson), *3:* 379
Silkworms, *8:* 1451–52
Sills, Beverly, *9:* **1714–16,** 1715 (ill.)
The Silmarillion (Tolkien), *10:* 1824
Silver Jubilee (Elizabeth II), *4:* 676–77
"Silver Sewer" Award, *2:* 206
Simon, Neil, *9:* **1716–19,** 1717 (ill.)
Simpson, O. J., *1:* 152
Sinatra, Frank, *9:* **1719–22,** 1720 (ill.)
Sinclair, Upton, *9:* **1722–24,** 1723 (ill.)
Singer, Isaac Bashevis, *9:* **1724–26,** 1725 (ill.)
Singers
    Anderson, Marian, *1:* 69–71
    Armstrong, Louis, *1:* 101–2
    Baez, Joan, *1:* 147–50
    Baker, Josephine, *1:* 152–54
    Beatles, *2:* 181–85
    Berry, Chuck, *2:* 213–15
    Brown, James, *2:* 291–94
    Callas, Maria, *2:* 340–42
    Calloway, Cab, *2:* 342–44
    Cole, Nat "King," *3:* 492–94
    Davis, Sammy, Jr., *3:* 563–65
    Domingo, Placido, *4:* 616–18
    Fitzgerald, Ella, *4:* 715–18
    Garland, Judy, *4:* 764–66
    Guthrie, Woody, *5:* 838–41
    Holiday, Billie, *5:* 918–20
    Horne, Lena, *5:* 940–43
    Jackson, Michael, *6:* 986–89
    John, Elton, *6:* 1011–12
    Jolson, Al, *6:* 1025–27
    Jones, Quincy, *6:* 1031
    King, B. B., *6:* 1086–89
    Madonna, *7:* 1197–1200
    McDaniel, Hattie, *7:* 1267–70
    Morrison, Jim, *7:* 1336–38
    Norman, Jessye, *8:* 1404–6
    Pavarotti, Luciano, *8:* 1456–59
    Presley, Elvis, *8:* 1517–20

U

Uganda, *1:* 59–62

Ukraine, *6:* 1085

Ulysses (Joyce), *6:* 1039

Umkhonto we Sizwe (Spear of the Nation), *7:* 1217

Uncertainty principle (Heisenberg) *5:* 868–70

Uncle Tom's Cabin (Stowe), *9:* 1767–68

Unconscious, *6:* 1043–44

Under Milk Wood (Thomas), *10:* 1813

Underground Railroad, *9:* 1596

Undersea exploration, *3:* 521–23

The Undersea World of Jacques-Yves Cousteau
(TV series), *3:* 522

UNICEF, *5:* 887–88

Unified field theory
Hawking, Stephen, *5:* 861
Heisenberg, Werner, *5:* 870

Union Pacific Railroad, *5:* 820

Unions. *See* Labor union activists, leaders, and
organizers; Labor union strikes

United Automobile Workers (UAW), *2:* 220; *4:* 728

United Church of Christ, *3:* 445

United Farm Workers Organizing Committee
(UFWOC), *3:* 437, 438

United Kingdom. *See* England; Great Britain;
Northern Ireland; Scotland

United Nations
Albright, Madeleine, *1:* 38
Annan, Kofi, *1:* 76–79
Aung San Suu Kyi, *1:* 131
Black, Shirley Temple, *2:* 228–29
Boutros-Ghali, Boutros, *2:* 263–64
Bunche, Ralph, *2:* 312–14
Bush, George, *2:* 324
Hepburn, Audrey, *5:* 887–88
Hussein, Saddam, *5:* 965
Qadhafi, Mu'ammar al-, *8:* 1545
Roosevelt, Eleanor, *9:* 1623

United States, *1:* 7–9, 12–15, 17–22, 25–27, 31–33,
37–39, 79–81, 88, 105–8; *2:* 204–6, 215–17,
244–50, 275–77, 294–97, 305–8, 312–17,
320–31, 346–49; *3:* 374–77, 379–83, 451–53,
461–64, 483–89, 527–29; *4:* 613–16, 626–29,
657–65, 690–93, 704–7, 710–13, 731–35;
5: 794–96, 816–18, 852–54, 883–86, 923–25;
6: 979–86, 994–97, 1016–19, 1061–69, 1071–74,
1091–97, 1104–7, 1150–54; *7:* 1185–88,
1191–97, 1210–14, 1243–46, 1264–67,
1298–1301; *8:* 1392–96, 1416–19, 1425–27,
1469–72, 1511–14, 1557–60, 1568–71, 1574–76;
9: 1580–83, 1621–31; *10:* 1807–10, 1834–37,
1840–43, 1906–10, 1916–19, 1951–54. *See also*
Colonial America; U.S.

Universal Negro Improvement Association and
African Communities League (UNIA-ACI),
4: 767–68

Universal science, *1:* 146–47

University of Chicago, *9:* 1606

University of Maryland Law School, *7:* 1244, 1246

Unsafe at Any Speed (Nader), *7:* 1375

Updike, John, *10:* **1855–57,** 1856 (ill.)

Uranium, *3:* 538–39

U.S. army
Eisenhower, Dwight D., *4:* 658
Seventh Cavalry, *1:* 58–59

U.S. Army Counter Intelligence Corps, *1:* 171–72

U.S. Bureau of Indian Affairs, *2:* 201

U.S. Bureau of Records, *1:* 176

U.S.-China relations, *6:* 1106

U.S. Coast Guard, *5:* 844

U.S. Constitution, *10:* 1908
Constitutional Convention (1787), *4:* 734–35;
5: 847; *7:* 1192, 1195
Nineteenth Amendment (women's right to
vote), *1:* 81
Thirteenth Amendment (abolition of slavery),
9: 1748

U.S. Department of Education, *2:* 205–6

U.S. Department of Justice, *1:* 172–73

U.S. Equal Opportunity Commission (EEOC),
10: 1809

U.S. foreign policy
Albright, Madeleine, *1:* 39
Kissinger, Henry, *6:* 1105–6

U.S. Interior Department, *1:* 58

U.S. Joint Chiefs of Staff, *8:* 1513

U.S. Lawn Tennis Association (USLTA), *1:* 111

U.S.-Myanmar relations, *1:* 132

U.S. Office of National Drug Control Policy, *2:* 206

U.S. Open
Ashe, Arthur, *1:* 111–12
King, Billie Jean, *6:* 1089–90
McEnroe, John, *7:* 1271–72

U.S. Postal Service, *4:* 733

U.S. presidents. *See* Presidents

U.S. secretaries of state. *See* Secretaries of state

U.S. Senate. *See* Senators

U.S.-Soviet relations, *2:* 282; *5:* 811

U.S. space programs, *1:* 104–5

U.S. Steel Corporation, *3:* 369

U.S. Supreme Court. *See* Supreme Court justices

U.S. vice presidents. *See* Vice presidents

U.S.-Vietnam relations, *3:* 486

Ut Unum Sintor (That They May Be One) (John Paul
II), *6:* 1015

Utopia (More), *7:* 1334–35

Utrect Caravaggists, *10:* 1863

V

Vaccines
    Pasteur, Louis, *1:* 1450–53
    Sabin, Albert, *9:* 1657–59
    Salk, Jonas, *9:* 1667–69
Vail, Alfred, *7:* 1342
Valley of the Kings (Egypt), *10:* 1846
Vampires, *9:* 1760
Van Dyck, Anthony, *9:* 1644
Van Gogh, Vincent, *4:* 774; *10:* **1859–62,**
    1861 (ill.)
Vanderbilt, Cornelius, *5:* 819–20
Vanity Fair (Thackeray), *10:* 1803
Vatican, *1:* 73
Vaudeville performers
    Astaire, Fred, *1:* 116
    Davis, Sammy, Jr., *3:* 563
    Garland, Judy, *4:* 764
    Grant, Cary, *5:* 830
    Hope, Bob, *5:* 936
    Jolson, Al, *6:* 1025–27
    Rogers, Will, *9:* 1615–17
Venice, *8:* 1498–1500
Venus, *9:* 1660–61
Ver, Fabian C., *1:* 86
The Verdict (Kafka), *6:* 1048
The Verdict (Mamet), *7:* 1215
Veritatis Splendor (The Resplendence of Truth) (John
    Paul II), *6:* 1015
Vermeer, Jan, *10:* **1862–64,** 1863 (ill.)
Verne, Jules, *10:* **1864–67,** 1865 (ill.)
Verrocchio, Andrea del, *6:* 1136
Versailles, treaty of, *10:* 1953–54
Verus, Lucius, *7:* 1236
Vespucci, Amerigo, *10:* **1867–69,** 1868 (ill.)
Vice presidents
    Adams, John, *1:* 14
    Agnew, Spiro, *1:* 31–33
    Burr, Aaron, *2:* 320–22
    Bush, George, *2:* 323–26
    Cheney, Dick, *3:* 451–53
    Gore, Al, *5:* 816–18
    Johnson, Lyndon B., *6:* 1018
    Nixon, Richard, *8:* 1392–96
    Roosevelt, Theodore, *9:* 1629
    Truman, Harry S., *10:* 1835
Victoria, Queen of Great Britain and Ireland and
    Empress of India, *10:* **1869–72,** 1870 (ill.)
Victorians
    Dickens, Charles, *4:* 600–603
    Hardy, Thomas, *5:* 859
Vidal, Gore, *10:* **1872–74,** 1873 (ill.)

Vienna, Austria
    Brahms, Johannes, *2:* 272–73
    Freud, Sigmund, *4:* 735–38
    Strauss, Johann, *9:* 1771–72
Vienna Psychoanalytic Society, *1:* 27
Vietnam, *5:* 913–15. *See also* Vietnam War
Vietnam Veterans' Memorial (Washington, D.C.),
    6: 1148–49
Vietnam War
    Ali, Muhammad, *1:* 48
    Bradley, Ed, *2:* 267, 268
    Bush, George W., *2:* 327
    Carter, Jimmy, *3:* 381
    Gore, Al, *5:* 816
    Graham, Katharine, *5:* 825
    Ho Chi Minh, *5:* 915
    Johnson, Lyndon B., *6:* 1018, 1019
    Kennedy, Edward, *6:* 1061
    Kennedy, John F., *6:* 1068
    Kissinger, Henry, *6:* 1106
    Nixon, Richard, *8:* 1394–95
    Powell, Colin, *8:* 1512
    Stone, Oliver, *9:* 1762
Vietnam War antiwar movement
    Abzug, Bella, *1:* 8
    Ali, Muhammad, *1:* 48
    Baez, Joan, *1:* 149
    Bernstein, Leonard, *2:* 212
    Bond, Julian, *2:* 245
    Carmichael, Stokely, *3:* 366
    Chisholm, Shirley, *3:* 463
    King, Coretta Scott, *6:* 1093
    King, Martin Luther, Jr., *6:* 1097
A View from Above (Chamberlain), *3:* 419
View of the Thames (Whistler), *10:* 1931
Villa, Pancho, *3:* 362
Violins
    Stradivari, Antonio, *9:* 1769–71
    Vivaldi, Antonio, *10:* 1877–78
Virgil, *10:* **1874–76,** 1875 (ill.)
Virgin of the Rocks (Leonardo da Vinci), *6:* 1137
Virginia
    Henry, Patrick, *5:* 883–86
    Jefferson, Thomas, *6:* 995
    Madison, James, *7:* 1194–97
    Pocahontas, *8:* 1488–90
    Washington, George, *10:* 1906
Virginia Revolutionary Conventions, *5:* 884, 885
Virologists
    Baltimore, David, *1:* 161–64
    Sabin, Albert, *9:* 1657–59
    Salk, Jonas, *9:* 1667–69
Viruses, *1:* 1450–53